THE AMERICAN WHIGS

THE AMERICAN WHIGS
AN ANTHOLOGY

Edited by
Daniel Walker Howe
Yale University

John Wiley & Sons, Inc.
New York • London • Sydney • Toronto

Copyright © 1973, by John Wiley & Sons, Inc.

All rights reserved. Published simultaneously in Canada.

No part of this book may be reproduced by any means, nor transmitted, nor translated into a machine language without the written permission of the publisher.

Library of Congress Cataloging in Publication Data:

Howe, Daniel Walker, comp.
    The American Whigs.

    (Wiley sourcebooks in American social thought)
    Bibliography: p.
    1. Whig Party. I. Title. II. Series.

JK2331.H66   329'.4   72–13144
ISBN 0–471–41670–3
ISBN 0–471–41671–1 (pbk)

Printed in the United States of America

10–9 8 7 6 5 4 3 2 1

CONTENTS

Part Four   SOCIAL   MORALITY

INTRODUCTION

The Whigs and the Democrats were the two major party rivals of what historians term the second American party system. The Federalists and Jeffersonian Republicans composed the first, the Republicans and Democrats, the third and present system. There were political factions of various kinds in colonial America as well, but since they were local and usually informal in organization they are not counted in enumerating the nationwide systems. The second party system took shape out of the factionalism of the late 1820s and early 1830s. It lasted until the mid-1850s, when the Whig party disintegrated and the modern Republican party was born. This period of about a generation is typically called "the age of Jackson." Thus one of the two parties dominates the image of the time, and only by an active effort do we recall that the Jacksonian Democrats had an opposition. Most textbooks and anthologies reinforce the general impression by emphasizing the significance of Andrew Jackson and his supporters. This volume attempts to redress the balance by reprinting some of the more important statements of Jackson's competitors.

There are of course reasons why the Whigs have been less well remembered than the Democrats. The most important is that the Whigs were less successful in competing for national office, and in history, as in life, nothing succeeds like success. Another is that the Democratic party still survives as an institution (it is the oldest political party in the world) while the Whig party does not. The Whigs were also the victims of sheer bad luck. American history is usually written from the vantage point of the White House; but the two presidents whom the Whigs elected, William Henry Harrison in 1840 and Zachary Taylor in 1848, both died in office after serving only one month and sixteen months, respectively. And although the great Whig senators Daniel Webster and Henry Clay have permanent places in the American memory, no purely congressional leader has ever been able to capture the public imagination as successfully as our most dynamic chief executives.

Nevertheless the Whigs should not be ignored by anyone seeking to understand America and its past. In fact, the Whig party was more powerful than a quick look at the presidential elections of the period (the Democrats won five to the Whigs' two) would indicate. The actual division between the two major parties in the days of the Whigs and Jacksonians was quite close. In most parts of the country only a few percentage points separated winners from losers at the polls. Indeed, the fairly even distribution of partisan strength is one of the distinctive characteristics of the second American party system. In the first and third party systems, there have been cities, states, and whole regions that were virtually one-party monopolies; in the second system it was rare for either party to enjoy such overwhelming dominance over any extensive area. The relative weakness of the Whig party in presidential politics gives little sign of its strength in congressional, state, and local politics.

As one of the two major parties in a constitutional democracy, the Whigs counted approximately half the voting population as at least occasional supporters. Such a large constituency was naturally very heterogeneous. There were Whigs in all occupational groups, economic classes, social strata, geographic regions, and religious denominations. Despite this diversity, one can hazard some generalizations about the kind of people who became Whigs, just as political scientists today (aided by far more complete data) can distinguish Republicans from Democrats in the population. Business and professional men tended to be Whigs. Industrial workers did not necessarily vote against their employers; frequently wage earners and others who felt they had a stake in the growth of manufacturing were also Whigs. With regard to people engaged in agriculture it is harder to judge, but there is reason to believe that farmers who produced for a commercial market were more likely to be Whigs than were those engaged in self-sustaining, or subsistence, agriculture. The Whig party was especially strong in southern New England as well as in parts of the country (such as eastern Tennessee) that hoped for government-aided economic development projects—"internal improvements" as they were called. People of New England extraction and members of the sects of New England Protestantism (Congregationalists, Unitarians, "New School" Presbyterians) also seem to have voted Whig in disproportionate numbers. Statistical evidence is sparse, but observers at the time usually assumed that people with greater income, education, and respectability were more likely to be Whig. Yet those at the very bottom of the social ladder also generally supported the Whigs: the blacks—insofar as they were permitted political participation—found the Whigs decidedly the lesser of white evils.

The generation when the Whig party existed was one of intense political excitement in the United States. Elections were frequent because there were many annual and biennial terms of office, and the voting days in different states were staggered throughout the year. Results of national elections trickled in slowly for weeks. United States senators were chosen by state legislatures that sometimes spent months reaching a decision. Thus political agitation was more or less constant, but the electorate was not (as yet) jaded. Indexes of voter turnout were high—higher than they were to be again for a century—and revealed widespread participation in the political process. The popular election of presidential electors was adopted everywhere except in South Carolina, and party nominating conventions replaced the congressional caucus as the means of selecting presidential candidates. Many state legislatures were reapportioned to make them more democratic. Virtually all property and religious qualifications for office and voting that remained were abolished in this period. Though women and most nonwhites were still excluded from the franchise, the political base was broader than it had been in any previous time or place.

Party politics was our first national sport, and the public played and watched the great game with enthusiasm. Torchlight parades, electioneering songs and slogans, debates, and speeches were popular entertainment. But there was a serious side to all this "politicking" that is sometimes overlooked. If the press was intensely partisan (on both sides) and many voters fervently committed, it was not simply out of longing for diversion. The fact is that the politicians were talking about important matters. The politics of the 1830s and 1840s centered on issues to a far greater extent than did the politics of, say, the post-reconstruction era.

The issues provide the logical place to begin a description of Whig thought. The chief reason for remembering the Whig party today is that it advanced a particular program of national development. The Whig economic platform called for purposeful intervention by the federal government to levy tariffs protecting domestic industry, to subsidize internal improvements like turnpikes and canals, and to charter a national bank that would regulate the currency and make tax revenues available for private investment. Taken together, the various facets of this program form a vision of America as an economically diversified country in which commerce and industry would take their place alongside agriculture. Practically all Americans expected and wanted their nation to grow and prosper, but they disagreed as to how progress might best be achieved. The Democrats inclined toward free trade and laissez-faire; when government action was required, they preferred to leave it to the states and local communities. The Whigs were more concerned with providing conscious, centralized direction to social change.

It would be a mistake, however, to identify the Whigs with what is called liberalism in the twentieth century. In the first place Whig policies did not have the objective of redistributing wealth or diminishing the influence of the privileged. Second, the Whigs thought of themselves as conservatives, preserving an identifiable social heritage in the strange environment of the New World. Furthermore, the Whigs distrusted the executive branch of the federal government (doubtlessly because they had been so disturbed by the conduct of Andrew Jackson in the White House), in sharp contrast to twentieth-century liberals who have generally endorsed a strong presidency. How these and other complications figured in the thinking of the Whigs will be revealed in the selections that follow, where the Whig leaders speak for themselves. Here I simply offer a few observations on how the Whigs' ideas compared with those of their Jacksonian opponents.

The Whig economic program entailed a political and constitutional theory emphasizing nationalism rather than states' rights. Much of the opposition to that program stemmed from doubts regarding its constitutionality, doubts the Whigs labored hard to alleviate. The relationship between the state and national governments was unclear in the early years of the republic; indeed, the leading precedents (the Dutch and Swiss confederations and the Holy Roman Empire) indicated that the central authority in a federal system was likely to remain weak. The Whigs, though seeking to limit the power of the president, were committed to enhancing the power of Congress and the federal judiciary in order to implement their economic program. The Democrats were usually more solicitous of the rights of the states, and construed the powers delegated to the federal government narrowly. But a somewhat different kind of nationalism was also emerging within the Democratic party. It was oriented toward foreign rather than domestic policy, and its slogan was "manifest destiny." During the 1840s it became clear that the Democrats were far more expansionist and belligerent toward foreign countries (whether Britain, France, or Mexico) than the Whigs.

Whig economic policies were integrated into a wide context of social thought; indeed, Whiggery was as much a cultural and moral posture as an economic or political program. The specific disagreements between Whigs and Democrats were rooted in larger differences about the nature and destiny of American society. The two parties disagreed not only over means but also over ends; they presented the electorate with rival images of national purpose. To put things very broadly, the Whigs proposed a society that would be economically diverse but culturally uniform; the Democrats preferred economic uniformity but were more tolerant of cultural and moral diversity.

Both Democrats and Whigs often praised the rural way of life—scarcely surprising in a country still predominantly agricultural—but the Whigs were more willing to confront the probability of increasing industrialization and division of labor. The Democrats regarded industrialization with misgivings; an economically homogeneous land of agriculturalists seemed preferable in many ways to them. Since changes were already under way, taking America farther and farther from the nation of yeomen farmers envisioned by Thomas Jefferson, it has been suggested that the Whigs were appealing to people's hopes and the Democrats to their fears. This distinction (proposed by the historian Marvin Meyers) holds well for economic policy, though in other realms the Whigs too had their apprehensions. On cultural and moral issues it was often the Whigs who were anxious and the Democrats who were optimistic or complacent.

As the first half of this anthology deals with economic and political thought, so the second half is devoted to illustrating Whig ideas on culture and social morality. Though the Whigs were a diverse lot, certain common preoccupations recur in their writings. The number of thematic "reverberations" in the political and social expression of the period is truly remarkable. While Jacksonian rhetoric emphasized "equality" (usually restricted in practice to equality of opportunity for white males), the Whigs stressed "morality." The values we associate with the "Puritan ethic," such as respect for hard work, honesty, and the deferment of gratification, can be found easily among both Whigs and Democrats, but the Whigs worried more about their enforcement. Whig morality was corporate as well as individual; the community, like its members, was expected to set an example of virtue. As a result the Whigs' cultural attitudes were highly prescriptive: Whigs looked to the family, the church, the school, voluntary associations, and the state to impose their values on others. Whig morality could take unlovely forms of intolerance, as it did at times in the nativist, sabbatarian, and temperance movements. On the other hand it also fueled a moral zeal for reforms that seem to have been sorely needed, like improvement of the treatment of the insane and opposition to slavery. The Democrats, one must record, had a less developed sense of public morality. Emphasizing as they did that one white man was as good as another, they were more willing to "live and let live," and consequently lacked both the vices and virtues that went with Whiggishness.

In the long run the Whigs' contribution to American society was at least as great as that of their Democratic contemporaries. The economic and technological changes going on in the nineteenth century ultimately produced an economy more like that envisioned by the Whigs than like the arcadia Jeffersonians and Jacksonians idealized. Most of the Whigs' economic platform was enacted by their successors: the Republican party firmly established a protective tariff and subsidized business enterprise; the Democrats under Wilson finally organized a nationwide banking system, though it operated on different principles from those the Whigs envisioned. The political evolution of the country has consistently increased the power of the federal government; "states' rights" retains less power as a political rallying cry than ever. Some of the social reforms the Whigs supported have passed into history so completely that by now we are more conscious of their shortcomings than of their achievements (free public education, for example). Other Whig objectives were never attained (such as respect for the rights of the Indians) or proved disastrous when finally implemented (like prohibition of liquor). As for the Democrats, the individualism and egalitarianism they preached have firmly taken root in the American character; the imposition of that cultural uniformity sought by the Whigs has long since become a lost cause. But as long as there are still people who strive to awaken a sense of public responsibility in politics and the arts, the spirit of the Whig reformers will not be altogether dead. Since America has become diversified both economically and culturally, perhaps one could say that the Whigs and Jacksonians have each had half their vision fulfilled.

A majority of the selections that follow were originally given as speeches; they were composed to be heard, not read. The techniques of oral delivery necessarily differ from those of literary communication. A speaker's audience cannot ponder or re-read a passage, so he usually restates his ideas, paraphrasing them until he is sure their import has been digested. This often makes speeches seem repetitious in print, particularly the speeches of a former and more leisurely era. Most of the pieces reprinted here have been cut, but I have sought in each case to retain the original flavor. Antebellum America was a time and place when eloquence was highly valued, when politicians, preachers, lawyers, and traveling lecturers all vied for the recognition that oratory won. Today our tastes are different, and the rhetoric of the Whigs often seems flowery or pompous. A certain integrity must be conceded, however, to the aesthetics of that period. One of the objectives of this anthology is to create some feeling for the sensibility of an age of elocution.

Part One

ECONOMIC PROGRAM

1

PROLOGUE TO WHIGGERY

John Quincy Adams
STATE OF THE UNION MESSAGE

John Quincy Adams (1767–1848) was probably America's greatest diplomat and one of our greatest defenders of civil liberties. His career in foreign affairs reached its climax when as secretary of state under President Monroe he was primarily responsible for formulating the policy known as the Monroe Doctrine. In later years "Old Man Eloquent" served long and honorably in the House of Representatives as a champion of free expression and a leader among the antislavery members. Adams' term as sixth president of the United States proved a bitter and frustrating interlude between these two careers. As his first "state of the union" message makes clear, Adams espoused a vigorous role for the federal government. But the objectives outlined here were not palatable to his political enemies who controlled Congress. They succeeded in blocking most of his initiatives and defeated him for reelection, installing Andrew Jackson in his place.

The vision of a strong central government promoting technology, education, and economic development persisted. The new Whig party that would come into being after Adams left the White House reaffirmed it. But because of the strong military and naval posture here advocated, the message may be read as foreshadowing the aggressive foreign policy of the Jacksonian Democrats as well as the domestic program of the Whigs.

Fellow-Citizens of the Senate and of the House of Representatives:
In taking a general survey of the concerns of our beloved country with reference to subjects interesting to the common welfare, the first sentiment which impresses itself upon the mind is of gratitude to the

SOURCE. John Quincy Adams, "First Annual Message, December 6, 1825," *Messages and Papers of the Presidents*, ed. James D. Richardson (Washington, D.C., 1900), II, 299–317.

11

Omnipotent Disposer of All Good for the continuance of the signal blessings of His providence, and especially for that health which to an unusual extent has prevailed within our borders, and for that abundance which in the vicissitudes of the seasons has been scattered with profusion over our land. Nor ought we less to ascribe to Him the glory that we are permitted to enjoy the bounties of His hand in peace and tranquillity—in peace with all the other nations of the earth, in tranquillity among ourselves. There has, indeed, rarely been a period in the history of civilized man in which the general condition of the Christian nations has been marked so extensively by peace and prosperity. . . .

It is with great satisfaction that I am enabled to bear witness to the liberal spirit with which the Republic of Colombia has made satisfaction for well-established claims . . . and among the documents now communicated to Congress will be distinguished a treaty of commerce and navigation with that Republic, the ratifications of which have been exchanged since the last recess of the Legislature. The negotiation of similar treaties with all the independent South American States has been contemplated and may yet be accomplished. The basis of them all, as proposed by the United States, has been laid in two principles—the one of entire and unqualified reciprocity, the other the mutual obligation of the parties to place each other permanently upon the footing of the most favored nation. These principles are, indeed, indispensable to the effectual emancipation of the American hemisphere from the thraldom of colonizing monopolies and exclusions, an event rapidly realizing in the progress of human affairs, and which the resistance still opposed in certain parts of Europe to the acknowledgment of the Southern American Republics as independent States will, it is believed, contribute more effectually to accomplish. . . .

Among the measures which have been suggested to them by the new relations with one another, resulting from the recent changes in their condition, is that of assembling at the Isthmus of Panama a congress, at which each of them should be represented, to deliberate upon objects important to the welfare of all. The Republics of Colombia, of Mexico, and of Central America have already deputed plenipotentiaries to such a meeting, and they have invited the United States to be also represented there by their ministers. The invitation has been accepted, and ministers on the part of the United States will be commissioned to attend at those deliberations, and to take part in them so far as may be compatible with that neutrality from which it is neither our intention nor the desire of the other American States that we should depart. . . .

Among the unequivocal indications of our national prosperity is the flourishing state of our finances. The revenues of the present year, from all their principal sources, will exceed the anticipations of the last. . . .

The amount of duties secured on merchandise imported since the commencement of the year is about twenty-five millions and a half, and that which will accrue during the current quarter is estimated at five millions and a half; from these thirty-one millions, deducting the drawbacks, estimated at less than seven millions, a sum exceeding twenty-four millions will constitute the revenue of the year, and will exceed the whole expenditures of the year. The entire amount of the public debt remaining due on the 1st of January next will be short of $81,000,000. . . .

The act of Congress of the 3d of March last, directing the Secretary of the Treasury to subscribe, in the name and for the use of the United States, for 1,500 shares of the capital stock of the Chesapeake and Delaware Canal Company, has been executed by the actual subscription for the amount specified; and such other measures have been adopted by that officer, under the act, as the fulfillment of its intentions requires. The latest accounts received of this important undertaking authorize the belief that it is in successful progress.

The payments into the Treasury from the proceeds of the sales of the public lands during the present year were estimated at $1,000,000. The actual receipts of the first two quarters have fallen very little short of that sum; it is not expected that the second half of the year will be equally productive, but the income of the year from that source may now be safely estimated at a million and a half. . . .

The organization and discipline of the Army are effective and satisfactory. To counteract the prevalence of desertion among the troops it has been suggested to withhold from the men a small portion of their monthly pay until the period of their discharge; and some expedient appears to be necessary to preserve and maintain among the officers so much of the art of horsemanship as could scarcely fail to be found wanting on the possible sudden eruption of a war, which should take us unprovided with a single corps of cavalry. The Military Academy at West Point, under the restrictions of a severe but paternal superintendence, recommends itself more and more to the patronage of the nation, and the numbers of meritorious officers which it forms and introduces to the public service furnishes the means of multiplying

the undertakings of public improvements to which their acquirements at that institution are peculiarly adapted. The school of
artillery practice established at Fortress Monroe is well suited to the
same purpose, and may need the aid of further legislative provision to
the same end. The reports of the various officers at the head of the
administrative branches of the military service, connected with the
quartering, clothing, subsistence, health, and pay of the Army, exhibit
the assiduous vigilance of those officers in the performance of their
respective duties, and the faithful accountability which has pervaded
every part of the system. . . .

On the 12th of February last a treaty was signed at the Indian
Springs between commissioners appointed on the part of the United
States and certain chiefs and individuals of the Creek Nation of
Indians, which was received at the seat of Government only a very
few days before the close of the last session of Congress and of the late
Administration. The advice and consent of the Senate was given to it
on the 3d of March, too late for it to receive the ratification of the then
President of the United States; it was ratified on the 7th of March,
under the unsuspecting impression that it had been negotiated in good
faith and in the confidence inspired by the recommendation of the
Senate. The subsequent transactions in relation to this treaty will
form the subject of a separate communication.[1]

The appropriations made by Congress for public works, as well in
the construction of fortifications as for purposes of internal improvement, so far as they have been expended, have been faithfully applied.
Their progress has been delayed by the want of suitable officers for
superintending them. An increase of both the corps of engineers,
military and topographical, was recommended by my predecessor at
the last session of Congress. The reasons upon which that recommendation was founded subsist in all their force and have acquired additional urgency since that time. It may also be expedient to organize
the topographical engineers into a corps similar to the present establishment of the Corps of Engineers. The Military Academy at West
Point will furnish from the cadets annually graduated there officers
well qualified for carrying this measure into effect.

The Board of Engineers for Internal Improvement, appointed for
carrying into execution the act of Congress of 30th of April, 1824, "to

---

[1]Adams had discovered that this treaty ceding lands to the whites had been
fraudulently obtained. Despite his efforts to rectify matters, however, the
Creeks did not recover their territory. Ed.

procure the necessary surveys, plans, and estimates on the subject of roads and canals," have been actively engaged in that service from the close of the last session of Congress. They have completed the surveys necessary for ascertaining the practicability of a canal from the Chesapeake Bay to the Ohio River, and are preparing a full report on that subject, which, when completed, will be laid before you. The same observation is to be made with regard to the two other objects of national importance upon which the Board have been occupied, namely, the accomplishment of a national road from this city to New Orleans, and the practicability of uniting the waters of Lake Memphramagog with Connecticut River and the improvement of the navigation of that river. The surveys have been made and are nearly completed. The report may be expected at an early period during the present session of Congress.

The acts of Congress of the last session relative to the surveying, marking, or laying out roads in the Teritories of Florida, Arkansas, and Michigan, from Missouri to Mexico, and for the continuation of the Cumberland road, are, some of them, fully executed, and others in the process of execution. Those for completing or commencing fortifications have been delayed only so far as the Corps of Engineers has been inadequate to furnish officers for the necessary superintendence of the works. . . . The light-houses and monuments for the safety of our commerce and mariners, the works for the security of Plymouth Beach and for the preservation of the islands in Boston Harbor, have received the attention required by the laws relating to those objects respectively. The continuation of the Cumberland road, the most important of them all, after surmounting no inconsiderable difficulty in fixing upon the direction of the road, has commenced under the most promising auspices, with the improvements of recent invention in the mode of construction, and with the advantage of a great reduction in the comparative cost of the work. . . .

The first service of a new frigate has been performed in restoring to his native soil and domestic enjoyments the veteran hero whose youthful blood and treasure had freely flowed in the cause of our country's independence, and whose whole life has been a series of services and sacrifices to the improvement of his fellow-men. The visit of General Lafayette, alike honorable to himself and to our country, closed, as it had commenced, with the most affecting testimonials of devoted attachment on his part, and of unbounded gratitude of this people to him in return. It will form hereafter a pleasing incident in the annals of our Union, giving to real history the intense interest of romance and signally marking the unpurchasable tribute of a great nation's social affections to the disinterested champion of the liberties of human-kind.

The constant maintenance of a small squadron in the Mediterranean is a necessary substitute for the humiliating alternative of paying tribute for the security of our commerce in that sea, and for a precarious peace, at the mercy of every caprice of four Barbary States, by whom it was liable to be violated. An additional motive for keeping a respectable force stationed there at this time is found in the maritime war raging between the Greeks and the Turks, and in which the neutral navigation of this Union is always in danger of outrage and depredation. A few instances have occurred of such depredations upon our merchant vessels by privateers or pirates wearing the Grecian flag, but without real authority from the Greek or any other Government. The heroic struggles of the Greeks themselves, in which our warmest sympathies as freemen and Christians have been engaged, have continued to be maintained with vicissitudes of success adverse and favorable.

Similar motives have rendered expedient the keeping of a like force on the coasts of Peru and Chile on the Pacific. The irregular and convulsive character of the war upon the shores has been extended to the conflicts upon the ocean. An active warfare has been kept up for years with alternate success, though generally to the advantage of the American patriots. . . .

The objects of the West India Squadron have been to carry into execution the laws for the suppression of the African slave trade; for the protection of our commerce against vessels of piratical character, though bearing commissions from either of the belligerent parties; for its protection against open and unequivocal pirates. These objects during the present year have been accomplished more effectually than at any former period. The African slave trade has long been excluded from the use of our flag, and if some few citizens of our country have continued to set the laws of the Union as well as those of nature and humanity at defiance by persevering in that abominable traffic, it has been only by sheltering themselves under the banners of other nations less earnest for the total extinction of the trade than ours. . . .

It were, indeed, a vain and dangerous illusion to believe that in the present or probable condition of human society a commerce so extensive and so rich as ours could exist and be pursued in safety without the continual support of a military marine—the only arm by which the power of this Confederacy can be estimated or felt by foreign nations, and the only standing military force which can never be dangerous to our own liberties at home. A permanent naval peace establishment, therefore, adapted to our present condition, and adaptable to that gigantic growth with which the nation is advancing in its career, is among the subjects which have already occupied the foresight of the last Congress, and which will deserve your serious deliberations. . . .

Upon this first occasion of addressing the Legislature of the Union, with which I have been honored, in presenting to their view the execution so far as it has been effected of the measures sanctioned by them for promoting the internal improvement of our country, I can not close the communication without recommending to their calm and persevering consideration the general principle in a more enlarged extent. The great object of the institution of civil government is the improvement of the condition of those who are parties to the social compact, and no government, in whatever form constituted, can accomplish the lawful ends of its institution but in proportion as it improves the condition of those over whom it is established. Roads and canals, by multiplying and facilitating the communications and intercourse between distant regions and multitudes of men, are among the most important means of improvement. But moral, political, intellectual improvement are duties assigned by the Author of Our Existence to social no less than to individual man. For the fulfillment of those duties governments are invested with power, and to the attainment of the end—the progressive improvement of the condition of the governed—the exercise of delegated powers is a duty as sacred and indispensable as the usurpation of powers not granted is criminal and odious. Among the first, perhaps the very first, instrument for the improvement of the condition of men is knowledge, and to the acquisition of much of the knowledge adapted to the wants, the comforts, and enjoyments of human life public institutions and seminaries of learning are essential. So convinced of this was the first of my predecessors in this office, now first in the memory, as, living, he was first in the hearts, of our countrymen, that once and again in his addresses to the Congresses with whom he cooperated in the public service he earnestly recommended the establishment of seminaries of learning, to prepare for all the emergencies of peace and war—a national university and a military academy. With respect to the latter, had he lived to the present day, in turning his eyes to the institution at West Point he would have enjoyed the gratification of his most earnest wishes; but in surveying the city which has been honored with his name he would have seen the spot of earth which he had destined and bequeathed to the use and benefit of his country as the site for an university still bare and barren.

In assuming her station among the civilized nations of the earth it would seem that our country had contracted the engagement to contribute her share of mind, of labor, and of expense to the improvement of those parts of knowledge which lie beyond the reach of individual acquisition, and particularly to geographical and astronomical science. Looking back to the history only of the half century since the declaration of our independence, and observing the generous emulation with which the Governments of France, Great Britain, and Russia have devoted the genius, the intelligence, the treasures of their respective nations to the common improvement of the species in these branches of science, is it not incumbent upon us to inquire whether we are not bound by obligations of a high and honorable character to contribute our portion of energy and exertion to the common stock? The voyages of discovery prosecuted in the course of that time at the expense of those nations have not only redounded to their glory, but to the improvement of human knowledge. We have been partakers of that improvement and owe for it a sacred debt, not only of gratitude, but of equal or proportional exertion in the same common cause. Of the cost of these undertakings, if the mere expenditures of outfit, equipment, and completion of the expeditions were to be considered the only charges, it would be unworthy of a great and generous nation to take a second thought. One hundred expeditions of circumnavigation like those of Cook and La Perouse would not burden the exchequer of the nation fitting them out so much as the ways and means of defraying a single campaign in war. But if we take into the account the lives of those benefactors of mankind of which their services in the cause of their species were the purchase, how shall the cost of those heroic enterprises be estimated, and what compensation can be made to them or to their countries for them? Is it not by bearing them in affectionate remembrance? Is it not still more by imitating their example—by enabling countrymen of our own to pursue the same career and to hazard their lives in the same cause?

In inviting the attention of Congress to the subject of internal improvements upon a view thus enlarged it is not my design to recommend the equipment of an expedition for circumnavigating the globe for purposes of scientific research and inquiry. We have objects of useful investigation nearer home, and to which our cares may be more beneficially applied. The interior of our own territories has yet been very imperfectly explored. Our coasts along many degrees of latitude upon the shores of the Pacific Ocean, though much frequented by our spirited commercial navigators, have been barely visited by our public ships. The River of the West, first fully discovered and navigated by a countryman of our own, still bears the name of the ship in which he ascended its waters, and claims the protection of our armed national flag at its mouth. With the establishment of a military post there or at some other point of that coast, recommended by my predecessor and already matured in the deliberations of the last Congress, I would suggest the expediency of connecting the equipment of a public ship for the exploration of the whole northwest coast of this continent.

The establishment of an uniform standard of weights and measures was one of the specific objects contemplated in the formation of our Constitution, and to fix that standard was one of the powers delegated by express terms in that instrument to Congress. The Governments of Great Britain and France have scarcely ceased to be occupied with inquiries and speculations on the same subject since the existence of our Constitution, and with them it has expanded into profound, laborious, and expensive researches into the figure of the earth and the comparative length of the pendulum vibrating seconds in various latitudes from the equator to the pole. These researches have resulted in the composition and publication of several works highly interesting to the cause of science. The experiments are yet in the process of performance. Some of them have recently been made on our own shores, within the walls of one of our own colleges, and partly by one of our own fellow-citizens. It would be honorable to our country if the sequel of the same experiments should be countenanced by the patronage of our Government, as they have hitherto been by those of France and Britain.

Connected with the establishment of an university, or separate from it, might be undertaken the erection of an astronomical observatory, with provision for the support of an astronomer, to be in constant attendance of observation upon the phenomena of the heavens, and for the periodical publication of his observations. It is with no feeling of pride as an American that the remark may be made that on the comparatively small territorial surface of Europe there are existing upward of 130 of these light-houses of the skies, while throughout the whole American hemisphere there is not one. If we reflect a moment upon the discoveries which in the last four centuries have been made in the physical constitution of the universe by the means of these buildings and of observers stationed in them, shall we doubt of their usefulness to every nation? And while scarcely a year passes over our heads without bringing some new astronomical discovery to light, which we must fain receive at second hand from Europe, are we not cutting ourselves off from the means of returning light for light while we have neither observatory nor observer upon our half of the globe and the earth revolves in perpetual darkness to our unsearching eyes? . . .

The laws relating to the administration of the Patent Office are deserving of much consideration and perhaps susceptible of some improvement. The grant of power to regulate the action of Congress upon this subject has specified both the end to be obtained and the means by which it is to be effected, "to promote the progress of science and useful arts by securing for limited times to authors and inventors the exclusive right to their respective writings and discoveries." If an honest pride might be indulged in the reflection that on the records of that office are already found inventions the usefulness of which has scarcely been transcended in the annals of human ingenuity, would not its exultation be allayed by the inquiry whether the laws have effectively insured to the inventors the reward destined to them by the Constitution—even a limited term of exclusive right to their discoveries?

On the 24th of December, 1799, it was resolved by Congress that a marble monument should be erected by the United States in the Capitol at the city of Washington; that the family of General Washington should be requested to permit his body to be deposited under it, and that the monument be so designed as to commemorate the great events of his military and political life. In reminding Congress of this resolution and that the monument contemplated by it remains yet without execution, I shall indulge only the remarks that the works at the Capitol are approaching to completion; that the consent of the family, desired by the resolution, was requested and obtained; that a monument has been recently erected in this city over the remains of another distinguished patriot of the Revolution, and that a spot has been reserved within the walls where you are deliberating for the benefit of this and future ages, in which the mortal remains may be deposited of him whose spirit hovers over you and listens with delight to every act of the representatives of his nation which can tend to exalt and adorn his and their country.

The Constitution under which you are assembled is a charter of limited powers. After full and solemn deliberation upon all or any of the objects which, urged by an irresistible sense of my own duty, I have recommended to your attention should you come to the conclusion that, however desirable in themselves, the enactment of laws for effecting them would transcend the powers committed to you by that venerable instrument which we are all bound to support, let no consideration induce you to assume the exercise of powers not granted to you by the people. But if the power to exercise exclusive legislation in all cases whatsoever over the District of Columbia; if the power to lay and collect taxes, duties, imposts, and excises, to pay the debts and provide for the common defense and general welfare of the United States; if the power to regulate commerce with foreign nations and among the several States and with the Indian tribes, to fix the standard of weights and measures, to establish post-offices and post-roads, to declare war, to raise and support armies, to provide and maintain a navy, to dispose of and make all needful rules and regulations respecting the territory or other property belonging to the United States, and to make all laws which shall be necessary and proper for carrying these powers into execution—if these powers and others enumerated in the Constitution may be effectually brought into action by laws promoting the improvement of agriculture, commerce, and manufactures, the cultivation and encouragement of the mechanic and of the elegant arts, the advancement of literature, and the progress of the sciences, ornamental and profound, to refrain from exercising them for the benefit of the people themselves would be to hide in the earth the talent committed to our charge—would be treachery to the most sacred of trusts.

The spirit of improvement is abroad upon the earth. It stimulates the hearts and sharpens the faculties not of our fellow-citizens alone, but of the nations of Europe and of their rulers. While dwelling with pleasing satisfaction upon the superior excellence of our political institutions, let us not be unmindful that liberty is power; that the nation blessed with the largest portion of liberty must in proportion to its numbers be the most powerful nation upon earth, and that the tenure of power by man is, in the moral purposes of his Creator, upon condition that it shall be exercised to ends of beneficence, to improve the condition of himself and his fellowmen. While foreign nations less blessed with that freedom which is power than ourselves are advancing with gigantic strides in the career of public improvement, were we to slumber in indolence or fold up our arms and proclaim to the world that we are palsied by the will of our constituents, would it not be to cast away the bounties of Providence and doom ourselves to perpetual inferiority? In the course of the year now drawing to its close we have beheld, under the auspices and at the expense of one State of this Union, a new university unfolding its portals to the sons of science and holding up the torch of human improvement to eyes that seek the light. We have seen under the persevering and enlightened enterprise of another State the waters of our western lakes mingle with those of the ocean. If undertakings like these have been accomplished in the compass of a few years by the authority of single members of our Confederation, can we, the representative authorities of the whole Union, fall behind our fellow-servants in the exercise of the trust committed to us for the benefit of our common sovereign by the accomplishment of works important to the whole and to which neither the authority nor the resources of any one State can be adequate?

Finally, fellow-citizens, I shall await with cheering hope and faithful cooperation the result of your deliberations, assured that, without encroaching upon the powers reserved to the authorities of the respective States or to the people, you will, with a due sense of your obligations to your country and of the high responsibilities weighing upon yourselves, give efficacy to the means committed to you for the common good. And may He who searches the hearts of the children of men prosper your exertions to secure the blessings of peace and promote the highest welfare of our country.

2

THE PROMISE OF INDUSTRIALIZATION

Edward Everett
FOURTH OF JULY ADDRESS AT LOWELL, MASSACHUSETTS

The career of Edward Everett (1794–1865) illustrates the wide range of opportunities available to the orator in nineteenth-century America. Everett was by turns a preacher, professor, politician, journalist, diplomat, and lecturer. The first American to earn a Ph.D. (in Germany, since no institution in this country as yet offered the degree), he served as governor of Massachusetts, president of Harvard, minister to Britain, and secretary of state. A whole generation embraced him as the ideal man of letters; enthralled by his eloquence, Ralph Waldo Emerson called him "our Cicero." What was to be the crowning glory of his career ended ironically: Everett delivered a two-hour oration at the dedication of the national cemetery at Gettysburg, only to be forever upstaged by Lincoln's brief closing remarks.

When Everett gave the following speech, he was a congressman from Massachusetts. In Lowell, one of the first textile mill towns, he took the occasion of Independence Day to discourse on the benefits of manufacturing to America. Everett always remained a loyal Whig and as late as 1860 ran as vice-presidential candidate of the Constitutional Union party, the Whigs' last gasp.

A considerable part of my time, since I was honored with your invitation, has been necessarily devoted by me to fulfilling a previous engagement. I therefore appear before you this morning under circumstances creating some claim to your indulgence.

It seemed, however, to me that this was peculiarly the occasion when a man ought to be ready and willing to appear before his

SOURCE. Edward Everett, "Fourth of July at Lowell" (1830), *Orations and Speeches on Various Occasions* (Boston, 1850), I, 47–66.

fellow-citizens with little or no preparation. It is, in fact, eminently the day for short notice. It could not well be shorter than that which our fathers had to gird on the harness for the great conflicts which led to the declaration of independence. Rarely, in the course of human affairs, is shorter notice of important events given than that which called the citizens of Middlesex to arms on the nineteenth of April, 1775. Their deeds were not those of veteran armies maneuvering for whole campaigns under skilful generals. The very name which they gave themselves is their best description. They were *minute men;* —they held themselves ready to move without any notice;—and their marching orders came at last from the alarm-bell, at midnight.

I might go a little farther, and say, fellow-citizens of Lowell, that your town itself, in its very existence, affords signal authority for doing things at short notice. If, on the fourth of July, 1820,—ten years ago only,—a painter had come to the confluence of the Merrimack and Concord Rivers, and sketched upon his canvas the panorama of such a city as this, and pronounced that, in ten years, such a settlement would be found on this spot, it would have been thought a very extravagant suggestion. If he had said, that, in the course of forty or fifty years, such a population would be gathered here, with all these manufacturing establishments, private dwellings, warehouses, schools, and churches, he would have been thought to indulge a bold, but pleasing, vision, not, perhaps, beyond the range of probability. . . .

Finally, my friends, without wishing to run down the idea, I may remark, that our whole country has taken her present position in the family of nations on very short notice. Our history seems a great political romance. In the annals of most other states, ancient and modern, there is a tardiness of growth, which, if our own progress be assumed as the standard of comparison, we hardly know how to explain. Greece had been settled a thousand years before she took any great part on the theatre of the world. Rome, at the end of five centuries from the foundation of the city, was not so powerful as the state of Massachusetts. It is not much short of two thousand years since the light of the ancient civilization—such as it was—began to dawn on Great Britain. Its inhabitants have been a Christianized people for nearly fifteen centuries. . . .

What do we witness in this country? Compare our present condition with that of this then barbarous wilderness two centuries ago. With what rapidity the civilization of Europe has been caught up, naturalized, and, in many points of material growth and useful art, carried beyond the foreign standard! Consider our rapid progress even in the last generation, not merely in appropriating the arts of the old world, but in others of our own invention or great improvement. Take the case of steam navigation as a striking example. It has been known, for a century or more, that the vapor of boiling water is the most powerful mechanical agent at our command. The steam engine was brought near to perfection, by Bolton and Watt, sixty years ago; and it is not much less than that time since attempts began to be made to solve the problem of steam navigation. Twenty years ago, there were steamers regularly plying on the North River and Staten Island Sound; but so lately as eleven years ago, I think, there was no communication by steam between Liverpool and Dublin, or between Dover and Calais; nor did the use of steamers spread extensively in any direction in Europe till they had covered the American waters.

Take another example, in the agricultural staple so closely connected with the industry of Lowell. The southern parts of Europe, Egypt, and many other portions of Africa, and a broad zone in Asia, possess a soil and climate favorable to the growth of cotton. It is, in fact, an indigenous product of Asia, Africa, or both. It has been cultivated in those countries from time immemorial: the oldest European historians speak of its use. It is, also, an indigenous product throughout a broad belt on the American continent; and was cultivated by the aborgines before the discovery of Columbus. Although it was the leading principle of the colonial system to encourage the cultivation in the colonies of all those articles which would be useful to the manufactures of the mother country, not a bale of cotton is known to have been exported from the United States to Great Britain before the revolution. Immediately after the close of the revolutionary war, attention began to be turned to this subject in several parts of the Southern States. The culture of cotton rapidly increased; and, since the invention of the cotton gin, has become, next to the cereal grains, the most important agricultural product. It is supposed, that, for the present year, the cotton crop of the United States will amount to one million of bales—five times, I presume, the amount raised for exportation in all the rest of the world.

Take another example, in commerce and navigation, and one peculiarly illustrative of the effect, on the industry of the country, of the political independence established on the day which we commemorate. The principles of the colonial system confined our trade and navigation to the intercourse of the mother country. The individuals are living, or recently deceased, who made the first voyages from this country to the Baltic, to the Mediterranean, or around either of the great capes of the world. . . . Nor is the progress less remarkable which has been made since [independence] in the interior of the continent. The settlement of our western country is a marvel in human affairs. . . .

This astonishing growth has evidently not only been subsequent to the declaration of independence, but consequent upon its establishment, as effect upon cause; and this both by a removal of specific obstacles to our progress, which were imposed by the colonial system, and by the general operation of the new political order of things on the mind and character of the country. The reason why England has long excelled every other country in Europe, in the extent of her available resources, and in the cultivation of most of the practical arts, is to be found in those principles of constitutional representative government, in that parliamentary freedom and popular energy which cannot exist under any form of despotism. The still more complete establishment of similar principles here, I take to be the chief cause of a still more accelerated march of improvement. It is usual to consider human labor as the measure of value. That which can be got by any one without labor, directly or indirectly performed, as the common daylight and air, has no exchangeable value. That which requires the greatest amount of labor for its production, other things being equal, is most valuable. But there is as much mere physical capacity for labor dormant in a population of serfs and slaves, or of the subjects of an Oriental despotism, as in an equal population of the freest country on earth. . . . It is the spirit of a free country which animates and gives energy to its labor; which puts the mass in action, gives it motive and intensity, makes it inventive, sends it off in new directions, subdues to its command all the powers of nature, and enlists in its service an army of machines, that do all but think and talk. Compare a hand loom with a power loom; a barge, poled up against the current of a river, with a steamer breasting its force. The difference is not greater between them than between the efficiency of labor under a free or despotic government; in an independent state or a colony. . . .

This is a general operation of the establishment of an independent government in the United States of America, which has not perhaps been enough considered among us. We have looked too exclusively to the mere political change, and the substitution of a domestic for a foreign rule, as an historical fact, flattering to the national vanity. There was also another consequence of very great practical importance, which, in celebrating the declaration of independence at

Lowell, ought not to pass unnoticed. While we were colonies of Great Britain, we were dependent on a government in which we were not represented. The laws passed by the Imperial Parliament were not passed for the benefit of the colony as their immediate object, but only so far as the interest of the colony was supposed to be consistent with that of the mother country. It was the principle of the colonial system of Europe, as it was administered before the revolution, to make the colonies subserve the growth and wealth of the parent state. The industry of the former was accordingly encouraged where it contributed to this object; it was discouraged and restrained where it was believed to have an opposite tendency. . . .

The establishment, therefore, of a prosperous manufacturing town like Lowell, regarded in itself, and as a specimen of other similar seats of American art and industry, may with propriety be considered as a peculiar triumph of our political independence. They are, if I may so express it, the complement of the revolution. They redress the peculiar hardships of the colonial system. They not only do that which was not done, but which was not permitted to be done before the establishment of an independent government. . . .

Connected with this is another benefit of the utmost importance, and not wholly dissimilar in kind. The population gathered at a manufacturing establishment is to be fed, and this gives an enhanced value to the land in all the neighboring region. In this new country the land often acquires a value in this way for the first time. A large number of persons in this assembly are well able to contrast the condition of the villages in the neighborhood of Lowell with what it was ten or twelve years ago, when Lowell itself consisted of two or three quite unproductive farms. It is the contrast of production with barrenness; of cultivation with waste; of plenty with an absence of every thing but the bare necessaries of life. The effect, of course, in one locality is of no great account in the sum of national production throughout the extent of the land. But wherever a factory is established this effect is produced; and every individual to whom they give employment ceases to be a producer, and becomes a consumer of agricultural produce. The aggregate effect is, of course, of the highest importance. . . .

It is a familiar remark, of which all, I believe, admit the justice, that a variety of pursuits is a great advantage to a community. It affords scope to the exercise of the boundless variety of talent and capacity which are bestowed by nature, and which are sure to be developed by an intelligent population, if encouragement and opportunity are presented. In this point of view, the establishment of manufacturing industry, in all its departments, is greatly to be desired in every country, and has had an influence in ours of a peculiar character. I have already alluded to the fact that, with the erection of an independent government, a vast domain in the west was for the first time thrown freely open to settlement. As soon as the Indian frontier was pacified by the treaty of Greenville, a tide of emigration began to flow into the territory north-west of the Ohio; and from no part of the country more rapidly than from Massachusetts. In many respects this was a circumstance by no means to be regretted. It laid the foundation of the settlement of this most important and interesting region by a kindred race; and it opened to the mass of enterprising adventurers from the older states a short road to competence. But it was a serious drain upon the population of good old Massachusetts. The temptation of the fee simple of some of the best land in the world for two dollars an acre, and that on credit (for such, till a few years ago, was the land system of the United States) was too powerful to be resisted by the energetic and industrious young men of the New England States, in which there is but a limited quantity of fertile land, and that little of course to be had only at a high price. The consequence was that although the causes of an increase of population existed in New England to as great a degree, with this exception, as in any other part of the world, the actual increase was far from rapid; scarcely amounting to one half of the average rate of the country. The singular spectacle was exhibited of a community abounding in almost all the elements of prosperity, possessing every thing calculated to engage the affections of her children, annually deserted by the flower of her population. These remarks apply with equal force to all the other New England States, with the exception of Maine, where an abundance of unoccupied fertile land counterbalances the attractions of the west.

But this process of emigration has already received a check, and is likely to be hereafter adequately regulated by the new demand for labor of every kind and degree, consequent upon the introduction of manufactures. This new branch of industry, introduced into the circle of occupations, is creating a demand for a portion of that energy and spirit of acquisition which have heretofore carried our young men beyond the Ohio, and beyond the Wabash. Obvious and powerful causes will continue to direct considerable numbers in the same path of adventure; but it will not be, as it was at the commencement of this century, almost the only outlet for the population of the older states. In short, a new alternative of career is now presented to the rising generation.

There is another point of importance, in reference to manufactures, which ought not to be omitted in this connection, and it is this—that in addition to what may be called their direct operation and influence, manufactures are a great school for all the practical arts. As they are aided themselves, in the progress of inventive sagacity, by hints and materials from every art and every science, and every kingdom of nature, so, in their turn, they create the skill and furnish the instruments for carrying on almost all the other pursuits. Whatever pertains to machinery, in all the great branches of industry, will probably be found to have its origin, directly or indirectly, in that skill which can be acquired only in connection with manufactures. Let me mention two striking instances, the one connected with navigation, and the other with agriculture. The greatest improvement in navigation, since the invention of the mariner's compass, is the application of steam for propelling vessels. Now, by whom was this improvement made? Not by the merchant, or the mariner, fatigued by adverse winds and weary calms. The steam engine was the production of the machine shops of Birmingham, where a breath of the sea breeze never penetrated; and its application as a motive power on the water, was a result wrought out by the sagacity of Fulton from the science and skill of the millwright and the machinist. The first elements of such a mechanical system as the steam engine, in any of its applications, must be wanting in a purely commercial or agricultural community. Again, the great improvement in the agriculture of our southern States, and in its results one of the greatest additions to the agricultural produce of the world, dates from the invention of the machine for separating the seed from the staple. This invention was not the growth of the region which enjoys its first benefits. The peculiar faculty of the mind to which these wonderful mechanical contrivances of modern art owe their origin, is not likely to be developed in the routine of agricultural operations. These operations have their effects on the intellectual character—salutary effects—but they do not cultivate the principle of mechanical contrivance, which peoples your factories with their lifeless but almost reasoning tenants.

I cannot but think that the loss and injury unavoidably accruing to a people, among whom a long-continued exclusive pursuit of other occupations has prevented the cultivation of the inventive faculty and the acquisition of mechanical skill, is greater in reference to the general affairs and business of life than in reference to the direct products of manufactures. The latter is a great economical loss, the nature and extent of which are described in the remarks which I have quoted from the great teacher of political economy; but a community in which the inventive and constructive principle is faintly developed is deprived of one of the highest capacities of reasoning mind. . . .

Another lesson has been taught at Lowell and our other well-conducted manufacturing establishments, which I deem vastly more important. It is well known that the degraded condition of the operatives in the old world had created a strong prejudice against the introduction of manufactures into this country. We were made acquainted, by sanitary and parliamentary reports, detailing the condition of the great manufacturing cities abroad, with a state of things revolting to humanity. It would seem that the industrial system of Europe required for its administration an amount of suffering, depravity, and brutalism, which formed one of the great scandals of the age. No form of serfdom or slavery could be worse. Reflecting persons, on this side of the ocean, contemplated with uneasiness the introduction, into this country, of a system which had disclosed such hideous features in Europe; but it must be frankly owned that these apprehensions have proved wholly unfounded. Were I addressing an audience in any other place, I could with truth say more to this effect than I will say on this occasion. But you will all bear me witness, that I do not speak the words of adulation when I say, that for physical comfort, moral conduct, general intelligence, and all the qualities of social character which make up an enlightened New England community, Lowell might safely enter into a comparison with any town or city in the land. Nowhere, I believe, for the same population, is there a greater number of schools and churches, and nowhere a greater number of persons whose habits and mode of life bear witness that they are influenced by a sense of character.

In demonstrating to the world that such a state of things is consistent with the profitable pursuit of manufacturing industry, you have made a discovery more important to humanity than all the wonderful machinery for weaving and spinning—than all the miracles of water or steam. You have rolled off from the sacred cause of labor the mountain reproach of ignorance, vice, and suffering under which it lay crushed. You have gained, for the skilled industry required to carry on these mighty establishments, a place of honor in the great dispensation by which Providence governs the world. You have shown that the home-bred virtues of the parental roof are not required to be left behind by those who resort for a few years to these crowded marts of social industry; and, in the fruits of your honest and successful labor, you are daily carrying gladness to the firesides where you were reared.

The alliance which you have thus established between labor and capital (which is nothing but labor saved) may truly be called a *holy alliance.* It realizes, in a practical way, that vision of social life and action which has been started abroad, in forms, as it appears to me, inconsistent with the primary instincts of our nature, and wholly incapable of being ingrafted upon our modern civilization. That no farther progress can be made in this direction, I certainly would not say. It would be contrary to the great laws of human progress to suppose that, at one effort, this hard problem in social affairs had reached its perfect solution. But I think it may be truly said, that in no other way has so much been done, as in these establishments, to mingle up the interests of society; to confer upon labor, in all its degrees of cultivation (from mere handiwork and strength up to inventive skill and adorning taste) the advantages which result from previous accumulations. Without shaking that great principle by which a man calls what he has *his own*, whether it is little or much (the corner stone of civilized life) these establishments form a mutually beneficial connection between those who have nothing but their muscular power and those who are able to bring into the partnership the masses of property requisite to carry on an extensive concern—property which was itself, originally, the work of men's hands, but has been converted, by accumulation and thrift, from labor into capital. This I regard as one of the greatest triumphs of humanity, morals, and, I will add, religion. The labor of a community is its great wealth—its most vital concern. To elevate it in the social scale, to increase its rewards, to give it cultivation and self-respect, should be the constant aim of an enlightened patriotism. There can be no other basis of a progressive Christian civilization. Woe to the land where labor and intelligence are at war! Happy the land whose various interests are united together by the bonds of mutual benefit and kind feeling!

But it is time, fellow-citizens, that I should close. . . . Your prosperous town is but another monument to the wisdom and patriotism of our fathers. It has grown up on the basis of the national independence. But for the deed which was done on the Fourth of July, 1776, your streets and squares would still be the sandy plain which nature made them.

3

ECONOMIC NATIONALISM

Henry Clay
THE AMERICAN SYSTEM

Henry Clay (1777–1852) was the most powerful leader in the Whig party. In a real sense the party was an extension of his personal ambition: he was largely responsible for creating it, and when he died it did not outlive him. Clay was elected to the Kentucky constitutional convention at the age of twenty-two and spent practically all the rest of his life in politics. "Harry of the West" was an ardent nationalist with views very similar to those of John Quincy Adams, though in temperament the two men were utterly different. By supporting Adams for the presidency in 1824 Clay earned the undying enmity of Andrew Jackson. Thereafter Clay and Jackson gradually built up two rival political coalitions that became the Whig and Democratic parties.

The core of Whig policy was Clay's program of government aid to business enterprise, which he called "the American system" to distinguish it from "the British system" of laissez-faire. Clay delivered the following speech under historic circumstances. South Carolina was threatening to nullify the existing federal tariff law, which she blamed (not altogether correctly) for economic hard times in the state. The Union itself seemed threatened. Clay designed his defense of the tariff less to convert the South Carolinians—a hopeless task—than to rally supporters elsewhere. In his lifetime Clay was regarded as a spellbinding orator; this speech took three days to deliver and has had to be cut considerably. Clay's reputation as a speaker was exceeded only by his reputation as the "Great Compromiser." It is typical of Clay that, after making this vigorous vindication of his position, he shrewdly arranged a compromise that gradually lowered tariff rates over the next several years and resolved the constitutional crisis.

SOURCE. Henry Clay, "Speech in Defence of the American System, in the Senate of the United States, Feb. 2d, 3d, and 6th, 1832," *The Life and Speeches of Henry Clay*, ed. Daniel Mallory (New York, 1844), II, 5–55.

Eight years ago, it was my painful duty to present to the other house of congress an unexaggerated picture of the general distress pervading the whole land. We must all yet remember some of its frightful features. We all know that the people were then oppressed, and borne down by an enormous load of debt; that the value of property was at the lowest point of depression; that ruinous sales and sacrifices were every where made of real estate; that stop laws, and relief laws, and paper money were adopted, to save the people from impending destruction; that a deficit in the public revenue existed, which compelled government to seize upon, and divert from its legitimate object, the appropriations to the sinking fund, to redeem the national debt; and that our commerce and navigation were threatened with a complete paralysis. In short, sir, if I were to select any term of seven years since the adoption of the present constitution which exhibited a scene of the most wide-spread dismay and desolation, it would be exactly that term of seven years which immediately preceded the establishment of the tariff of 1824.

I have now to perform the more pleasing task of exhibiting an imperfect sketch of the existing state of the unparalleled prosperity of the country. On a general survey, we behold cultivation extended, the arts flourishing, the face of the country improved, our people fully and profitably employed, and the public countenance exhibiting tranquillity, contentment, and happiness. And if we descend into particulars, we have the agreeable contemplation of a people out of debt; land rising slowly in value, but in a secure and salutary degree; a ready though not extravagant market for all the surplus productions of our industry; innumerable flocks and herds browsing and gamboling on ten thousand hills and plains, covered with rich and verdant grasses; our cities expanded, and whole villages springing up, as it were, by enchantment; our exports and imports increased and increasing; our tonnage, foreign and coastwise, swelling and fully occupied; the rivers of our interior animated by the perpetual thunder and lightning of countless steamboats; the currency sound and abundant; the public debt of two wars nearly redeemed; and, to crown all, the public treasury overflowing, embarrassing congress, not to find subjects of taxation, but to select the objects which shall be liberated from the impost. If the term of seven years were to be selected, of the greatest prosperity which this people have enjoyed since the establishment of their present constitution, it would be exactly that period of seven years which immediately followed the passage of the tariff of 1824.

This transformation of the condition of the country from gloom and distress to brightness and prosperity, has been mainly the work of American legislation, fostering American industry, instead of allowing it to be controlled by foreign legislation, cherishing foreign industry. . . .

If the system of protection be founded on principles erroneous in theory, pernicious in practice, above all, if it be unconstitutional, as is alleged, it ought to be forthwith abolished, and not a vestige of it suffered to remain. But, before we sanction this sweeping denunciation, let us look a little at this system, its magnitude, its ramifications, its duration, and the high authorities which have sustained it. . . . Why, sir, there is scarcely an interest, scarcely a vocation in society, which is not embraced by the beneficence of this system. . . .

It extends to almost every mechanic art—to tanners, cordwainers, tailors, cabinet-makers, hatters, tinners, brass-workers, clock-makers, coach-makers, tallow-chandlers, trace-makers, rope-makers, cork-cutters, tobacconists, whip-makers, paper-makers, umbrella-makers, glass-blowers, stocking-weavers, butter-makers, saddle and harness-makers, cutlers, brush-makers, book-binders, dairy-men, milk-farmers, black-smiths, type-founders, musical instrument-makers, basket-makers, milliners, potters, chocolate-makers, floor-cloth-makers, bonnet-makers, hair-cloth-makers, copper-smiths, pencil-makers, bellows-makers, pocket-book-makers, card-makers, glue-makers, mustard-makers, lumber-sawyers, saw-makers, scale-beam-makers, scythe-makers, wood-saw-makers, and many others. . . .

Such are some of the items of this vast system of protection, which it is now proposed to abandon. We might well pause and contemplate, if human imagination could conceive the extent of mischief and ruin from its total overthrow, before we proceed to the work of destruction. Its duration is worthy also of serious consideration. Not to go behind the constitution, its date is coeval with that instrument. It began on the ever-memorable fourth day of July—the fourth day of July, 1789. The second act which stands recorded in the statute-book, bearing the illustrious signature of George Washington, laid the corner-stone of the whole system. That there might be no mistake about the matter, it was then solemnly proclaimed to the American people and to the world, that it was *necessary* for "the encouragement and *protection* of manufactures," that duties should be laid. It is in vain to urge the small amount of the measure of the protection then extended. The great principle was then established by the fathers of the constitution, with the father of his country at their head. And it cannot now be questioned, that, if the government had not then been new and the subject untried, a greater measure of protection would have been applied, if it had been supposed necessary. Shortly after, the master minds of Jefferson and Hamilton were brought to act on this interesting subject. Taking views of it appertaining to the departments of foreign affairs and of the treasury, which they respectively filled, they presented, severally, reports which yet remain monuments of their profound wisdom, and came to the same conclusion of protection to American industry. Mr. Jefferson argued that foreign restrictions, foreign prohibitions, and foreign high duties, ought to be met at home by American restrictions, American prohibitions, and American high duties. Mr. Hamilton, surveying the entire ground, and looking at the inherent nature of the subject, treated it with an ability, which, if ever equalled, has not been surpassed, and earnestly recommended protection.

The wars of the French revolution commenced about this period, and streams of gold poured into the United States through a thousand channels, opened or enlarged by the successful commerce which our neutrality enabled us to prosecute. We forgot or overlooked, in the general prosperity, the necessity of encouraging our domestic manufactures. Then came the edicts of Napoleon, and the British orders in council; and our embargo, non-intercourse, non-importation, and war, followed in rapid succession. These national measures, amounting to a total suspension, for the period of their duration, of our foreign commerce, afforded the most efficacious encouragement to American manufactures; and accordingly they every where sprung up. . . .

Peace, under the treaty of Ghent, returned in 1815, but there did not return with it the golden days which preceded the edicts levelled at our commerce by Great Britain and France. It found all Europe tranquilly resuming the arts and the business of civil life. It found Europe no longer the consumer of our surplus, and the employer of our navigation, but excluding, or heavily burdening, almost all the productions of our agriculture, and our rivals in manufactures, in navigation, and in commerce. It found our country, in short, in a situation totally different from all the past—new and untried. It became necessary to adapt our laws, and especially our laws of impost, to the new circumstances in which we found ourselves. Accordingly, that eminent and lamented citizen, then at the head of the treasury (Mr. Dallas), was required, by a resolution of the house of representatives, under date of the twenty-third of February, 1815, to prepare and report to the succeeding session of congress, a system of revenue conformable with the actual condition of the country. . . . The measure of protection which he proposed was not adopted, in regard to some leading articles, and there was great difficulty in ascertaining what it ought to have been. But the *principle* was then distinctly asserted and fully sanctioned.

The subject of the American system was again brought up in 1820, by the bill reported by the chairman of the committee of manufactures, now a member of the bench of the supreme court of the United States, and the principle was successfully maintained by the representatives of the people; but the bill which they passed was defeated in the senate. It was revived in 1824; the whole ground carefully and deliberately explored, and the bill then introduced, receiving all the sanctions of the constitution, became the law of the land. An amendment of the system was proposed in 1828, to the history of which I refer with no agreeable recollections. The bill of that year, in some of its provisions, was framed on principles directly adverse to the declared wishes of the friends of the policy of protection. . . . Subsequent legislation has corrected the error then perpetrated, but still that measure is vehemently denounced by gentlemen who contributed to make it what it was.

Thus, sir, has this great system of protection been gradually built, stone upon stone, and step by step, from the fourth of July, 1789, down to the present period. In every stage of its progress it has received the deliberate sanction of congress. A vast majority of the people of the United States has approved and continue to approve it. Every chief magistrate of the United States, from Washington to the present, in some form or other, has given to it the authority of his name; and, however the opinions of the existing president are interpreted south of Mason and Dixon's line, on the north they are at least understood to favor the establishment of a *judicious* tariff.

The question, therefore, which we are now called upon to determine, is not, whether we shall establish a new and doubtful system of policy, just proposed, and for the first time presented to our consideration, but whether we shall break down and destroy a long established system, patiently and carefully built up and sanctioned, during a series of years, again and again, by the nation and its highest and most revered authorities. . . .

I shall not discuss the constitutional question. Without meaning any disrespect to those who raise it, if it be debatable, it has been sufficiently debated. . . .

[Here the vice-president [John C. Calhoun] interposed, and remarked, that, if the senator from Kentucky alluded to him, he must say that his opinion was, that the measure was unconstitutional.)

When, sir, I contended with you, side by side, and with perhaps less zeal than you exhibited, in 1816, I did not understand you then to consider the policy forbidden by the constitution.

(The vice-president again interposed, and said that the constitutional question was not debated at that time, and that he had never expressed an opinion contrary to that now intimated.)

I give way with pleasure to these explanations, which I hope will always be made when I say any thing bearing on the individual opinions of the chair. I know the delicacy of the position, and sympathize with the incumbent, whoever he may be. It is true, the question was not debated in 1816; and why not? Because it was not debatable; it was then believed not fairly to arise. It never has been made as a distinct, substantial, and leading point of objection. It never was made until the discussion of the tariff of 1824, when it was rather hinted at as against the *spirit* of the constitution, than formally announced as being contrary to the provisions of that instrument. What was not dreamed of before, or in 1816, and scarcely thought of in 1824, is now made, by excited imaginations, to assume the imposing form of a serious constitutional barrier.

Such are the origin, duration, extent, and sanctions, of the policy which we are now called upon to subvert. Its beneficial effects, although they may vary in degree, have been felt in all parts of the union. To none, I verily believe, has it been prejudicial. In the north, every where, testimonials are borne to the high prosperity which it has diffused. There, all branches of industry are animated and flourishing. Commerce, foreign and domestic, active; cities and town springing up, enlarging and beautifying; navigation fully and profitably employed, and the whole face of the country smiling with improvement, cheerfulness, and abundance. The gentleman from South Carolina has supposed that we in the west derive no advantages from this system. He is mistaken. Let him visit us, and he will find, from the head of La Belle Riviere, at Pittsburgh, to America, at its mouth, the most rapid and gratifying advances. He will behold Pittsburgh itself, Wheeling, Portsmouth, Maysville, Cincinnati, Louisville, and numerous other towns, lining and ornamenting the banks of the noble river, daily extending their limits, and prosecuting, with the greatest spirit and profit, numerous branches of the manufacturing and mechanic arts. If he will go into the interior, in the state of Ohio, he will there perceive the most astonishing progress in agriculture, in the useful arts, and in all the improvements to which they both directly conduce. Then let him cross over into my own, my favorite state, and contemplate the spectacle which is there exhibited. He will perceive numerous villages, not large, but neat, thriving, and some of them highly ornamented; many manufactories of hemp, cotton, wool, and other articles. In various parts of the country, and especially in the Elkhorn region, an endless succession of natural parks; the forests thinned; fallen trees and undergrowth cleared away; large herds and flocks feeding on luxuriant grasses; and interspersed with comfortable, sometimes elegant mansions, surrounded by extensive lawns. The honorable gentleman from South Carolina says, that a profitable trade was carried on from the west, through the Seleuda gap, in mules, horses, and other live stock, which has been checked by the operation of the tariff. It is true, that such a trade was carried on between Kentucky and South Carolina, mutually beneficial to both parties; but, several years ago, resolutions, at popular meetings, in Carolina, were adopted, not to purchase the produce of Kentucky, by way of punishment for her attachment to the tariff. They must have supposed us as stupid as the sires of one of the descriptions of the stock of which that trade consisted, if they imagined that their resolutions would affect our principles. Our drovers cracked their whips, blew their horns, and passed the Seleuda gap, to other markets, where better humors existed, and equal or greater profits were made. . . .

Nor has the system which has been the parent source of so much benefit to other parts of the union, proved injurious to the cotton-growing country. I cannot speak of South Carolina itself, where I have never been, with so much certainty; but of other portions of the union in which cotton is grown, especially those bordering on the Mississippi, I can confidently speak. If cotton-planting is less profitable than it was, that is the result of increased production; but I believe it to be still the most profitable investment of capital of any branch of business in the United States. . . .

When gentlemen have succeeded in their design of an immediate or gradual destruction of the American system, what is their substitute? Free trade? Free trade! The call for free trade is as unavailing, as the cry of a spoiled child in its nurse's arms, for the moon, or the stars that glitter in the firmament of heaven. It never has existed, it never will exist. Trade implies at least two parties. To be free, it should be fair, equal, and reciprocal. But if we throw our ports wide open to the admission of foreign productions, free of all duty, what ports of any other foreign nation shall we find open to the free admission of our surplus produce? We may break down all barriers to free trade on our part, but the work will not be complete, until foreign powers shall have removed theirs. There would be freedom on one side, and restrictions, prohibitions, and exclusions, on the other. The bolts and the bars and the chains of all other nations will remain undisturbed. . . .

Gentlemen deceive themselves. It is not free trade that they are recommending to our acceptance. It is, in effect, the British colonial system that we are invited to adopt; and, if their policy prevail, it will lead substantially to the recolonization of these states, under the commercial dominion of Great Britain. . . .

But it is contended . . . that the south cannot, from physical and other causes, engage in the manufacturing arts. I deny the premises, and I deny the conclusion. I deny the fact of inability; and, if it existed, I deny the conclusion, that we must, therefore, break down our manufactures, and nourish those of foreign countries. The south possesses, in an extraordinary degree, two of the most important elements of manufacturing industry—water-power and labor. The former gives to our whole country a most decided advantage over Great Britain. But a single experiment, stated by the gentleman from South Carolina, in which a faithless slave put the torch to a manufacturing establishment, has discouraged similar enterprises. We have in Kentucky the same description of population, and we employ them, almost exclusively, in many of our hemp manufactories. A neightbor of mine, one of our most opulent and respectable citizens, has had one, two, if not three, manufactories burnt by incendiaries; but he persevered, and his perseverance has been rewarded with wealth. We found that it was less expensive to keep night-watches than to pay premiums for insurance, and we employed them.

Let it be supposed, however, that the south cannot manufacture; must those parts of the union which can, be therefore prevented? Must we support those of foreign countries? . . .

I regret, Mr. President, that one topic has, I think, unnecessarily been introduced into this debate. I allude to the charge brought against the manufacturing system, as favoring the growth of aristocracy. If it were true, would gentlemen prefer supporting foreign accumulations of wealth, by that description of industry, rather than in their own country? But is it correct? The joint stock companies of the north, as I understand them, are nothing more than associations, sometimes of hundreds, by means of which the small earnings of many are brought into a common stock, and the associates, obtaining corporate privileges, are enabled to prosecute, under one superintending head, their business to better advantage. Nothing can be more essentially democratic or better devised to counterpoise the influence of individual wealth. In Kentucky, almost every manufactory known to me, is in the hands of enterprising and self-made men, who have acquired whatever wealth they possess by patient and diligent labor. Comparisons are odious, and but in defence would not be made by me. But is there more tendency to aristocracy in a manufactory, supporting hundreds of freemen, or in a cotton plantation, with its not less numerous slaves, sustaining perhaps only two white families—that of the master and the overseer? I pass, with pleasure, from this disagreeable topic. . . .

The next article to which I would call the attention of the senate, is that of cotton fabrics. . . . The introduction of calico printing into the United States constitutes an important era in our manufacturing industry. It commenced about the year 1825, and has since made such astonishing advances, that the whole quantity now annually printed is but little short of forty millions of yards—about two thirds of our whole consumption. It is a beautiful manufacture, combining great mechanical skill with scientific discoveries in chemistry. The engraved cylinders for making the impression require much taste, and put in requisition the genius of the fine arts of design and engraving. Are the fine graceful forms of our fair countrywomen less lovely when enveloped in the chintzes and calicoes produced by native industry, than when clothed in the tinsel of foreign drapery? . . .

Will gentlemen believe the fact, which I am authorized now to state, that the United States, at this time, manufacture one half the quantity of cotton which Great Britain did in 1816! We possess three great advantages; first, the raw material; second, water-power instead of that of steam, generally used in England; and, third, the cheaper labor of females. In England, males spin with the mule and weave; in this country, women and girls spin with the throstle, and superintend the power-loom. And can there be any employment more appropriate? Who has not been delighted with contemplating the clock-work regularity of a large cotton manufactory? I have often visited them at Cincinnati and other places, and always with increased admiration. The women, separated from the other sex, work in apartments, large, airy, well warmed, and spacious. Neatly dressed, with ruddy complexions, and happy countenances, they watch the work before them, mend the broken threads, and replace the exhausted balls or broaches. At stated hours they are called to their meals, and go and return light and cheerful step. At night they separate, and repair to their respective houses, under the care of a mother, guardian, or friend. "Six days shalt thou labor and do all that thou hast to do, but the seventh day is the sabbath of the Lord thy God." Accordingly, we behold them, on that sacred day, assembled together in His temples, and in devotional attitudes and with pious countenances offering their prayers to heaven for all its blessings; of which it is not the least, that a system of policy has been adopted by their country, which admits of their obtaining a comfortable subsistence. Manufactures have brought into profitable employment a vast amount of female labor, which, without them, would be lost to the country. . . .

Under the operation of the American system, the products of our agriculture command a higher price than they would do without it, by the creation of a home market; and by the augmentation of wealth produced by manufacturing industry, which enlarges our powers of consumption both of domestic and foreign articles. The importance of the home market is among the established maxims which are universally recognised by all writers and all men. However some may differ as to the relative advantages of the foreign and the home market, none deny to the latter great value and high consideration. It is nearer to us; beyond the control of foreign legislation; and undisturbed by those vicissitudes to which all international intercourse is more or less exposed. The most stupid are sensible of the benefit of a residence in the vicinity of a large manufactory, or of a market town, of a good road, or of a navigable stream, which connects their farms with some great capital. If the pursuits of all men were perfectly the same, although they would be in possession of the greatest abundance of the particular produce of their industry, they might, at the same time, be in extreme want of other necessary articles of human subsistence. The uniformity of the general occupation would preclude all exchanges, all commerce. It is only in the diversity of the vocations of the members of a community that the means can be found for those salutary exchanges which conduce to the general prosperity. And the greater that diversity, the more extensive and the more animating is the circle of exchange. . . .

Gentlemen are greatly deceived as to the hold which this system has in the affections of the people of the United States. They represent that it is the policy of New England, and that she is most benefited by it. If there be any part of this union which has been most steady, most unanimous, and most determined in its support, it is Pennsylvania. Why is not that powerful state attacked? Why pass her over, and aim the blow at New England? New England came reluctantly into the policy. In 1824, a majority of her delegation was opposed to it. From the largest state of New England there was but a solitary vote in favor of the bill. That enterprising people can readily accommodate their industry to any policy, provided it be *settled*. They supposed this was fixed, and they submitted to the decrees of government. And the progress of public opinion has kept pace with the developments of the benefits of the system. Now, all New England, at least in this house (with the exception of one small still voice) is in favor of the system. In 1824, all Maryland was against it; now the majority is for it. Then, Louisiana, with one exception, was opposed to it; now, without any exception, she is in favor of it. The march of public sentiment is to the south. Virginia will be the next convert; and in less than seven years, if there be no obstacles from political causes, or prejudices industriously instilled, the majority of eastern Virginia will be, as the majority of western Virginia now is, in favor of the American system. North Carolina will follow later, but not less certainly. Eastern Tennessee is now in favor of the system. And, finally, its doctrines will pervade the whole union, and the wonder will be, that they ever should have been opposed. . . .

It is for the great body of the people, and especially for the poor, that I have ever supported the American system. It affords them profitable employment, and supplies the means of comfortable subsistence. It *secures* to them, certainly, necessaries of life, manufactured at home and places within their reach, and enables them to acquire a reasonable share of foreign luxuries; while the system of gentlemen *promises* them necessaries made in foreign countries, and which are beyond their power, and *denies* to them luxuries, which they would possess no means to purchase. . . .

And now, sir, I would address a few words to the friends of the American system in the senate. The revenue must, ought to be reduced. The country will not, after by the payment of the public debt ten or twelve millions of dollars become unnecessary, bear such an annual surplus. Its distribution would form a subject of perpetual contention. Some of the opponents of the system understand the stratagem by which to attack it, and are shaping their course accordingly. It is to crush the system by the accumulation of revenue, and by the effort to persuade the people that they are unnecessarily taxed, while those would really tax them who would break up the native sources of supply, and render them dependent upon the foreign. But the revenue ought to be reduced, so as to accommodate it to the fact of the payment of the public debt. And the alternative is or may be, to preserve the protecting system, and repeal the duties on the unprotected articles, or to *preserve* the duties on *unprotected* articles, and endanger if not destroy the system. Let us then adopt the measure before us, which will benefit all classes; the farmer, the professional man, the merchant, the manufacturer, the mechanic; and the cotton planter more than all. A few months ago there was no diversity of opinion as to the expediency of this measure. All, then, seemed to unite in the selection of these objects for a repeal of duties which were not produced within the country. Such a repeal did not touch our domestic industry, violated no principle, offended no prejudice.

Can we not all, whatever may be our favorite theories, cordially unite on this neutral ground? When that is occupied, let us look beyond it, and see if any thing can be done in the field of protection, to modify, to improve it, or to satisfy those who are opposed to the system. Our southern brethren believe that it is injurious to them, and ask its repeal. We believe that its abandonment will be prejudicial to them, and ruinous to every other section of the union. However strong their convictions may be, they are not stronger than ours. Between the points of the preservation of the system and its absolute repeal, there is no principle of union. If it can be shown to operate immoderately on any quarter; if the measure of protection to any article can be demonstrated to be undue and inordinate; it would be the duty of congress to interpose and apply a remedy. And none will cooperate more heartily than I shall in the performance of that duty. It is quite probable that beneficial modifications of the system may be made without impairing its efficacy. But to make it fulfil the purposes of its institution, the measure of protection ought to be adequate. If it be not, all interests will be injuriously affected. The manufacturer, crippled in his exertions, will produce less perfect and dearer fabrics, and the consumer will feel the consequence. This is the spirit, and these are the principles only, on which it seems to me that a settlement of the great question can be made, satisfactorily to all parts of our union.

4

ECONOMIC CENTRALIZATION IN A DEMOCRACY

George Tucker
THE NATIONAL BANK

The second Bank of the United States—patterned after the first Bank of the United States, which had existed from 1791 to 1811—was chartered in 1816 for a period of twenty years. The Bank was a mixed public-private corporation, with five directors representing the federal government and twenty directors chosen by its private stockholders. As the most powerful financial institution in the country, the Bank exerted considerable control over the amount of credit available and consequently came under severe criticism from time to time. In the famous case of McCulloch v. Maryland (1819), the U.S. Supreme Court upheld the power of Congress to incorporate the Bank, but many people, including Andrew Jackson, continued to doubt its constitutionality. In 1832 Clay, thinking to defeat Jackson for reelection, persuaded Bank president Nicholas Biddle to make the rechartering of the BUS a campaign issue. The plan did not succeed and, amidst stormy controversy, the Bank's federal charter was allowed to expire in 1836. For a number of years thereafter the Whig party advocated the revival of a national bank.

George Tucker (1775–1861), an economist and moral philosopher, taught at the University of Virginia. His defense of the operation of the national Bank is orthodox Whiggery. He tries with particular care to rebut the favorite charge of the Jacksonians that the Bank was an undemocratic institution conferring excessive influence on the wealthy elite. His argument is of course partisan pleading and cannot be taken as an impartial estimate of the Bank's role in politics. A lifelong friend and admirer of his fellow Virginian Thomas Jefferson, Tucker shows that support for the Bank was by no means confined to northeasterners or former Federalists.

SOURCE. George Tucker, "Examination of the Political Objections to a National Bank," *The Theory of Money and Banks Investigated* (Boston, 1839), pp. 306–327.

One of the political objections urged against a national bank is that it tends to increase the power of the moneyed classes, and, by thus embodying it and imparting to it unity of action, enable it to impede and even thwart, the government in its most salutary and important functions.

The objection supposes that corporations composed of men associated for the purpose of making money are capable of uniting, and likely to unite, for political objects. On this subject, we must be guided by experience. We know that the stockholders of a national bank, as well as of every other, may consist of men of all sects and parties; and while, as individuals, they all have their several political preferences and animosities, we also know that these do not induce them to lend money to one man, or to refuse it to another, on account of his politics. Why, indeed, should this be the case in a banking company, more than in an insurance, a canal, or a railroad company? The character and extent of the means, as well as the inducements, may be the same in both cases; yet such an objection has never yet been made to any other corporation than that of a bank. The motive of self-interest which is admitted to predominate in the case of the other corporations, is supposed, in the case of a bank, to be made subservient to political objects.

A course of action so anomalous ought not to be assented to without the clearest proof. The principal part of the stockholders are either men who have accumulated capital, and retired from business; or wealthy planters, who have saved money from their incomes; or salaried officers, or widows, or orphans; none of whom are likely to be ardent politicians, and are certain not to be of one way of thinking. Nor, if they were, can they be presumed willing to sacrifice their pecuniary interests to their party sympathies. To suppose they would consent to see the profits of the bank used for that purpose, is in opposition to all experience of men's acts. Such of them as may be willing to spend their money in electioneering, would rather have the credit and the pleasure of disbursing it themselves, than suffer it to be so used by the officers of the bank.

Some will here refer to the evidences of political feeling exhibited by the stockholders, officers, and all others interested in the late bank of the United States; and it will be asked if there was an individual, or at least if there was one out of fifty of the whole number, including a great part of the debtors to the bank, who was not in opposition to the administration. Admitting this to be the fact, it must be recollected that they were then struggling for the existence of an institution which they all deemed important, and that they might very naturally have thought that its preservation was of more importance to them, and to the country, too, than whether the executive functions of the government should be administered by one set of politicians or another. Men must always be expected to withhold their favor from those who oppose their interests; and we every day see elections turning on questions of mere local or even personal concerns,—such as the promotion of a particular canal or rail-road, and sometimes for very inferior objects. In like manner, administrations are supported or opposed, as they are supposed to favor foreign commerce, manufactures, and the like, according to the several interests of the voters. . . .

To ascertain what was the political influence inherent in the bank, let us ask what it was before general Jackson and his cabinet determined to put down that institution. The answer is—it was literally nothing. The bank kept the noiseless tenor of its way, meddling as little in the political concerns of the country as any other corporate body of the nation, and was entirely unnoticed by the politician, until, in an evil hour, as some think, and fortunately, according to others, the president of the United States, seven years before the bank charter was to expire, invited the consideration of congress to the question of its renewal, and in opposition to what was then the opinion of nine tenths of those who had any opinion on the matter, stated that it had failed to furnish the country with the uniform currency that had been expected. In this statement, he was contradicted by a large majority of both houses of congress, at the very time when a majority of both consisted of his friends.

When the interests of the stockholders were thus directly attacked by the president, and when, as they no doubt honestly believed, on unjust or mistaken grounds, because such was the opinion of others who had no particular interest in the bank, it was natural that they should feel not well affected towards him, and should oppose his reelection. It was to this extent that the bank and its adherents offended, and to this extent every supposable private interest always will offend. Where is the man of the forty or fifty thousand, who hold office under the federal government, who, if he believes that on the success of one party, he will continue in office, and, on its failure, he will be removed, does not desire the success of the party with whom his own interest is identified, and who will not use his endeavors to promote it? . . .

The questions of national policy that decide very many, perhaps most, of the elections, are perpetually changing. At one time, the inquiry was, whether the candidate inclined to one or the other of the great European belligerents; at another, whether he supported or opposed the war with Great Britain; and, at a third, whether he supported or opposed a protecting tariff. In one corner of the union, the doctrine of nullification was made a test question; in another, the expulsion of the Indians; and in yet another, the preemption rights of squatters. If some regarded the recharter of a national bank as a cardinal measure of national policy, there were others who took up a violent antipathy to certain societies,[1] whose members, time out of mind, had held secret meetings for their own exclusive amusement and instruction—who, once a year, walked in procession with little silk or leather aprons, carrying candlesticks and other mysterious symbols—and a part of whom were thought to have hanged or drowned a roguish brother, who betrayed them; and so dangerous did they consider this society that they would vote for no man who belonged to it; nay, more—for no man, whether member or not, who would not join in the crusade against these same odious freemasons; and they were numerous enough to bestow seven of the electoral votes for president and vice president on two of their proselytes. In these cases, individuals must be left to the unrestricted exercise of the electoral franchise, according to their own sense of duty and rectitude.

On all these questions, indeed, many take sides for no other reason than that of supporting or of opposing the administration, according to their respective feelings; and, without doubt, many were in favor of a national bank because the president was unfriendly to it. But the number of those who opposed it for the same reason must have been much larger. Of those who were actuated by their private interests in supporting the bank, the number . . . could not exceed 15,000, and probably was not 10,000; while those who supported the administration from the same motive amounted to 40 or 50,000.

One of the proofs of the dangerous and corrupting influence of the bank was that it had used the money of the stockholders to buy up editors, and to circulate throughout the union pamphlets written in its behalf. When the bank was charged with various acts of malfeasance, by reason of which it ought not to be rechartered, if it had employed advocates to defend it before the public, it would seem to have committed no very flagrant offence, but to have used a very natural and justifiable effort of self-preservation. But, when it is recol-

---

[1]The Freemasons, who were widely disliked in the 1820s and 1830s. Ed.

lected, that it was established for the public benefit, to furnish the community with a better currency, and to be the financial agent of the general government; and that it was urged by the chief magistrate of the nation; that it had not fulfilled the purposes for which it was established; and that its financial duties could be discharged as well, or better, by the state banks—the truth of these charges, and the soundness of these views, became the concern of the nation no less than that of the bank.

The bank had the right, always belonging to the party accused, of defending itself; and the public had the right to hear what could be said on both sides of a question in which it had so deep a stake; and, while the voice of its accusers was transmitted to every quarter of the union, with all the aids of the franking privilege, and an obsequious post-office, it became necessary, to enable the people to form a correct judgment on the merits of the question, that correspondent measures should be adopted for circulating the arguments urged in defence of the bank. That was accordingly done. It published arguments to show that the bank had truly performed all that could have been reasonably expected; that it rendered the currency both stable and uniform; that it had so discharged all its financial duties, that the government had not sustained the loss of a single dollar; and, lastly, that the danger from the treasury bank, which the president proposed to substitute, was as real as that from the existing bank was chimerical.

The issue was thus fairly made up between the friends and the opponents of the bank, and the people sat in judgment. Yet men, calling themselves just, were unwilling that both sides should be heard; and, believing themselves republicans, sought to stifle public discussion. The bank was censured not merely for securing a friendly avenue to the public mind, by granting accommodations to some three or four of the thousand editors of journals, but also for publishing such arguments as had been volunteered in its defence. . . .

The mass of those who opposed the president's course towards the bank did so because they believed, from more than forty years' experience, that such an institution was highly useful, if not indispensable. This was particularly the case with the mercantile part of the community, who, as a class, do not meddle much in politics, except where the interests of commerce are affected. When, too, we recollect how many were opposed to the bank on the ground that it was unconstitutional, it seems fair to infer that a large majority of the people believed a national bank to be an institution of great public utility and importance; and, but for the constitutional scruples of many, they would have continued its existence, in spite of all the efforts of the administration. . . .

[It is charged] that the bank tends to favor a moneyed aristocracy, as well as to add to the natural influence of wealth, and is so far repugnant to republican principles. This objection, if it be merely that the bank tends to make the rich richer, applies to every useful and profitable enterprise that can be mentioned; to manufactories, canals, railroads, and to all banks whatever, whether state, or national; and it is to this very circumstance that they principally owe their value, since, unless they were profitable to the capitalists who establish them, they would never have existed; and the community would lose all the benefits they confer, which often is many times greater than that which is received by their proprietors.

If, however, the objection go farther, and maintain, as some have rashly asserted, that a bank also tends to make the poor poorer, then the proposition may be unhesitatingly denied. It is not seen how a bank can be injurious to any class of productive industry. If it quickens enterprise, increases the demand for the productions of agriculture, commerce, and manufactures, and facilitates their transmission from the producers to the consumers, as we have seen, then it adds to the fund from which all classes are maintained; and the poor, as well as the rich, have their proportional share increased.

One of the best proofs that the benefits afforded by banks are not exclusive is, if we may trust to the sagacity of self-interest, that mechanics and small dealers are generally as desirous of a bank in their neighborhood as any other class. It is a fact of general notoriety, that a great stimulus is given to building, and other local improvements, by the establishment of banks; and this fact necessarily implies that a greater number of mechanics obtain employment, and receive better rewards. Those who have any thing to sell find it easier to obtain cash for it by reason of the bank; and those who go into the market as buyers, are likely to buy upon somewhat better terms; as the bank, by enabling merchants to enlarge their business, tends to lessen the rate of profit. In these two classes are comprehended the whole community.

It would seem to be quite sufficient, in our country, for the recommendation of any course of policy, that it adds to the mass of the national wealth; and, as to the distribution of that wealth, we may safely leave it to the relative industry, talent, and prudence of individuals, together with the laws which regulate successions, to give to each one the share to which he is justly entitled. Unless it could be shown that banks prevent industry, talents, or skill, from obtaining employment, or from receiving a fair remuneration, the objection must be considered as resting on false and superficial views, or as designedly seeking to take advantage of the ignorance and discontent which are the presumed accompaniments of poverty.

This objection, it must be remembered, applies equally to all banks, and has more force against the state banks than against the national bank, as they may be presumed greatly to exceed it in capital, in every state in the union. But it is unfounded as to all. They all, if well conducted, add to the stock of national wealth, and those individuals obtain the largest share of the addition, who exert the most industry, talent, prudence, and enterprise. If, indeed, there is any difference as to the classes of society, these institutions may be said to favor the poor yet more than the rich, inasmuch as they enable those who are without capital, to obtain the temporary use and profits of it by means of their credit, which is a far greater benefit than merely adding to the capital that is already possessed.

So far, too, as the power which banks possess of distributing the spare capital of the community, may be considered to give them an undue influence in managing the public concerns (though this seems to have been egregiously overrated), it is better that it should be weakened by division than be concentrated in the state banks; and those to whom power and influence of every description is ever an object of jealousy and apprehension may see in a national bank the means of neutralizing the power of the state banks.

It may be remarked, in conclusion, that the political objections which have been made to banks in the United States seem never yet to have been made in the country whose civil institutions most nearly resemble our own, and whose people are little behind us in political jealousy. From this fact we may infer that most of the apprehended evils, being too minute to be distinctly seen, are, for the most part, the creatures of imagination.

Part Two
POLITICAL THOUGHT

1

THE ORIGINS OF POLITICAL AUTHORITY

Daniel Webster
SECOND REPLY TO HAYNE

Daniel Webster (1782–1853) was the greatest of Whig orators and second only to Clay in stature within the party. His forensic abilities as a lawyer and legislator have made him an American legend. Born in rural New England, Webster became the spokesman of urban business interests. From 1813 to 1817 he served in the House of Representatives, during which time he generally took states' rights and free trade positions. After he returned to Congress in 1823, however, Webster experienced a change of heart. Industry had begun to develop in New England, and in keeping with the new economic interests of his section he espoused the twin causes of nationalism and protectionism.

The Webster-Hayne debate, from which the next selection is taken, was one of the most dramatic confrontations in American political history. It began as an argument over federal land policy, but other sectional issues quickly surfaced, and soon the very nature of the Constitution was at issue. Senator Robert Hayne of South Carolina expounded the theory of state rights and nullification while its great formulator vice president John C. Calhoun looked on. Webster responded with a rival theory of the Constitution in which state nullification of federal laws was treason. So eloquently did Webster argue his case that his second reply to Hayne was recognized at once as a classic of American nationalism. For generations schoolchildren memorized the peroration.

There yet remains to be performed, Mr. President, by far the most grave and important duty, which I feel to be devolved on me by this occasion. It is to state, and to defend, what I conceive to be the true principles of the Constitution under which we are here assembled. I might well have desired that so weighty a task should have fallen into

SOURCE. Daniel Webster, "Second Speech on Foot's Resolution. Delivered in the Senate of the United States on the 26th of January, 1830." *Works,* 19th ed. (Boston, 1885), III, 317–342.

other and abler hands. I could have wished that it should have been executed by those whose character and experience give weight and influence to their opinions, such as cannot possibly belong to mine. But, Sir, I have met the occasion, not sought it; and I shall proceed to state my own sentiments, without challenging for them any particular regard, with studied plainness, and as much precision as possible.

I understand the honorable gentleman from South Carolina to maintain, that it is a right of the State legislatures to interfere, whenever, in their judgment, this government transcends its constitutional limits, and to arrest the operation of its laws.

I understand him to maintain this right, as a right existing *under* the Constitution, not as a right to overthrow it on the ground of extreme necessity, such as would justify violent revolution.

I understand him to maintain an authority, on the part of the States, thus to interfere, for the purpose of correcting the exercise of power by the general government, of checking it, and of compelling it to conform to their opinion of the extent of its powers.

I understand him to maintain, that the ultimate power of judging of the constitutional extent of its own authority is not lodged exclusively in the general government, or any branch of it; but that, on the contrary, the States may lawfully decide for themselves, and each State for itself, whether, in a given case, the act of the general government transcends its power.

I understand him to insist, that, if the exigency of the case, in the opinion of any State government, require it, such State government may, by its own sovereign authority, annul an act of the general government which it deems plainly and palpably unconstitutional.

This is the sum of what I understand from him to be the South Carolina doctrine, and the doctrine which he maintains. I propose to consider it, and compare it with the Constitution. . . .

That there are individuals besides the honorable gentleman who do maintain these opinions, is quite certain. I recollect the recent expression of a sentiment, which circumstances attending its utterance and publication justify us in supposing was not unpremeditated. "The sovereignty of the State,—never to be controlled, construed, or decided on, but by her own feelings of honorable justice."

[Mr. Hayne here rose and said, that, for the purpose of being clearly understood, he would state that his proposition was in the words of the Virginia resolution,[1] as follows:

[1]A classic assertion of states' rights, written by James Madison and adopted by the Virginia legislature in 1798 in protest against the federal Alien and Sedition Acts. Ed.

"That this assembly doth explicitly and peremptorily declare, that it views the powers of the federal government, as resulting from the compact to which the States are parties, as limited by the plain sense and intention of the instrument constituting that compact, as no farther valid than they are authorized by the grants enumerated in that compact; and that, in case of a deliberate, palpable, and dangerous exercise of other powers, not granted by the said compact, the States who are parties thereto have the right, and are in duty bound, to interpose, for arresting the progress of the evil, and for maintaining within their respective limits the authorities, rights, and liberties appertaining to them."

Mr. Webster resumed:)

I am quite aware, Mr. President, of the existence of the resolution which the gentleman read, and has now repeated, and that he relies on it as his authority. I know the source, too, from which it is understood to have proceeded. I need not say that I have much respect for the constitutional opinions of Mr. Madison; they would weigh greatly with me always. But before the authority of his opinion be vouched for the gentleman's proposition, it will be proper to consider what is the fair interpretation of that resolution, to which Mr. Madison is understood to have given his sanction. As the gentleman construes it, it is an authority for him. Possibly, he may not have adopted the right construction. That resolution declares, that, *in the case of the dangerous exercise of powers not granted by the general government, the States may interpose to arrest the progress of the evil.* But how interpose, and what does this declaration purport? Does it mean no more than that there may be extreme cases, in which the people, in any mode of assembling, may resist usurpation, and relieve themselves from a tyrannical government? No one will deny this. . . . We all know that civil institutions are established for the public benefit, and that when they cease to answer the ends of their existence they may be changed. But I do not understand the doctrine now contended for to be that, which, for the sake of distinction, we may call the right of revolution. I understand the gentleman to maintain, that, without revolution, without civil commotion, without rebellion, a remedy for supposed abuse and transgression of the powers of the general government lies in a direct appeal to the interference of the State governments.

(Mr. Hayne here rose and said: He did not contend for the mere right of revolution, but for the right of constitutional resistance. What he maintained was, that in case of a plain, palpable violation of the Constitution by the general government, a State may interpose; and that this interposition is constitutional.

Mr. Webster resumed:)

So, Sir, I understood the gentleman, and am happy to find that I did not misunderstand him. What he contends for is, that it is constitutional to interrupt the administration of the Constitution itself, in the hands of those who are chosen and sworn to administer it, by the direct interference, in form of law, of the States, in virtue of their sovereign capacity. The inherent right in the people to reform their government I do not deny; and they have another right, and that is, to resist unconstitutional laws, without overturning the government. It is no doctrine of mine that unconstitutional laws bind the people. The great question is, Whose prerogative is it to decide on the constitutionality or unconstitutionality of the laws? On that, the main debate hinges. The proposition, that, in case of a supposed violation of the Constitution by Congress, the States have a constitutional right to interfere and annul the law of Congress, is the proposition of the gentleman. I do not admit it. . . . I say, the right of a State to annul a law of Congress cannot be maintained, but on the ground of the inalienable right of man to resist oppression; that is to say, upon the ground of revolution. I admit that there is an ultimate violent remedy, above the Constitution and in defiance of the Constitution, which may be resorted to when a revolution is to be justified. But I do not admit, that, under the Constitution and in conformity with it, there is any mode in which a State government, as a member of the Union, can interfere and stop the progress of the general government, by force of her own laws, under any circumstances whatever.

This leads us to inquire into the origin of this government and the source of its power. Whose agent is it? Is it the creature of the State legislatures, or the creature of the people? If the government of the United States be the agent of the State governments, then they may control it, provided they can agree in the manner of controlling it; if it be the agent of the people, then the people alone can control it, restrain it, modify, or reform it. It is observable enough, that the doctrine for which the honorable gentleman contends leads him to the necessity of maintaining, not only that this general government is the creature of the States, but that it is the creature of each of the States severally, so that each may assert the power for itself of determining whether it acts within the limits of its authority. It is the servant of four-and-twenty masters, of different wills and different purposes, and yet bound to obey all. This absurdity (for it seems no less) arises from a misconception as to the origin of this government and its true character. It is, Sir, the people's Constitution, the people's government, made for the people, made by the people, and answerable to the people. The people of the United States have declared that this Constitution shall be the supreme law. We must either admit the proposition, or dispute their authority. The States are, unquestionably, sovereign, so far as their sovereignty is not affected by this supreme law. But the State legislatures, as political bodies, however sovereign, are yet not sovereign over the people. So far as the people have given power to the general government, so far the grant is unquestionably good, and the government holds of the people, and not of the State governments. We are all agents of the same supreme power, the people. The general government and the State governments derive their authority from the same source. Neither can, in relation to the other, be called primary, though one is definite and restricted, and the other general and residuary. The national government possesses those powers which it can be shown the people have conferred on it, and no more. All the rest belongs to the State governments, or to the people themselves. So far as the people have restrained State sovereignty, by the expression of their will, in the Constitution of the United States, so far, it must be admitted, State sovereignty is effectually controlled. I do not contend that it is, or ought to be, controlled farther. The sentiment to which I have referred propounds that State sovereignty is only to be controlled by its own "feeling of justice"; that is to say, it is not to be controlled at all, for one who is to follow his own feelings is under no legal control. Now, however men may think this ought to be, the fact is, that the people of the United States have chosen to impose control on State sovereignties. There are those, doubtless, who wish they had been left without restraint; but the Constitution has ordered the matter differently. To make war, for instance, is an exercise of sovereignty; but the Constitution declares that no State shall make war. To coin money is another exercise of sovereign power; but no State is at liberty to coin money. Again, the Constitution says that no sovereign State shall be so sovereign as to make a treaty. These prohibitions, it must be confessed, are a control on the State sovereignty of South Carolina, as well as of the other States, which does not arise "from her own feelings of honorable justice." The opinion referred to, therefore, is in defiance of the plainest provisions of the Constitution. . . .

And now, Sir, what I have first to say on this subject is, that at no time, and under no circumstances, has New England, or any State in New England, or any respectable body of persons in New England, or any public man of standing in New England, put forth such a doctrine as this Carolina doctrine.

The gentleman has found no case, he can find none, to support his own opinions by New England authority. New England has studied the Constitution in other schools, and under other teachers. She looks upon it with other regards, and deems more highly and reverently both of its just authority and its utility and excellence. The history of her legislative proceedings may be traced. The ephemeral effusions of temporary bodies, called together by the excitement of the occasion, may be hunted up; they have been hunted up. The opinions and votes of her public men, in and out of Congress, may be explored. It will all be in vain. The Carolina doctrine can derive from her neither countenance nor support. She rejects it now; she always did reject it; and till she loses her senses, she always will reject it. . . .

Sir, the human mind is so constituted, that the merits of both sides of a controversy appear very clear, and very palpable, to those who respectively espouse them; and both sides usually grow clearer as the controversy advances. South Carolina sees unconstitutionality in the tariff; she sees oppression there also, and she sees danger. Pennsylvania, with a vision not less sharp, looks at the same tariff, and sees no such thing in it; she sees it all constitutional, all useful, all safe. The faith of South Carolina is strengthened by opposition, and she now not only sees, but *resolves*, that the tariff is palpably unconstitutional, oppressive, and dangerous; but Pennsylvania, not to be behind her neighbors, and equally willing to strengthen her own faith by a confident asseveration *resolves*, also, and gives to every warm affirmative of South Carolina, a plain, downright, Pennsylvania negative. South Carolina, to show the strength and unity of her opinion, brings her assembly to a unanimity, within seven voices; Pennsylvania, not to be outdone in this respect any more than in others, reduces her dissentient fraction to a single vote. Now, Sir, again, I ask the gentleman, What is to be done? Are these States both right? Is he bound to consider them both right? If not, which is in the wrong? or rather, which has the best right to decide? And if he, and if I, are not to know what the Constitution means, and what it is, till those two State legislatures, and the twenty-two others, shall agree in its construction, what have we sworn to, when we have sworn to maintain it? I was forcibly struck, Sir, with one reflection, as the gentleman went on in his speech. He quoted Mr. Madison's resolutions, to prove that a State may interfere, in a case of deliberate, palpable, and dangerous exercise of a power not granted. The honorable member supposes the tariff law to be such an exercise of power; and that consequently a case has arisen in which the State may, if it see fit, interfere by its own law. Now it so happens, nevertheless, that Mr. Madison deems this same tariff law quite constitutional. Instead of a clear and palpable violation, it is, in his judgment, no violation at all. So that, while they use his authority for a hypothetical case, they reject it in the very case before them. All this, Sir, shows the inherent futility, I had almost used a stronger word, of conceding this power of interference to the State, and then attempting to secure it from abuse by imposing qualifications of which the States themselves are to judge. One of two things is true; either the laws of the Union are beyond the discretion and beyond the control of the States; or else we have no constitution of general government, and are thrust back again to the days of the Confederation. . . .

I wish now, Sir, to make a remark upon the Virginia resolutions of 1798. I cannot undertake to say how these resolutions were understood by those who passed them. Their language is not a little indefinite. In the case of the exercise by Congress of a dangerous power not granted to them, the resolutions assert the right, on the part of the State, to interfere and arrest the progress of the evil. This is susceptible of more than one interpretation. It may mean no more than that the States may interfere by complaint and remonstrance, or by proposing to the people an alteration of the Federal Constitution. This would all be quite unobjectionable. Or it may be that no more is meant than to assert the general right of revolution, as against all governments, in cases of intolerable oppression. This no one doubts, and this, in my opinion, is all that he who framed the resolutions could have meant by it; for I shall not readily believe that he was ever of opinion that a State, under the Constitution and in conformity with it, could, upon the ground of her own opinion of its unconstitutionality, however clear and palpable she might think the case, annul a law of Congress, so far as it should operate on herself, by her own legislative power.

I must now beg to ask, Sir, Whence is this supposed right of the States derived? Where do they find the power to interfere with the laws of the Union? Sir, the opinion which the honorable gentleman maintains is a notion founded in a total misapprehension, in my judgment, of the origin of this government, and of the foundation on which it stands. I hold it to be a popular government, erected by the people; those who administer it, responsible to the people; and itself capable of being amended and modified, just as the people may choose it should be. It is as popular, just as truly emanating from the people, as the State governments. It is created for one purpose; the State governments for another. It has its own powers; they have theirs. There is no more authority with them to arrest the operation of a law of Congress, than with Congress to arrest the operation of their laws. We are here to administer a Constitution emanating immediately from the people, and trusted by them to our administration. It is not the creature of the State governments. It is of no moment to the argument, that certain acts of the State legislatures are necessary to fill our seats in this body. That is not one of their original State powers, a part of the sovereignty of the State. It is a duty which the people, by the Constitution itself, have imposed on the State legislatures; and which they might have left to be performed elsewhere, if they had seen fit. So they have left the choice of President with electors; but all this does not affect the proposition that this whole government, President, Senate, and House of Representatives, is a popular government. It leaves it still all its popular character. The governor of a State (in some of the States) is chosen, not directly by the people, but by those who are chosen by the people, for the purpose of performing, among other duties, that of electing a governor. Is the government of the State, on that account, not a popular government? This government, Sir, is the independent offspring of the popular will. It is not the creature of State legislatures; nay, more, if the whole truth must be told, the people brought it into existence, established it, and have hitherto supported it, for the very purpose, amongst others, of imposing certain salutary restraints on State sovereignties. The States cannot now make war; they cannot contract alliances; they cannot make, each for itself, separate regulations of commerce; they cannot lay imposts; they cannot coin money. If this Constitution, Sir, be the creature of State legislatures, it must be admitted that it has obtained a strange control over the volitions of its creators.

The people, then, Sir, erected this government. They gave it a Constitution, and in that Constitution they have enumerated the powers which they bestow on it. They have made it a limited government. They have defined its authority. They have restrained it to the exercise of such powers as are granted; and all others, they declare, are reserved to the States or the people. But, Sir, they have not stopped here. If they had, they would have accomplished but half their work. No definition can be so clear, as to avoid possibility of doubt; no limitation so precise, as to exclude all uncertainty. Who, then, shall construe this grant of the people? Who shall interpret their will, where it may be supposed they have left it doubtful? With whom do they repose this ultimate right of deciding on the powers of the government? Sir, they have settled all this in the fullest manner. They have left it with the government itself, in its appropriate branches. Sir, the very chief end, the main design, for which the whole Constitution was framed and adopted, was to establish a government that should not be obliged to act through State agency, or depend on State opinion and State discretion. The people had had quite enough of that kind of government under the Confederation. Under that system, the legal action, the application of law to individuals, belonged exclusively to the States. Congress could only recommend; their acts were not of binding force, till the States had adopted and sanctioned them. Are we in that condition still? Are we yet at the mercy of State discretion and State construction? Sir, if we are, then vain will be our attempt to maintain the Constitution under which we sit.

But, Sir, the people have wisely provided, in the Constitution itself, a proper, suitable mode and tribunal for settling questions of constitutional law. There are in the Constitution grants of powers to Congress, and restrictions on these powers. There are, also, prohibitions on the States. Some authority must, therefore, necessarily exist, having the ultimate jurisdiction to fix and ascertain the interpretation of these grants, restrictions, and prohibitions. The Constitution has itself pointed out, ordained, and established that authority. How has it accomplished this great and essential end? By declaring, Sir, that *"the Constitution, and the laws of the United States made in pursuance thereof, shall be the supreme law of the land, any thing in the constitution or laws of any State to the contrary notwithstanding."*

This, Sir, was the first great step. By this the supremacy of the Constitution and laws of the United States is declared. The people so will it. No State law is to be valid which comes in conflict with the Constitution, or any law of the United States passed in pursuance of it. But who shall decide this question of interference? To whom lies the last appeal? This, Sir, the Constitution itself decides also, by declaring, *"that the judicial power shall extend to all cases arising under the Constitution and laws of the United States."* These two provisions cover the whole ground. They are, in truth, the keystone of the arch! With these it is a government; without them it is a confederation. In pursuance of these clear and express provisions, Congress established, at its very first session, in the judicial act, a mode for carrying them into full effect, and for bringing all questions of constitutional power to the final decision of the Supreme Court. It then, Sir, became a government. It then had the means of self-protection; and but for this, it would, in all probability, have been now among things which are past. Having constituted the government, and declared its powers, the people have further said, that, since somebody must decide on the extent of these powers, the government shall itself decide; subject, always, like other popular governments, to its responsibility to the people. . . .

And, Sir, if we look to the general nature of the case, could any thing have been more preposterous, than to make a government for the whole Union, and yet leave its powers subject, not to one interpretation, but to thirteen or twenty-four interpretations? Instead of one tribunal, established by all, responsible to all, with power to decide for all, shall constitutional questions be left to four-and-twenty popular bodies, each at liberty to decide for itself, and none bound to respect the decisions of others; and each at liberty, too, to give a new construction on every new election of its own members? Would any thing, with such a principle in it, or rather with such a destitution of all principle, be fit to be called a government? No, Sir. It should not be denominated a Constitution. It should be called, rather, a collection of topics for everlasting controversy; heads of debate for a disputatious people. It would not be a government. It would not be adequate to any practical good, or fit for any country to live under.

To avoid all possibility of being misunderstood, allow me to repeat again, in the fullest manner, that I claim no powers for the government by forced or unfair construction. I admit that it is a government of strictly limited powers; of enumerated, specified, and particularized powers; and that whatsoever is not granted, is withheld. But notwithstanding all this, and however the grant of powers may be expressed, its limit and extent may yet, in some cases, admit of doubt; and the general government would be good for nothing, it would be incapable of long existing, if some mode had not been provided in which those doubts, as they should arise, might be peaceably, but authoritatively, solved.

And now, Mr. President, let me run the honorable gentleman's doctrine a little into its practical application. Let us look at his probable *modus operandi*. If a thing can be done, an ingenious man can tell *how* it is to be done, and I wish to be informed *how* this State interference is to be put in practice without violence, bloodshed, and rebellion. We will take the existing case of the tariff law. South Carolina is said to have made up her opinion upon it. If we do not repeal it (as we probably shall not), she will then apply to the case the remedy of her doctrine. She will, we must suppose, pass a law of her legislature, declaring the several acts of Congress, usually called the tariff laws, null and void, so far as they respect South Carolina, or the citizens thereof. So far, all is a paper transaction, and easy enough. But the collector at Charleston is collecting the duties imposed by these tariff laws. He, therefore, must be stopped. The collector will seize the goods if the tariff duties are not paid. The State authorities will undertake their rescue, the marshal, with his posse, will come to the collector's aid, and here the contest begins. The militia of the State will be called out to sustain the nullifying act. They will march, Sir, under a very gallant leader; for I believe the honorable member himself commands the militia of that part of the State. He will raise the NULLIFYING ACT on his standard, and spread it out as his banner! . . . Arrived at the custom-house, he will tell the collector that he must collect no more duties under any of the tariff laws. This he will be somewhat puzzled to say, by the way, with a grave countenance, considering what hand South Carolina herself had in that of 1816. But, Sir, the collector would not, probably, desist, at his bidding. He would show him the law of Congress, the treasury instruction, and his own oath of office. He would say, he should perform his duty, come what might.

Here would ensue a pause; for they say that a certain stillness precedes the tempest. The trumpeter would hold his breath awhile, and before all this military array should fall on the custom-house, collector, clerks, and all, it is very probable some of those composing it would request of their gallant commander-in-chief to be informed a little upon the point of law. . . . What would be the nature of their offence, they would wish to learn, if they, by military force and array, resisted the execution in Carolina of a law of the United States, and it should turn out, after all, that the law *was constitutional?* He would answer, of course, Treason. No lawyer could give any other answer. . . . Is it your opinion, gallant commander, they would then say, that, if we should be indicted for treason, that same floating banner of yours would make a good plea in bar? "South Carolina is a sovereign State," he would reply. That is true; but would the judge admit our plea? "These tariff laws," he would repeat, "are unconstitutional, palpably, deliberately, dangerously." That may all be so; but if the tribunal should not happen to be of that opinion, shall we swing for it? We are ready to die for our country, but it is rather an awkward business, this dying without touching the ground! After all, that is a sort of hemp tax worse than any part of the tariff.

Mr. President, the honorable gentleman would be in a dilemma, like that of another great general. He would have a knot before him which he could not untie. He must cut it with his sword. He must say to his followers, "Defend yourselves with your bayonets"; and this is war—civil war.

Direct collision, therefore, between force and force, is the unavoidable result of that remedy for the revision of unconstitutional laws which the gentleman contends for. It must happen in the very first case to which it is applied. Is not this the plain result? To resist by force the execution of a law, generally, is treason. Can the courts of the United States take notice of the indulgence of a State to commit treason? The common saying, that a State cannot commit treason herself, is nothing to the purpose. Can she authorize others to do it? . . .

The honorable gentleman argues, that if this government be the sole judge of the extent of its own powers, whether that right of judging be in Congress or the Supreme Court, it equally subverts State sovereignty. This the gentleman sees, or thinks he sees, although he cannot perceive how the right of judging, in this matter, if left to the exercise of State legislatures, has any tendency to subvert the government of the Union. The gentleman's opinion may be, that the right *ought not* to have been lodged with the general government; he may like better such a constitution as we should have under the right of State interference; but I ask him to meet me on the plain matter of fact. I ask him to meet me on the Constitution itself. I ask him if the power is not found there, clearly and visibly found there?

But, Sir, what is this danger, and what are the grounds of it? Let it be remembered, that the Constitution of the United States is not unalterable. It is to continue in its present form no longer than the people who established it shall choose to continue it. If they shall become convinced that they have made an injudicious or inexpedient partition and distribution of power between the State governments and the general government, they can alter that distribution at will.

If any thing be found in the national Constitution, either by original provision or subsequent interpretation, which ought not to be in it, the people know how to get rid of it. If any construction, unacceptable to them, be established, so as to become practically a part of the Constitution, they will amend it, at their own sovereign pleasure. But while the people choose to maintain it as it is, while they are satisfied with it, and refuse to change it, who has given, or who can give, to the State legislatures a right to alter it, either by interference, construction, or otherwise? Gentlemen do not seem to recollect that the people have any power to do any thing for themselves. They imagine there is no safety for them, any longer than they are under the close guardianship of the State legislatures. Sir, the people have not trusted their safety, in regard to the general Constitution, to these hands. They have required other security, and taken other bonds. They have chosen to trust themselves, first, to the plain words of the instrument, and to such construction as the government themselves, in doubtful cases, should put on their own powers, under their oaths of office, and subject to their responsibility to them; just as the people of a State trust their own State governments with a similar power. Secondly, they have reposed their trust in the efficacy of frequent elections, and in their own power to remove their own servants and agents whenever they see cause. Thirdly, they have reposed trust in the judicial power, which, in order that it might be trustworthy, they have made as respectable, as disinterested, and as independent as was practicable. Fourthly, they have seen fit to rely, in case of necessity, or high expediency, on their known and admitted power to alter or amend the Constitution, peaceably and quietly, whenever experience shall point out defects or imperfections. And, finally, the people of the United States have at no time, in no way, directly or indirectly, authorized any State legislature to construe or interpret *their* high instrument of government; much less, to interfere, by their own power, to arrest its course and operation. . . .

But, Sir, although there are fears, there are hopes also. The people have preserved this, their own chosen Constitution, for forty years, and have seen their happiness, prosperity, and renown grow with its growth, and strengthen with its strength. They are now, generally, strongly attached to it. Overthrown by direct assault, it cannot be; evaded, undermined, NULLIFIED, it will not be, if we, and those who shall succeed us here, as agents and representatives of the people, shall conscientiously and vigilantly discharge the two great branches of our public trust, faithfully to preserve, and wisely to administer it.

Mr. President, I have thus stated the reasons of my dissent to the doctrines which have been advanced and maintained. I am conscious of having detained you and the Senate much too long. I was drawn into the debate with no previous deliberation, such as is suited to the discussion of so grave and important a subject. But it is a subject of which my heart is full, and I have not been willing to suppress the utterance of its spontaneous sentiments. I cannot, even now, persuade myself to relinquish it, without expressing once more my deep conviction, that, since it respects nothing less than the Union of the States, it is of most vital and essential importance to the public happiness. I profess, Sir, in my career hitherto, to have kept steadily in view the prosperity and honor of the whole country, and the preservation of our Federal Union. It is to that Union we owe our safety at home, and our consideration and dignity abroad. It is to that Union that we are chiefly indebted for whatever makes us most proud of our country. That Union we reached only by the discipline of our virtues in the severe school of adversity. It had its origin in the necessities of disordered finance, prostrate commerce, and ruined credit. Under its benign influences, these great interests immediately awoke, as from the dead, and sprang forth with newness of life. Every year of its duration has teemed with fresh proofs of its utility and its blessings; and although our territory has stretched out wider and wider, and our population spread farther and farther, they have not outrun its protection or its benefits. It has been to us all a copious fountain of national, social, and personal happiness.

I have not allowed myself, Sir, to look beyond the Union, to see what might lie hidden in the dark recess behind. I have not coolly weighed the chances of preserving liberty when the bonds that unite us together shall be broken asunder. I have not accustomed myself to hang over the precipice of disunion, to see whether, with my short sight, I can fathom the depth of the abyss below; nor could I regard him as a safe counsellor in the affairs of this government, whose thoughts should be mainly bent on considering, not how the Union may be best preserved, but how tolerable might be the condition of the people when it should be broken up and destroyed. While the Union lasts, we have high, exciting, gratifying prospects spread out before us, for us and our children. Beyond that I seek not to penetrate the veil. God grant that in my day, at least, that curtain may not rise! God grant that on my vision never may be opened what lies behind! When my eyes shall be turned to behold for the last time the sun in heaven, may I not see him shining on the broken and dishonored fragments of a once glorious Union; on States dissevered, discordant, belligerent; on a land rent with civil feuds, or drenched, it may be, in fraternal blood! Let their last feeble and lingering glance rather behold the gorgeous ensign of the republic, now known and honored throughout the earth, still full high advanced, its arms and trophies streaming in their original lustre, not a stripe erased or polluted, nor a single star obscured, bearing for its motto, no such miserable interrogatory as "What is all this worth?" nor those other words of delusion and folly, "Liberty first and Union afterwards"; but everywhere, spread all over in characters of living light, blazing on all its ample folds, as they float over the sea and over the land, and in every wind under the whole heavens, that other sentiment, dear to every true American heart—Liberty AND Union, now and for ever, one and inseparable!

2

THE LIMITS OF POLITICAL AUTHORITY

William Henry Harrison
INAUGURAL ADDRESS

William Henry Harrison (1773–1841) was a western territorial administrator and army officer. He became a hero by defeating the great Indian chief Tecumseh at the battle of Tippecanoe in 1811. The Whig party took advantage of his fame to nominate him for the presidency in 1840. The ensuing campaign marked the emergence of modern mass politics in America. The techniques of publicity developed then—campaign slogans ("Tippecanoe and Tyler too"), banners, processions, and the like—have been prominent features of American political life ever since. Harrison won the election and promptly summoned a special session of Congress to enact the Whig economic program, including the recharter of the national Bank.

Though the Whigs believed in a strong central government, they were anxious to limit the power of the presidential office, which they felt Jackson had abused. They also firmly believed that the sovereignty of the people needed to be limited by respect for law. Harrison's inaugural address, longer and more philosophical than most of its kind, stresses both these themes. It may be regarded as a counterpoint to the preceding oration by Webster. Webster himself edited Harrison's draft of the speech, so it bears his imprimatur. Just one month after delivering this address, President Harrison died of pneumonia. The Whig triumph was suddenly turned to ashes.

Called from a retirement which I had supposed was to continue for the residue of my life to fill the chief executive office of this great and free nation, I appear before you, fellow-citizens, to take the oaths which the Constitution prescribes as a necessary qualification for the performance of its duties; and in obedience to a custom coeval with our government and what I believe to be your expectations I proceed to present to you a summary of the principles which will govern me in

SOURCE. William Henry Harrison, "Inaugural Address" (March 4, 1841), *Messages and Papers of the Presidents*, ed. James D. Richardson (Washington, D.C., 1900), IV, 5–21.

the discharge of the duties which I shall be called upon to perform.

It was the remark of a Roman consul in an early period of that celebrated republic that a most striking contrast was observable in the conduct of candidates for offices of power and trust before and after obtaining them, they seldom carrying out in the latter case the pledges and promises made in the former. However much the world may have improved in many respects in the lapse of upward of two thousand years since the remark was made by the virtuous and indignant Roman, I fear that a strict examination of the annals of some of the modern elective governments would develop similar instances of violated confidence. . . .

The broad foundation upon which our Constitution rests being the people—a breath of theirs having made, as a breath can unmake, change, or modify it—it can be assigned to none of the great divisions of government but to that of democracy. If such is its theory, those who are called upon to administer it must recognize as its leading principle the duty of shaping their measures so as to produce the greatest good to the greatest number. But with these broad admissions, if we would compare the sovereignty acknowledged to exist in the mass of our people with the power claimed by other sovereignties, even by those which have been considered most purely democratic, we shall find a most essential difference. All others lay claim to power limited only by their own will. The majority of our citizens, on the contrary, possess a sovereignty with an amount of power precisely equal to that which has been granted to them by the parties to the national compact, and nothing beyond. We admit of no government by divine right, believing that so far as power is concerned the Beneficent Creator has made no distinction amongst men; that all are upon an equality, and that the only legitimate right to govern is an express grant of power from the governed. The Constitution of the United States is the instrument containing this grant of power to the several departments composing the government. On an examination of that instrument it will be found to contain declarations of power granted and of power withheld. The latter is also susceptible of division into power which the majority had the right to grant, but which they did not think proper to intrust to their agents, and that which they could not have granted, not being possessed by themselves. In other words, there are certain rights possessed by each individual American citizen which in his compact with the others he has never surrendered. Some of them, indeed, he is unable to surrender, being, in the language of our system, unalienable. The boasted privilege of a Roman citizen was to him a shield only against a petty provincial ruler, whilst the proud democrat of Athens would console himself under a sentence of death for a supposed violation of the national faith—which no one understood and which at times was the subject of the mockery of all—or the banishment from his home, his family, and his country with or without an alleged cause, that it was the act not of a single tyrant or hated aristocracy, but of his assembled countrymen. Far different is the power of our sovereignty. It can interfere with no one's faith, prescribe forms of worship for no one's observance, inflict no punishment but after well-ascertained guilt, the result of investigation under rules prescribed by the Constitution itself. These precious privileges, and those scarcely less important of giving expression to his thoughts and opinions, either by writing or speaking, unrestrained but by the liability for injury to others, and that of a full participation in all the advantages which flow from the Government, the acknowledged property of all, the American citizen derives from no charter granted by his fellow-man. He claims them because he is himself a man, fashioned by the same Almighty hand as the rest of his species and entitled to a full share of the blessings with which He has endowed them. Notwithstanding the limited sovereignty possessed by the people of the United States and the restricted grant of power to the government which they have adopted, enough has been given to accomplish all the objects for which it was created. It has been found powerful in war, and hitherto justice has been administered, an intimate union effected, domestic tranquillity preserved, and personal liberty secured to the citizen. As was to be expected, however, from the defect of language and the necessarily sententious manner in which the Constitution is written, disputes have arisen as to the amount of power which it has actually granted or was intended to grant.

This is more particularly the case in relation to that part of the instrument which treats of the legislative branch, and not only as regards the exercise of powers claimed under a general clause giving that body the authority to pass all laws necessary to carry into effect the specified powers, but in relation to the latter also. It is, however, consolatory to reflect that *most* of the instances of alleged departure from the letter or spirit of the Constitution have ultimately received the sanction of a majority of the people. And the fact that many of our statesmen most distinguished for talent and patriotism have been at one time or other of their political career on both sides of each of the most warmly disputed questions forces upon us the inference that the errors, if errors there were, are attributable to the intrinsic difficulty in many instances of ascertaining the intentions of the framers of the

Constitution rather than the influence of any sinister or unpatriotic motive. But the great danger to our institutions does not appear to me to be in a usurpation by the government of power not granted by the people, but by the accumulation in one of the departments of that which was assigned to others. Limited as are the powers which have been granted, still enough have been granted to constitute a despotism if concentrated in one of the departments. This danger is greatly heightened, as it has been always observable that men are less jealous of encroachments of one department upon another than upon their own reserved rights. When the Constitution of the United States first came from the hands of the Convention which formed it, many of the sternest republicans of the day were alarmed at the extent of the power which had been granted to the federal government, and more particularly of that portion which had been assigned to the executive branch. There were in it features which appeared not to be in harmony with their ideas of a simple representative democracy or republic, and knowing the tendency of power to increase itself, particularly when exercised by a single individual, predictions were made that at no very remote period the government would terminate in virtual monarchy. It would not become me to say that the fears of these patriots have been already realized; but as I sincerely believe that the tendency of measures and of men's opinions for some years past has been in that direction, it is, I conceive, strictly proper that I should take this occasion to repeat the assurances I have heretofore given of my determination to arrest the progress of that tendency if it really exists and restore the government to its pristine health and vigor, as far as this can be effected by any legitimate exercise of the power placed in my hands.

I proceed to state in as summary a manner as I can my opinion of the sources of the evils which have been so extensively complained of and the correctives which may be applied. Some of the former are unquestionably to be found in the defects of the Constitution; others, in my judgment, are attributable to a misconstruction of some of its provisions. Of the former is the eligibility of the same individual to a second term of the Presidency. The sagacious mind of Mr. Jefferson early saw and lamented this error, and attempts have been made, hitherto without success, to apply the amendatory power of the States to its correction. . . . Until an amendment of the Constitution can be effected public opinion may secure the desired object. I give my aid to it by renewing the pledge heretofore given that under no circumstances will I consent to serve a second term.

But if there is danger to public liberty from the acknowledged defects of the Constitution in the want of limit to the continuance of the Executive power in the same hands, there is, I apprehend, not much less from a misconstruction of that instrument as it regards the powers actually given. I can not conceive that by a fair construction any or either of its provisions would be found to constitute the President a part of the legislative power. It can not be claimed from the power to recommend, since, although enjoined as a duty upon him, it is a privilege which he holds in common with every other citizen; and although there may be something more of confidence in the propriety of the measures recommended in the one case than in the other, in the obligations of ultimate decision there can be no difference. In the language of the Constitution, "all the legislative powers" which it grants "are vested in the Congress of the United States." It would be a solecism in language to say that any portion of these is not included in the whole.

It may be said, indeed, that the Constitution has given to the Executive the power to annul the acts of the legislative body by refusing to them his assent. So a similar power has necessarily result-ed from that instrument to the judiciary, and yet the judiciary forms no part of the Legislature. There is, it is true, this difference between these grants of power: The Executive can put his negative upon the acts of the Legislature for other cause than that of want of conformity to the Constitution, whilst the judiciary can only declare void those which violate that instrument. But the decision of the judiciary is final in such a case, whereas in every instance where the veto of the Executive is applied it may be overcome by a vote of two-thirds of both Houses of Congress. The negative upon the acts of the legislative by the executive authority, and that in the hands of one individual, would seem to be an incongruity in our system. Like some others of a similar character, however, it appears to be highly expedient, and if used only with the forbearance and in the spirit which was intended by its authors it may be productive of great good and be found one of the best safeguards to the Union. At the period of the formation of the Constitution the principle does not appear to have enjoyed much favor in the State governments. It existed but in two, and in one of these there was a plural executive. If we would search for the motives which operated upon the purely patriotic and enlightened assembly which framed the Constitution for the adoption of a provision so apparently repugnant to the leading democratic principle that the majority should govern, we must reject the idea that they anticipated from it any benefit to the ordinary course of legislation. They knew too well the high degree of intelligence which existed among the people and the enlightened character of the State legislatures not to have the fullest confidence that the two bodies elected by them would be worthy representatives of such constituents, and, of course, that they would require no aid in conceiving and maturing the measures which the circumstances of the country might require. And it is preposterous to suppose that a thought could for a moment have been entertained that the President, placed at the capital, in the center of the country, could better understand the wants and wishes of the people than their own immediate representatives, who spend a part of every year among them, living with them, often laboring with them, and bound to them by the triple tie of interest, duty, and affection. To assist or control Congress, then, in its ordinary legislation could not, I conceive, have been the motive for conferring the veto power on the President. This argument acquires additional force from the fact of its never having been thus used by the first six Presidents—and two of them were members of the Convention, one presiding over its deliberations and the other bearing a larger share in consummating the labors of that august body than any other person. But if bills were never returned to Congress by either of the Presidents above referred to upon the ground of their being inexpedient or not as well adapted as they might be to the wants of the people, the veto was applied upon that of want of conformity to the Constitution or because errors had been committed from a too hasty enactment.

There is another ground for the adoption of the veto principle, which had probably more influence in recommending it to the Convention than any other. I refer to the security which it gives to the just and equitable action of the Legislature upon all parts of the Union. It could not but have occurred to the Convention that in a country so extensive, embracing so great a variety of soil and climate, and consequently of products, and which from the same causes must ever exhibit a great difference in the amount of the population of its various sections, calling for a great diversity in the employments of the people, that the legislation of the majority might not always justly regard the rights and interests of the minority, and that acts of this character might be passed under an express grant by the words of the Constitution, and therefore not within the competency of the judiciary to declare void; that however enlightened and patriotic they might suppose from past experience the members of Congress might be, and however largely partaking, in the general, of the liberal feelings of the people, it was impossible to expect that bodies so constituted should not sometimes be controlled by local interests and sectional feelings. It was proper, therefore, to provide some umpire from whose situation and mode of appointment more independence and freedom from such influences might be expected. Such a one was afforded by the executive department constituted by the Constitution. A person elected to that high office, having his constituents in every section, State, and subdivision of the Union, must consider himself bound by the most solemn sanctions to guard, protect, and defend the rights of all and of every portion, great or small, from the injustice and oppression of the rest. I consider the veto power, therefore, given by the Constitution to the Executive of the United States solely as a conservative power, to be used only, first, to protect the Constitution from violation; secondly, the people from the effects of hasty legislation where their will has been probably disregarded or not well understood, and, thirdly, to prevent the effects of combinations violative of the rights of minorities. In reference to the second of these objects I may observe that I consider it the right and privilege of the people to decide disputed points of the Constitution arising from the general grant of power to Congress to carry into effect the powers expressly given; and I believe with Mr. Madison that "repeated recognitions under varied circumstances in acts of the legislative, executive, and judicial branches of the government, accompanied by indications in different modes of the concurrence of the general will of the nation," as affording to the President sufficient authority for his considering such disputed points as settled. . . .

By making the President the sole distributer of all the patronage of the Government the framers of the Constitution do not appear to have anticipated at how short a period it would become a formidable instrument to control the free operations of the State governments. Of trifling importance at first, it had early in Mr. Jefferson's Administration become so powerful as to create great alarm in the mind of that patriot from the potent influence it might exert in controlling the freedom of the elective franchise. If such could have then been the effects of its influence, how much greater must be the danger at this time, quadrupled in amount as it certainly is and more completely under the control of the Executive will than their construction of their powers allowed or the forbearing characters of all the early Presidents permitted them to make. But it is not by the extent of its patronage alone that the executive department has become dangerous, but by the use which it appears may be made of the appointing power to bring under its control the whole revenues of the country. The Constitution has declared it to be the duty of the President to see that the laws are executed, and it makes him the Commander in Chief of the Armies and Navy of the United States. If the opinion of the most approved writers upon that species of mixed government which in modern Europe is termed *monarchy* in contradistinction to *despotism* is correct, there was wanting no other addition to the powers of our Chief Magistrate to stamp a monarchical character on our government but the control of the public finances; and to me it appears strange indeed that anyone should doubt that the entire control which the President possesses over the officers who have the custody of the public money, by the power of removal with or without cause, does, for all mischievous purposes at least, virtually subject the treasure also to his disposal. . . . It was certainly a great error in the framers of the Constitution not to have made the officer at the head of the Treasury Department entirely independent of the Executive. He should at least have been removable only upon the demand of the popular branch of the Legislature. I have determined never to remove a Secretary of the Treasury without communicating all the circumstances attending such removal to both Houses of Congress.[1] . . .

Connected with this subject is the character of the currency. The idea of making it exclusively metallic, however well intended, appears to me to be fraught with more fatal consequences than any other scheme having no relation to the personal rights of the citizens that has ever been devised. If any single scheme could produce the effect of arresting at once that mutation of condition by which thousands of our most indigent fellow-citizens by their industry and enterprise are raised to the possession of wealth, that is the one. If there is one measure better calculated than another to produce that state of things so much deprecated by all true republicans, by which the rich are daily adding to their hoards and the poor sinking deeper into penury, it is an exclusive metallic currency. Or if there is a process by which the character of the country for generosity and nobleness of feeling may be destroyed by the great increase and necessary toleration of usury, it is an exclusive metallic currency.

Amongst the other duties of a delicate character which the President is called upon to perform is the supervision of the government of the Territories of the United States. Those of them which are destined to become members of our great political family are compensated by their rapid progress from infancy to manhood for the partial and temporary deprivation of their political rights. It is in this District only where American citizens are to be found who under a settled policy are deprived of many important political privileges

---

[1]President Jackson had dismissed two secretaries of the treasury in the course of his quarrel with the BUS. Ed.

without any inspiring hope as to the future. . . . The people of the District of Columbia are not the subjects of the people of the States, but free American citizens. Being in the latter condition when the Constitution was formed, no words used in that instrument could have been intended to deprive them of that character. . . . The legislation of Congress should be adapted to their peculiar position and wants and be conformable with their deliberate opinions of their own interests.

I have spoken of the necessity of keeping the respective departments of the government, as well as all the other authorities of our country, within their appropriate orbits. This is a matter of difficulty in some cases, as the powers which they respectively claim are often not defined by any distinct lines. Mischievous, however, in their tendencies as collisions of this kind may be, those which arise between the respective communities which for certain purposes compose one nation are much more so, for no such nation can long exist without the careful culture of those feelings of confidence and affection which are the effective bonds to union between free and confederated states. . . . No participation in any good possessed by any member of our extensive Confederacy, except in domestic government, was withheld from the citizen of any other member. By a process attended with no difficulty, no delay, no expense but that of removal, the citizen of one might become the citizen of any other, and successively of the whole. The lines, too, separating powers to be exercised by the citizens of one State from those of another seem to be so distinctly drawn as to leave no room for misunderstanding. The citizens of each State unite in their persons all the privileges which that character confers and all that they may claim as citizens of the United States, but in no case can the same person at the same time act as the citizen of two separate States, and *he is therefore positively precluded from any interference with the reserved powers of any State but that of which he is for the time being a citizen.* He may, indeed, offer to the citizens of other States his advice as to their management, and the form in which it is tendered is left to his own discretion and sense of propriety. . . .

Our citizens must be content with the exercise of the powers with which the Constitution clothes them. The attempt of those of one State to control the domestic institutions of another can only result in feelings of distrust and jealousy, the certain harbingers of disunion, violence, and civil war, and the ultimate destruction of our free institutions. Our Confederacy is perfectly illustrated by the terms and principles governing a common copartnership. There is a fund of power to be exercised under the direction of the joint councils of the allied members, but that which has been reserved by the individual members is intangible by the common government or the individual members composing it. To attempt it finds no support in the principles of our Constitution.

It should be our constant and earnest endeavor mutually to cultivate a spirit of concord and harmony among the various parts of our Confederacy. Experience has abundantly taught us that the agitation by citizens of one part of the Union of a subject not confided to the General Government, but exclusively under the guardianship of the local authorities, is productive of no other consequences than bitterness, alienation, discord, and injury to the very cause which is intended to be advanced. Of all the great interests which appertain to our country, that of union—cordial, confiding, fraternal union—is by far the most important, since it is the only true and sure guaranty of all others. . . .

Unpleasant and even dangerous as collisions may sometimes be between the constituted authorities of the citizens of our country in relation to the lines which separate their respective jurisdictions, the results can be of no vital injury to our institutions if that ardent patriotism, that devoted attachment to liberty, that spirit of moderation and forbearance for which our countrymen were once distinguished, continue to be cherished. If this continues to be the ruling passion of our souls, the weaker feeling of the mistaken enthusiast will be corrected, the utopian dreams of the scheming politician dissipated, and the complicated intrigues of the demagogue rendered harmless. The spirit of liberty is the sovereign balm for every injury which our institutions may receive. On the contrary, no care that can be used in the construction of our government, no division of powers, no distribution of checks in its several departments, will prove effectual to keep us a free people if this spirit is suffered to decay; and decay it will without constant nurture. To the neglect of this duty the best historians agree in attributing the ruin of all the republics with whose existence and fall their writings have made us acquainted. The same causes will ever produce the same effects, and as long as the love of power is a dominant passion of the human bosom, and as long as the understandings of men can be warped and their affections changed by operations upon their passions and prejudices, so long will the liberties of a people depend on their own constant attention to its preservation. The danger to all well-established free governments arises from the unwillingness of the people to believe in its existence or from the influence of designing men diverting their attention from the quarter whence it approaches to a source from which it can never come. This is the old trick of those who would usurp the government of their country. In the name of democracy they speak, warning the people against the influence of wealth and the danger of aristocracy. History, ancient and modern, is full of such examples. Caesar became the master of the Roman people and the senate under the pretense of supporting the democratic claims of the former against the aristocracy of the latter; Cromwell, in the character of protector of the liberties of the people, became the dictator of England, and Bolivar possessed himself of unlimited power with the title of his country's liberator. There is, on the contrary, no instance on record of an extensive and well-established republic being changed into an aristocracy. The tendencies of all such governments in their decline is to monarchy, and the antagonist principle to liberty there is the spirit of faction—a spirit which assumes the character and in times of great excitement imposes itself upon the people as the genuine spirit of freedom, and, like the false Christs whose coming was foretold by the Savior, seeks to, and were it possible would, impose upon the true and most faithful disciples of liberty. . . .

Before concluding, fellow-citizens, I must say something to you on the subject of the parties at this time existing in our country. To me it appears perfectly clear that the interest of that country requires that the violence of the spirit by which those parties are at this time governed must be greatly mitigated, if not entirely extinguished, or consequences will ensue which are appalling to be thought of.

If parties in a republic are necessary to secure a degree of vigilance sufficient to keep the public functionaries within the bounds of law and duty, at that point their usefulness ends. Beyond that they become destructive of public virtue, the parent of a spirit antagonist to that of liberty, and eventually its inevitable conqueror. . . . Always the friend of my countrymen, never their flatterer, it becomes my duty to say to them from this high place to which their partiality has exalted me that there exists in the land a spirit hostile to their best interests—hostile to liberty itself. It is a spirit contracted in its views, selfish in its objects. It looks to the aggrandizement of a few even to the destruction of the interests of the whole. The entire remedy is with the people. Something, however, may be effected by the means which they have placed in my hands. It is union that we want, not of a party for the sake of that party, but a union of the whole country for the sake of the whole country, for the defense of its interests and its honor against foreign aggression, for the defense of those principles for which our ancestors so gloriously contended. As far as it depends upon me it shall be accomplished. All the influence that I possess shall be exerted to prevent the formation at least of an Executive party in the halls of the legislative body. I wish for the support of no member of that body to any measure of mine that does not satisfy his judgment and his sense of duty to those from whom he holds his appointment, nor any confidence in advance from the people but that asked for by Mr. Jefferson, "to give firmness and effect to the legal administration of their affairs."

I deem the present occasion sufficiently important and solemn to justify me in expressing to my fellow-citizens a profound reverence for the Christian religion and a thorough conviction that sound morals, religious liberty, and a just sense of religious responsibility are essentially connected with all true and lasting happiness; and to that good Being who has blessed us by the gifts of civil and religious freedom, who watched over and prospered the labors of our fathers and has hitherto preserved to us institutions far exceeding in excellence those of any other people, let us unite in fervently commending every interest of our beloved country in all future time.

Fellow-citizens, being fully invested with that high office to which the partiality of my countrymen has called me, I now take an affectionate leave of you.

3

THE WHIG INTERPRETATION OF HISTORY

John Pendleton Kennedy
DEFENCE OF THE WHIGS

The original political faction that gathered around Henry Clay's American System and Nicholas Biddle's Bank called themselves the National Republicans. But in 1834, as their ranks increased with accessions from disaffected former Jacksonians, Clay's followers began to use the term "Whigs." This was a word replete with historical significance in the Anglo-American political tradition. This selection explains why the opponents of Andrew Jackson adopted this name, and what it reveals about their self-image.

John Pendleton Kennedy (1795–1870) was a Maryland lawyer who gave up his practice for careers in literature and politics. His chief accomplishment as a writer is the novel The Swallow Barn *(1832), a classic, somewhat idealized, depiction of southern plantation life. As a Whig congressman he fought successfully for the appropriation enabling Samuel F.B. Morse to develop the telegraph. As secretary of the Navy he sent Commodore Perry to open trade with Japan. The following selection is taken from a campaign pamphlet he produced to help the Whig cause in 1844. It is interesting that Kennedy hearkens back nostalgically to the "era of good feelings" before the rise of the second party system. Many Whigs long nursed such misgivings about a partisan political system, even while working hard for success within it.*

THE BASIS OF PARTIES

We may discern in the progress of all representative government professing to be established on the basis of popular freedom, two parties fundamentally distinguished from each other by their views as to the nature of delegated power. These parties are more or less developed at different epochs, as the events of the day have furnished them excitement.

In English history they have sometimes been denominated the

SOURCE. [John Pendleton Kennedy,] *Defence of the Whigs, by a Member of the Twenty-Seventh Congress* (New York, 1844), pp. 12–24.

Court Party and the Country Party, but more generally by the names of Tories and Whigs.

The Court Party is chiefly distinguished as the friends of the Executive Power.

The Country Party, without being classed in the category of actual enemies to that Power, are noted for their distrust of it.

This is a division of parties which naturally grows out of the constitution of the public mind, and is as much native to our republican government as to the monarchy of Great Britain.

All experience has taught us that the possessor of the authority and patronage of magistracy may find it convenient to employ these resources for the advancement of himself or his friends. A knowledge of this seduces many to become the champions and apologists of the executive in every country. There are designing men, there are corrupt men, poor men, or idle men, who hope to find, in the good will of the ruling magistrate, the means of promoting their schemes or of adding to their comforts: they become, therefore, his dependents both in opinion and conduct.

There are others, quite honest, who conscientiously believe that a strong executive is absolutely necessary to maintain order in the state. For this reason they also take sides with the executive.

These two descriptions of men combine to enlist a large support amongst the people in favor of the administrative arm of the government.

Their opponents, fearing this administrative arm, and believing that the safety of free institutions is best secured by watching and restraining the executive, disdain to seek its favor by any act of adulation or by any relaxation of their distrust. These naturally put great faith in the National Legislature. They see in the executive the fountain of political honors, rank, emolument, consideration with the world: that it is prone to be selfish, ambitious, crafty: that it has a motive to reward subserviency: that in dispensing the offices necessary to conduct government, it may so dispense them as to gratify those who defend and applaud it: that it may convert public servants into political minions: that it may work in secret and corrupt enterprises, and gloss them over with pretences of public good. In all these attributes and propensities of executive power they find strong motive to regard it with jealousy.

On the other hand, they see in the Legislature none of these attributes. Public Liberty is very seldom damaged by the activity of a Representative Legislature; though it is just to say that history is not without its example of a wicked phrensy in this law-making power.

Such example, happily, is rare. In the main, not from the active purpose of Legislative bodies has Liberty sustained hurt: but from their tardiness sometimes, from their dissensions sometimes, and from their omissions, mischief has arisen. The imperfection of the Legislature is in its occasional failure, whether from ignorance, division or sloth, to do what the public good requires; very seldom in corrupt action or deliberate wickedness of object. It has no personal ambition, vanity or selfishness, because, in fact, it has no person, but is an aggregate of many persons, and these of many minds. Neither has it patronage to gratify a love of making dependents. Two or three hundred representatives may make bad laws, or fail to make good ones, but they have scant motive to flatter any man's pride, stimulate any man's usurpation. The usurper always begins by turning the Legislature out of doors, knowing that whilst they are free he is not.

Their special duty is to become acquainted with the condition of the body politic: to inquire into what is done in every department: to inspect every public servant: to look into every corner and crevice of public service and learn what is doing there; and then to report all that they have seen, heard, learned. What they find out of place it is their duty to set in place; what knavery they suspect, to proclaim; what they discover to be weak, to make strong.

To this end they are called, and are, the Grand Inquest of the nation; are clothed with all power to *inquire* and *report*; are empowered to make laws to remedy what is defective, repeal what is hurtful, punish what is delinquent. Thus free Legislation is built upon free Inquiry.

Upon these grounds of favor towards executive and Legislative Power have parties divided ever since men have practised a representative government.

The people have taken part sometimes with the one, sometimes with the other; generally as their passions have been more or less skilfully excited by the one or the other.

In the days of Charles the First the great body of the English people went with the Parliament, and stood up for Privilege against Prerogative. A turn of the wheel of fortune exhibited them, in a few years afterward, applauding Cromwell for silencing the voice of a free representation, and justifying his assumption of prerogatives more dangerous than those for which Charles had suffered. At the Restoration, the Executive Power found its chief support in the popular advocacy; and it was not long after this, that the great champions of Privilege against Prerogative, Russell and Sidney, suffered on the scaffold, almost unwept by the millions of Englishmen whose descendants now turn to that scaffold as to the very altar of Liberty.

Looking, therefore, to the strength which these parties—Court and Country, as I have called them—have gained from time to time, and from their nature are apt to gain, it may be said of them that that strength depends in great measure upon the intelligence, and talent to propagate their doctrines, in the political leaders who give tone to public opinion; and that they who, from supineness or from incapacity, are content to give themselves little trouble with their political sentiments, and to take them at second hand, will still, as heretofore, find themselves ranged on the side of Prerogative or Privilege, will belong to the Court or Country party, will be Whigs or Tories, according to the accidents of the day, or as they may be practised upon by the craft of those who have an interest in giving a particular ply to the floating public opinion of the time. Let this reflection admonish us, that every citizen of a free government should study public affairs for himself, think and determine for himself.

The Revolution of 1688, famous in British history for the overthrow of the Stuarts and the introduction of the House of Brunswick to the throne, gave a prominent distinction to this division of parties. The Whigs of the reign of William the Third and of Queen Anne are notable, above all other things, for their jealousy of executive and their faith in Legislative Power. They have done more to establish British Liberty, and by deduction from that, more to establish American Liberty, than any other political organization of modern times. I need not recount their struggles to clip the wings of Prerogative and enlarge the limits of Privilege, which give so much interest to the Parliamentary history of that time. The principle of specific annual appropriation; the restraint of members of Parliament against holding office, under the crown; the triennial Parliament and annual meeting; the regulation of trials for treason; the protection of the liberty of the Press—among many other improvements of the practice and principles of the British Constitution, bear witness to the enlightened estimate of human happiness and due appreciation of rational freedom made in that day by the Whigs.

It is not to be supposed that these men reached at once the most perfect arrangement of the sureties for civil liberty. But with great sagacity they announced the fundamental doctrines upon which that liberty has been subsequently built up. They were in a perpetual struggle to wrest from Prerogative what they deemed unsafe appendages to executive power, and to strengthen Parliament with all the faculties requisite to render it a vigilant and effective guardian of popular rights. The Tories labored, on the other side, to impress the nation with the belief that Government could only be healthfully administered by a hand strong enough to overbear and repress what was deemed the licentiousness of the people and their representatives.

The Whig party succeeded—not in preserving their ascendency in the councils of the nation—but in stamping their principles upon the British Constitution. Through many reverses and mischances they won success. Often baffled and turned back, always misrepresented or misunderstood, frequently derided and reviled, and but seldom in the actual administration of affairs—still the progress of their principles was onward, and they had the satisfaction to see the cause of human liberty gradually intrenching itself behind the bulwarks they had erected: even to witness this consummation at the moments when party rage and the fanaticism of political zeal excluded them from all share in the management of government—a noble homage to the wisdom and fidelity of their labors!

Not without hostility from the people, in whose behalf they had so long and faithfully toiled, was this conquest achieved. It is one degree of virtue to pursue, with steady sagacity, good ends, when all the means are at hand and the mass of mankind look on, approve, and assist: it is a still higher degree of virtue to persevere in a good work, when means are scant and they who should be allies and partners in the endeavor, are indifferent spectators: far nobler than this to persevere when the beneficiaries of our toil are open opponents or vindictive foes. History is full of instruction and admonition to the great community of every nation, how deep is the stake of human happiness dependent upon a just conviction by the people,

First, Of what is true liberty, and

Second, Of what are the real aims and personal objects of those who climb to the head of a party.

THE MADISONIAN PLATFORM

Our own Revolution of 1776, which a careful student of political history may trace to that of 1688, brought to view the same division of parties. We had our Tories and Whigs, our friends of Prerogative and our friends of Privilege. Again the battle was fought and won by the Whigs.

The war of the Revolution was waged against the encroachments of Executive Power. Witness that beadroll of complaints set forth in the manifesto of Congress declaring our Independence:

"He has refused his assent to laws the most wholesome and necessary for the public good.

"He has forbidden his governors to pass laws of immediate and pressing importance, unless suspended in their operation until his assent should be obtained; and when so suspended he has utterly neglected to attend to them.

"He has refused to pass other laws for the accommodation of large districts of people, unless those people would relinquish the right of representation in the Legislature, a right inestimable to them and formidable to tyrants only.

"He has called together Legislative bodies at places unusual, uncomfortable and distant from the depository of their public records, for the sole purpose of fatiguing them into compliance with his measures.

"He has dissolved Representative houses repeatedly, for opposing with manly firmness his invasions on the rights of the people.

"He has refused for a long time after such dissolutions to cause others to be elected, whereby the Legislative powers, incapable of annihilation, have returned to the people at large for their exercise, the state remaining, in the mean time, exposed to the dangers of invasion from without and convulsions within."

"He has obstructed the administration of justice by refusing his assent to laws for establishing judiciary powers."

"He has erected a multitude of new offices, and sent hither swarms of new officers to harass our people and eat out our substance.

"He has kept among us in times of peace standing armies without the consent of our Legislatures."

These, and others of the like character, are the grievances for which the Whigs took up arms. The purpose of that war was to rid the nation of this domineering Executive, and secure to themselves a free Legislature.

Before separation or independence entered the thoughts of our people, the contest stood substantially upon the same ground—the Privilege of a Representative Legislature against the Executive Prerogative. It was in fact a revival of the old quarrel of Parliament with the Stuarts on the question of loans, benevolences and ship money.

Many men of the colonies in that day, whom we must admit to have been honest and attached to the country, did not concur in this general zeal against Executive Encroachment. Many, besides, who held office under the crown, or who hoped for office under the crown, saw no danger to public liberty in the restraints put upon domestic legislation. They who hold office and they who expect it, will always be the last in any country to see danger in the executive power.

These opponents to the Revolution principles were the Tories of that day. They were vanquished by the Whigs.

When the war came to an end, it may be said there was but one party in the country. The Whig principle was established and all resistance to it was withdrawn. The next task of those who had conducted the war was to erect a form of government which should embody the political doctrines of the Revolution. Every man then desired to see a government so constructed as to secure the faculty of administering to the happiness of the people with the least possible hazard from executive power.

The first general conception of a guarantee against oppression, and upon which there was no division of opinion, was in a strong Representative Legislature.

As to the amount of power which might be confided to an executive—upon that point all the old jealousy was awakened. In all the embarrassments growing out of the old Confederation, this fear of the Executive ever stood in the way of change. In all the discussions upon the formation of the Constitution of 1787, this fear of the executive was the chief stumbling block. I will not stop to indicate the points of these discussions. They are common history.

There were enlightened patriots of that epoch upon both sides of the question. No longer divided in opinion as Whig and Tory, they were, nevertheless, as friends of a popular Representative Republic, divided in opinion as to the quantum of power which it was safe to trust even to an Elective Republican Magistrate.

It is impossible that men could be more honest or more in earnest than these. Then, there was a question of the conflict between Federal and State power; a question which is not yet settled, though fast growing to be so.

Naturally some men's minds incline towards Prerogative, from an idea that the popular impulses require to be checked by a strong hand. A powerful party grew up in the nation upon this opinion. The same habit of thinking which made men friendly to the Federal, as distinguished from the State power, inclined their minds to the fancy of a strong executive; and thus it came that the Federalists were, to a certain extent, identified with the supporters of the executive power.

Then again, naturally, and by complexion of character, many men run into extremes in regard to the removing of all restraints upon popular action; and they fall into mischievous conclusions in that direction of opinion. The French Revolution, whose fires were discernible, even within this remote horizon of ours, witnessed some of these extremes and taught them to our citizens.

Thus a contest arose of ultraisms in our political schools; and, for years, the harmony of public administration was disturbed, and sometimes embittered by the strife of parties, which having, in the main, no other than patriotic aims, maintained their antagonist positions without material injury to any interest in the State. In fact, being nearly balanced in power and equally distinguished in talent, they promoted that degree of watchfulness of each other which, with good reason, has been said to be a surety for the healthful administration of affairs.

In this strife the active politicians, only, took a deep interest. The great body of the nation felt secure in the conviction that the public liberty was in good hands. Some flatterers of the administration, some incumbents and many expectants of office were, doubtless, active—as such persons always are—to give the greatest degree of significancy to the opinions of their party. On the other hand, some demagogues, seeking favor from the great body of electors, and lauding the people in that fulsome phrase which only demagogues will utter, and which is never employed by a man who has a true respect for the good sense of his fellow-citizens—on their side strove, by like devices, to exalt the value of party opinion. Each of these fomented division; exaggerated the weight of their political influence; magnified frivolous distinctions; engendered, no doubt, much useless hatred.

But in the midst of this strife, looking on, not anxiously caring for the issue, but still watchful of events, was a large mass of substantial citizens, deeply implicated in all that concerned the prosperity of the country; men having inheritances of good name to support; having close alliance with all that constituted the strength, the wealth, the labor, the success, the glory of their country; the men employed in the business of this nation, and who hoped to hand it over to their children as something to be proud of—all these stood by, caring something, perhaps, for the ascendency of the parties of the day, but caring more that the generation to which they belonged should in no jot detract from or impair those sacred principles of human right and civil liberty which had been won by their ancestors in 1688, and still more securely knit together and confirmed by their ancestors of 1776.

Thus, in no visible array or manifest organization, but unembodied and comparatively in repose, the Whigs of this Union remained spectators of events, content to take such various interest in public measures as the passing questions of the time might excite, yet but little inclined to party agitation as long as the fundamental Whig principle was likely to sustain no detriment in the conduct of those at the head of affairs.

Such was the state of the nation toward the close of Mr. Madison's administration. There had been turbulent feeling before this, because political opinion had been passing through an exciting transition, from the date of the election of Mr. Jefferson to the close of the war, and many hot ferments had been engendered. The calm and philosophic temper of Mr. Madison, the purity of his character, the sincerity of his patriotism, and the sagacity of his intellect had inspired universal trust—except, perhaps, in a few Federalists, in whose minds an ancient grudge yet rankled. With this exception, a balmy peace reigned throughout our political world. The extremes of Federalism had been tempered with an infusion of democratic flavor; the extremes of Democracy had been melted in an amalgam of Federalism. Both were the better for it. Above all, the Constitution was settled; its Whig basis strengthened; and many men thought that, from that day, it was a book interpreted and certain. Truly, I think that the Constitution of the United States, as expounded and practised by Marshall and Madison, is the very Constitution of our forefathers! I desire no farther commentary: from that day forth it has been to me an article of faith: my creed therein is written.

This was the glory of Mr. Madison's administration, that it made peace between parties; that it established the true import of our fundamental law; and that it marked out the administrative policy of this people, both in their outward relations and in their domestic affairs. The Madisonian basis of the American government and policy may be regarded as one established by the almost universal consent of the country. It was wise, being the product of careful thought and just consideration of the temper and aims of our people: it was likely to be permanent, because it grew out of a calm and dispassionate state of public feeling, auspicious to durable settlements. An experience of twelve years, from 1816 to 1829, has proved it to be eminently calculated to advance the comfort, the prosperity, and the strength of the people.

First. It settled the construction and practice of the Constitution on the foundation of the Whig doctrines: this construction and practice was chiefly manifested in the high respect and confidence of the nation in the Legislative Power, and the scrupulous adherence of the executive to its orbit.

Second. It settled the policy of the Government. Witness these measures:

It regulated the Currency by the control of a National Bank, and, through this instrumentality, checked and finally removed the mischief of excessive State Banking.

It protected the Domestic Industry of our people, by the establishment of a Tariff of Duties specially directed to that object.

It promoted Internal Improvements in the nation, by giving the aid of government to useful enterprises which were beyond the capacity of individual States; a policy which, if it had not been since abandoned, would have saved the country that load of State debt which has become of late almost equally our misfortune and our disgrace.

It enlarged the sphere of our Commerce and Navigation, by tendering to foreign nations reciprocal privileges of trade restricted within certain limits defined in the legislation of 1815, and in the Convention of London of that year.

It devised the plan for paying off the public debt.

It placed the public expenditures upon the footing of a strict economy.

It discountenanced and subdued all attempts to connect office with the means of political influence; and left the public servant free from that odious inquisition into his opinions which has since made him either the victim or the confederate of spies and informers.

In short, its whole scheme of administration was national, American, liberal and honorable. It infused that sentiment into the mind of the people, and rendered them, everywhere, throughout all classes, honorable, high-minded, and patriotic.

This was the inheritance to which Mr. Monroe, and, in due succession, Mr. Adams succeeded. They conscientiously adhered to this truly republican, equal and beneficent system of administration. The consequence was a progressive increase in every element of national happiness. Under the working of this system the nation gradually arose to a state of unexampled vigor. The havoc of the war was slowly but surely repaired. The currency, from a state of extraordinary derangement, was brought into singular purity. Manufactures and the mechanic arts were rapidly trained from a feeble infancy to a robustness almost incredible. Commerce and navigation were increased; the war debt was paid; and that series of internal improvements begun which, however they may have involved those who constructed them in debt, are worth more to this Union than ten times the cost expended upon them. They are works from which the National Treasury should never have been withheld: they are works which now belong more to the people of the United States than to the States in whose borders they lie, and for which the People of the Union are equitably and honorably the true debtors: they are works which, by a policy as cruel as it was unstatesmanlike, were ever committed to the unassisted enterprise of the States.

This is the outline of the Whig doctrine in reference to the fundamental characteristics of our government, and also of its policy.

The Whigs stand emphatically upon the Madisonian platform.

4

WHIG IMAGE-MAKING

Calvin Colton
DEMOCRACY

Calvin Colton (1789–1857) was one of the leading propagandists and theoreticians of the Whig party. He wrote on a wide variety of subjects, defending the state of American civilization against the sneers of Europeans, yet criticizing his fellow countrymen for their treatment of the Indians. A Presbyterian minister who became disillusioned with religious revivalism and converted to the antirevival Episcopal church, Colton always remained deeply concerned with the social implications of various religious positions. He was devoted to Henry Clay, editing his speeches for posterity and preparing a eulogistic biography that cast the great Kentuckian as a folk hero. In the last years of his life he taught economics and produced an elaborate defense of the protective tariff.

Like the preceding selection, this one is taken from a Whig campaign tract of 1844. Colton reminds his readers that four years earlier the Whigs had gained victory by depicting William Henry Harrison as a "log cabin" and "hard cider" candidate. Actually Harrison lived in a comfortable house, had enjoyed a classical education (displayed in his inaugural address), and was by no means an uncouth backwoodsman. But Colton understood the arts of political persuasion and was sensitive to what he called the "poetry of symbols."

A STORY

A Member of the House of Representatives, in Congress, a friend of Mr. Van Buren, met a Whig Senator in a steamboat in the early part of the Presidential campaign of 1840, when the former said to the latter, "Your Log Cabin and Hard Cider is no go. We shall beat you." "How so?" asked the Senator. "Mr. Van Buren," answered the Member, "relies upon the words *Democracy—Democrat—*and *Democratic.* We

SOURCE. [Calvin Colton,] *Democracy. Number VI of The "Junius" Tracts.* (New York, 1844).

all rely upon them, as a party. While we wear this name, you can not beat us, but we shall beat you." This is a story of *fact,* told us, with some other details, by the Senator himself. It happened, however, for that occasion, that there was more democracy in "Log Cabin and Hard Cider," than there was in *"Democracy"* itself. The Member of the House was right, and the very reason he gave, prevailed on the other side. Mr. Van Buren was beaten.

THE LESSON

As the above is a story of fact, and as it doubtless tells a truth, and confesses a secret, though perfectly obvious to all observing minds, the Whigs will be very simple, if they do not profit by the lesson. All know that these self-styled "Democrats" place their chief reliance on this word, in its different forms of application. Not only so, but they rely equally on stigmatizing their opponents with the name of "Federalists." Look at the Globe and the other papers of that party throughout the Union. Is it not so? With an unwavering constancy they adhere to this rule, in print and in speech. They are aware of the importance of it. They *"rely"* upon it.

ETYMOLOGY

The word *Democracy* is formed of the Greek words *Demos,* people, and *Krateo,* to rule. Compounded, it signifies a *people*-government, in distinction from *Monarchy,* or *One Man* government. The word *Monarchy* is compounded of the Greek words *Monos,* sole, and *Arkos,* ruler, and means as above defined. In grammatical construction, therefore, these words, *Monarchy* and *Democracy,* stand opposed to each other, thus: Monarchy means the government of *One Man,* and Democracy a government by *the people.* There is a perfect grammatical purity and propriety in both, and they announce and declare precisely what they are intended to do.

HISTORICAL ORIGIN

The term *Democracy,* we believe, was first applied to the small republics of Greece, where the people ruled in primary assemblies. Hence the word is of pure Greek origin. That was the purest kind of democracy, where the people avoided the representative forms of a republic, as much as possible, and enacted their laws, and made their decrees, in primary assemblies of the people, though it is obvious that the executive functions of the Government were necessarily, for the most part, performed by individual and selected agents. The word Democracy is therefore of very ancient historical use, and has never since been laid aside, because men, in different parts of the world, have been constantly struggling for liberty, for a *people*-government, in opposition to the claims of Monarchy, or One Man Power. Democracy and Monarchy, Democrat and Monarchist, Democratic and Monarchical, in their several substantive and adjective forms, have passed down through all languages, in all countries, from their pure Greek origin, with little variation in form or meaning, always and everywhere standing opposed to each other, as correlative terms. The fact of this uniform and general use of these terms, with a uniform meaning, among all nations, for so many ages, three thousand years, more or less, is conclusive evidence, not only of the uninterrupted and equally extensive agitation of the political questions which they involve, but of the general tendency of society, all the world over, and of the persevering aims of mankind, for the universal establishment of Democracy, or a *people*-government.

THE POLITICAL POSITION OF THESE TERMS

This, we should think, ought to be considered as settled by the etymological derivation and historical origin and use above given. Such facts have a character of high and emphatic teaching. They have a potent influence over the mind of the world, high and low, in political philosophy, as well as in the hearts of those, who have felt the iron hand of monarchical power, and are struggling for release, or who have obtained their freedom. It is for *democracy* as opposed to *monarchy*, which the whole world are striving for, and which they are resolved to have.

DE TOCQUEVILLE

De Tocqueville's "American Democracy" is very instructive, not alone for the objects he had in view, but it is especially pertinent to our present purpose, which he never thought of, simply because he never thought it could be made a question. He took for granted that the word, Democracy, in all history and in all countries, with all political sects, in political philosophy, and in the common mind, occupies precisely the same position as it does in grammar, to wit, as opposed to Monarchy. Hence he everywhere treats of democracy as standing in this relation, and only in this general and comprehensive sense. He assumes, that there are different kinds of democracy, as of monarchy, and undertakes to treat of *American* democracy as one of the varieties. We hardly need say, that, by American Democracy, De Tocqueville means our *popular form* of government, such as it actually is.

OTHER AUTHORITIES

In the same manner, all political writers of the old world give the same meaning to these terms respectively, and uniformly use them in their relative grammatical sense. All attempts to put down monarchical power, and elevate the people, they call *Democracy*. It is the same in England. The antagonist of Monarchy there is Democracy, and the growth of popular influence in the Government, and in general society, is used synonymously and interchangeably with the progress of Democratic power. . . .

REPUBLICANISM

It is a remarkable fact, that, while DEMOCRACY is a word of high and pure significancy in the European world, representing simply what we have already indicated, to wit, a *people*-government, in distinction from Monarchy, the words, *Republicanism* and *Republicans*, have fallen under deep reproach. It results entirely from the atrocities of the French Revolution of 1790–1793, the authors and actors of which, as is well known, were called *Republicans*. We are known to the world as a Republic, and the phrase, "a republican form of government," is used in the Constitution of the United States, as guaranteed by that instrument to every new State; but the denomination of *republican* has never adhered long to any political party of the country. The cause is not apparent, unless it be supposed to result from the fact that there is no obvious meaning in the term itself indicative of the precise character of our institutions. It is well understood, however, to denote a popular government, acting by representative agents. . . .

OUR GOVERNMENT A DEMOCRACY

We are aware that some have denied this; but we think it is from want of an enlarged and philosophical view of the question. The grammatical and historical facts, already adduced, would certainly seem to decide, beyond controversy, in favor of our position. We think this question, if any choose to make controversy about it, is to be decided by the position which the term Democracy holds in the public mind of the world at large, and in the records of history, and not by the narrow views of our own political sectarians, nor by a nice scrutiny of the constitutional structure of our Government, as compared with an original and pure theoretical democracy, sitting and governing themselves in primary assemblies of the people. This latter picture is doubtless the purest theory of a democracy; but it is an impracticable mode of government. We choose rather to regard the more notable and fixed character, and to adopt the names, which history and immemorial usage have given to the different forms of government, as they actually appear from time to time, in different countries, and these are generally classed under the heads of Monarchies and Republics, or Monarchies and Democracies, Republics and Democracies being used as synonymous and convertible terms. Each of these two classes, as before observed, has its varieties. But the representative forms of popular governments, however one may differ from another, if all the powers of government originate in the people and periodically return to them, or if those powers may be constitutionally resumed and modified by the people, cannot divest them of their democratic character. They are still Democracies in distinction from Monarchies. With the first of these classes, the government of these United States is properly, and for aught we can see, necessarily ranked. It is a *Democracy*. And ours is a *very* democratic government, in its practical operation, as compared with any that has ever existed permanently by its own inherent strength. Who does not know how the slightest breezes of a political nature, moving over the popular mind, may affect and change the policy of the Government? Will any deny that this is *democracy*?

ARISTOCRACY

As it is not found convenient for monarchies to stand alone, and being socially at a lofty remove from the level of the people, it has been thought necessary to surround a throne with orders and ranks of nobility, having chartered privileges, large endowments of wealth, hereditary rights, patented honorary distinctions, &c., &c., each occupying a mediate stage between the sovereign and the people, till the chasm is filled up; and the interests of these numerous parties are so connected and identified with each other, and with the throne, that all are interested in maintaining the rights of the Monarchy against the claims of the Democracy. With the sanction of time and usage for their position, with their wealth, and with the physical force at their command, they support their power, and the supremacy of the sovereign. An aristocracy, in form or substance, is considered a necessary appendage of monarchy.

OLIGARCHY

An Oligarchy, or government of a *few*, associate and equal, is considered the most odious of all governments, and is doubtless capable of the most cruel despotism. Venice existed for centuries under this form of government, flourished as a commercial and warlike state, but was finally dissolved, and tumbled to ruins, by the atrocities of its Administration.

DEMOCRACY AS A PARTY IN THE REPUBLIC

A democratic party in a democratic state, would seem to be an anomaly. The curiosity of a stranger would naturally demand, What, then, can the other party be?—Are they monarchists? or what? An exclusive claim of one of two parties to democracy, in a democratic country like this, is, to say the least, not a very modest pretension, and a scrutiny as to the propriety and grounds of such a claim, must of course be expected.

A RETROSPECTIVE GLANCE

It is a well-known fact that in the time of the elder Adams, a party of high standing and great influence existed in the republic, called Federalists, the leaders of which were accused—we do not decide whether justly or unjustly—of aristocratic aspirations and monarchical schemes. It is also known that the passage of the Alien and Sedition laws was the signal for the uprising and organization of a party, which assumed the name and was called *democratic*, as being opposed to these imputed monarchical designs. With this color of propriety to start with, sounding their alarms, and urging their cause, they succeeded, under the lead of Thomas Jefferson, in 1801, in obtaining the government of the country, and the Federalists were thoroughly routed, so that they never appeared again, with any effect, as an organized party, were soon scattered, and after a few years, were merged in other parties, some going one way and some another. It is remarkable, however, that no small portion of the most prominent, most pretending, and apparently most influential leaders of the present *self*-styled "Democratic party," came from the Federal ranks. It is a fact to be *observed*.

A YOUNG CHAMPION OF THIS ORIGINAL DEMOCRACY

Henry Clay, of Kentucky, roused by his eloquence, marshalled by his skill, and led on by his valor, the democratic army of that Commonwealth, as their chosen captain. He was recognised and honored, as such, by Mr. Jefferson, throughout his Administration. He was neither the least, nor second, among the leaders of the Democracy under the administration of Mr. Madison. From the beginning of his political career, down to this hour, he has been a true, consistent, *American* Democrat, "original, dyed in the wool," as we shall by and by have occasion to see.

A HINT

Nothing is more obvious, than the truth, that, *since* the decline and dispersion of the Federal party, no other party in this country could, with propriety, modesty, or decency, claim the exclusive title of *democratic*, even if it were proper *before*. It was first assumed for the occasion, and continued to be applied from habit; but even the Federalists, as is well known, denied the charges which were alleged against them; and if, indeed, there were traitors to the country then, not a few of the worst and most dangerous of them are now figuring largely and prominently in the self-styled "Democratic" ranks.

A LIKENESS

The history of political parties in this country has been very much like the movements of flocks of wild pigeons and shoals of fishes. A cloud of these birds comes sweeping through the air, in a dense mass and long train, apparently following one leader, and anon, they divide into two, or three, or four armies, separating and circling away to different quarters of the heavens, under as many captains. They may form a junction again, in whole, or in part, or they may not. The chances are, they will never *all* get together in the same order. The same is it with shoals of fishes. Now a solid body moves steadily on, when all at once, they branch off, and dart away, no one knows where. It is supposed they have gone off under new leaders.

THE STATE OF PARTIES UNDER MR. MONROE'S ADMINISTRATION

There has been one period of comparative repose in our political history when all parties were apparently blended in a common mass. It was under Mr. Monroe.

THE NEW "DEMOCRACY" NO DEMOCRACY

After a calm, comes a storm. The evoking of new political parties, of such character and force, out of such a state of things as existed under Mr. Monroe, can be accounted for only by special influences. A violence was done to the repose of the public mind, and that violence was supported by a long protracted fraud. Principles were laid aside, and a MAN set up. The influence was PERSONAL, not political.

In this there could be NO Democracy, but the very opposite. When Napoleon rose, it was all for *liberty*, for the *people,* for *France*. It is always so, when MEN rise, in the place of PRINCIPLES. They call things by names directly opposite to the FACTS; and it becomes necessary to insist upon it, with an emphasis and an energy, proportionate to the falseness of the pretensions, and the danger of detection. Popular deception can not be carried on and carried through, without heaps upon heaps of false asseveration. Democracy and a democratic party *had* been popular in the country. What more prudent, or more politic, than to call this new development by the same name? They had all power, could do as they pleased, and would be believed. They called it *Democracy!* An implicit giving up of the control and management of everything to ONE MAN, *democracy!* Such is not the decision of grammar, nor the utterance of history, nor is it very nearly allied to common apprehension.

What resemblance, or what connexion there was between the *self-*styled "Democracy," which ruled in the land from 1830 to 1840, and that which rose in 1801, and long presided over the destinies of the country, we are utterly unable to see. Jeffersonian democracy, for aught that appears, was the power of the PEOPLE. Jackson "Democracy" was the ascendant star of ONE MAN. The first grew out of an alarm for the safety of popular rights; the last sprung from an obsequious regard for a Military Chieftain.

THE DEMOCRACY OF MR. CLAY

The position of Mr. Clay in the democratic party which triumphed in 1801, and long swayed the sceptre of this republic, has already been recognised. He was first, most eloquent, and most influential in the ranks of the Kentucky democracy of that era; he had the entire confidence of Mr. Jefferson; he was the main pillar of Mr. Madison's administration, and to no man is the country more indebted than to him for the success of our arms in the last war with Great Britain, and for an honorable and advantageous peace. A true *American* democrat from the beginning, rising from the humblest origin, poor and friendless, and depending alone on his personal industry and energy, he was ready, and full armed, for the service of his country. . . .

MODERN DEMOCRACY A NEW THING

We speak of that which is modern in our own history, as compared with its earlier dates. There is scarcely a feature of resemblance between the democracy, which preceded the amalgamation of parties under Mr. Monroe, and the *self-*styled "Democracy" that has sprung up since, and for twelve years held the reins of power. *This* is entirely a *new* thing. It is as remote from grammatical, historical, and philosophical democracy, and from *any* democracy ever recognised as such, as Monarchy itself. It involves the two principles of Monarchy and Oligarchy, with a strong smell of Aristocracy; but we have never found in it a single element of a *Constitutional* democracy. The people have had a part in it, without doubt; but it was only *to do as they were told.* They were mustered and organized under the *personal* popularity of *One Man*, and the *original*, afterward *transmitted* vitality of the party, consisted in *obsequiousness* to one man's will. Does any man need to be told that General Jackson's will was the *law* of his party; or that the party was a body of which he was the *soul*? It was a party formed around him *personally* as a nucleus, centre, and source of influence. Is it not apparent at a single glance, and from moral necessity, that such a party could not be *democratic*? The head was *monarch* of the party, *sole and absolute*. And as all monarchs require privileged and rewarded agents, he put his finger upon, appointed, and endowed such as would answer his purposes, and captains of tens, of fifties, of hundreds, and of thousands, were made all over the land. It was a strictly *disciplined* party, under *one Chief*, who was also at the head of the nation. It had a *military* character in its organization, discipline, and effect. . . .

AN ANECDOTE

"How many legs will a calf have," asked a fellow of another, whose depth and shrewdness he wanted to prove, "if you call his *tail* a leg?" "Five," was the answer. "O no, that's impossible." "But certainly, he will have five." "Does your *calling* his tail a leg, *make* it a leg?" "Well, now, I never thought of that."

It is strange, indeed, that it should have taken the people of this country so long to find out that a calf's tail could never be made into a calf's leg, by the act of *calling* it a leg; or that One-Man Power could not be converted into democracy, by *calling* it democracy. We have already partly suggested the reason why this misnomer was given, and the manner in which it was done. Democracy *had* been in good repute. And why should it not be, in a democratic country? But, as this *new* "Democracy" was known to be spurious, it was necessary to insist on its genuine character with special urgency—to affirm it over and over again. A falsehood is allowed to be made good, by telling it often and strong, and swearing to it, if necessary. . . .

THE DESIGN AND IMPORTANCE OF PARTY NAMES

We have already suggested, what we think can not be too well considered, that no party in this country is fairly entitled to the exclusive name of *democratic*. The government of the United States comes under the category of *Democracies*, in the general classification of the political forms of human society, and all the people of all parties are, or ought to be, *democrats*. They are not *monarchists*. Technically and specifically we are a Republic and Republicans; but for the general and more common purposes of language, both in political philosophy, and in the common speech of the world, we are a *Democracy and Democrats*. These are national designations, not party titles. The assumption of these titles by a political party, is a robbery of the other party of their national character. It is investing a sect—in such a case *self*-invested—for their exclusive use, with the honors which belong to the entire Democratic communion, in this country and elsewhere.

WHIGS AND LOCOFOCOS

Positively we know no such parties in this country as *Whigs and Democrats*. We deny that there are such. There are Whigs, and we maintain that the Whigs are THE Democrats, if there must be a party of that name. Certainly, they are the *true* Democrats, if there be any such in the land. We mean no disrespect to the *Locofocos*[1] by this party designation. They came by it accidentally, as the name of Whig was first acquired. Under these names, or any others not national and generically comprehensive, the issue is fairly made, and always stands, as is proper and important, which of the two is *more truly*, or *more* Democratic than the other, according to the democratic standard of our Government and its institutions? Neither party, so far as we know, proposes any other standard. But if either of these divisions of the people is permitted to wear the name of *democrats*, as an exclusive party designation, and if they are fairly entitled to it, the question is conceded, and the argument at an end, as to which is democratic, or more truly so. . . .

THE OBJECT OF THE POLITICAL REVOLUTION OF 1840

It was solely and alone to restore the democracy of the country—to *restore* it. For many years it had been giving way and was being

[1] "Locofoco" was the name given to a northeastern urban faction within the Democratic party. The Locofocos were especially hostile to the BUS and the business community in general; they had a reputation as the most radical of the Jacksonians. Colton, by pinning their label on all Democrats, is trying to stigmatize his opponents as extremists. Ed.

swallowed up by Executive power. One encroachment after another had been made on the rights of the popular and legislative branch of the Government, abuses multiplied, usurpations thickened, till the powers of legislation, directly or indirectly, by influence or mandate, chiefly emanated from the Executive chair. Congress, instead of originating public policy and public measures and giving form and substance to them by its own independent action, became a mere registrar of Executive decrees, a mechanics' workhouse for a master at the other end of the Avenue. The Democracy of the nation was prostrate—it was nearly annihilated. It was to *restore* the Democratic prerogatives of Congress, to reassert and reconfirm the independence of the national legislature, that the great struggle of 1840 was undertaken, and the aim triumphantly achieved. The people *saw* that their power was gone, and must be recovered, and they came to the rescue. . . .

THE DUTY OF THE PRESS, AND OF COMMON SPEECH

It is perhaps true, that *half* of the Whig press, and *half* the Whigs in the land, are at this time in the habit of calling the Locofocos *Democrats,* of speaking of them as the *Democracy,* of honoring their party with the title of *Democratic,* and of using the word in all its forms in this application. Are they aware of the consequence, and that they are probably doing more to help the Locofocos by this recognition of their claims, than all the counter influence they can throw into the other scale, by any means whatever? We are sure, if they thought as we do, believed as we do, they would from principle, from a sense of duty, abstain at once and for ever from such an application of these terms. It is unjust to all parties—to the Locofocos themselves; for they, of all men, are least entitled to it. . . . They have a name, *Locofoco,* accidentally acquired, as the name of Whig was originally, and there is no discourtesy in using that designation. They then stand upon their naked principles and practices, and the issue is fairly made before the people, Which are the true and best Democrats?

THE IMPORTANCE OF THIS QUESTION IN ITS RELATION TO IMMIGRANTS

It appears by official records, that the number of immigrants who arrived at the port of New York, from August, 1832, to August, 1842, ten years, was 507,131. We have not the means of knowing what proportion this bears to the *entire* immigration of foreigners into the country; but we have noticed immigrations, by way of Canada, for some years, which, at the same rate, would make an aggregate in ten years, but little short of this statement for New York. But suppose the average immigration into the country is *fifty thousand* a year, which was the average for ten years, at New York alone, as above; and suppose that one half of these become voters by naturalization; we then have an aggregate acquisition of voters, from foreign parts, every four years, not much short of the majority which elected General Harrison! We have before shown, that all these, or nearly all, come here for *Democracy* as opposed to *Monarchy*, and that they will be *Democrats*. Most of them are ignorant of our language, all are ignorant of our state of society, they know nothing of the principles which distinguish political parties here, but they are governed chiefly by the *names* which parties bear. The party that is *called* democratic, if there be such a party, they are sure to join. What other rule can they go by? And such, we generally find, is the result. Is not this fact *alone* sufficient for all the purposes of our argument? . . .

"DEMOCRATS" THE FRIENDS OF THE LABORING AND POORER CLASSES

This has not only been a standing text, but there has been much effective preaching from it, by the Locofoco "Democracy." But the laboring and poorer classes have made an important discovery in three particulars. 1. That they have been made *tools of* [by] the Locofoco party. . . . 2. That Whig policy and Whig measures are best for them. 3. They like that democracy which does them most good; which gives them food, clothing, and a comfortable home, instead of *promises*. They have at least *begun* to make this discovery, and are advancing in it rapidly. The tariff, a great Whig measure, is diffusing its blessings everywhere, and gladdening the hearts of the laboring and poorer classes. We have just noticed the remarkable fact that a little girl, in a cotton bag factory at Cincinnati, earns *six dollars* for five and a half days' labor every week, and that there are fifty-five females and forty-five males working in the same factory, with similar results.

Take away the *name*, by which the Locofocos have deceived the people, and their power is gone. . . .

THE CONFUSION OF POLITICAL PARTIES

As was sagaciously and shrewdly calculated upon by those most interested, a majority of the people of this country, honest and unsophisticated, took for granted, that the leaders of a party, coming into the field, would not call themselves *democrats,* if they were not so; and it was generally supposed, that this *new* party was only a continuation of the *old* democratic party, and that it occupied the same position; whereas, it was the *reverse,* or *opposite* position. What Mr. Clay said, in reply to Mr. Calhoun, that "it does not hold a *solitary principle in common* with the Republican (democratic) party of 1798," was perfectly true. It was in the antipodes, at the opposite pole, in relation to that party. It was moreover true, that this *new* party had adopted—it is equally true, that it has uniformly carried out—the most obnoxious principle of the old Federal party, viz.: "A strong, powerful, and energetic Executive," and that with this party still resides *all* the Federalism there is in the land, which in their case is a *reality,* whatever may have been the *fact* in the first case.

It was also supposed by the people, that the party, since called Whig, was *anti-*democratic, and that they succeeded to the Federalists, and inherited their principles; whereas, they were the only legitimate successors of the Jeffersonian, afterward Madisonian school, and were opposed to this new *self-*styled "democracy," because they were opposed to *Federalism,* and the worst *kind* of Federalism, as it was developed under the Locofoco Dynasty.

Such has been the entire and absolute *confusion* of political parties in this country, growing out of the *fraud* practised in the assumption of the name of *"Democrats"* by the Locofocos, who were able, by the irresistible sway of a popular Chieftain to maintain it for a protracted period. On this account, the two great parties have all this while been in *false* positions before the people, and it was not till 1840, that this fact began to be understood; nor is it perfectly understood even now. . . .

HOW TO SET IT RIGHT

1. Let the Whig press be reformed in this particular. It would do much less hurt by advocating Locofoco *principles,* than by calling Locofocos *Democrats.* The principles, *in their naked form,* will not bear scrutiny, and are generally a sufficient answer to themselves. But wrap them up in the name of *Democracy,* and they will mislead the majority of the people, simply because the people are honest, and take things by their *names.* 2. Let the Whig press endeavor to set this whole matter in its true light, debate the question, and dispute the point. 3. Let all Whigs, everywhere, scrupulously abstain from apply-

ing these terms to Locofocos, show why it ought not to be done, and if necessary to counterbalance the fraud of their opponents, let them take and wear the name themselves, as their right. It has already been done extensively. Let it be done universally, and it will be an approximation to justice. In the end it will cure the evil. 4. Show Mr. Clay's position, historically, in the ranks of true democracy; where he was under the Administration of Mr. Jefferson; where under Mr. Madison; and how faithfully he has fought the battles of Democracy, under the Locofoco Dynasty, against One-Man Power, against Executive encroachments on the democratic prerogatives of the Constitution, as vested in the Representatives of the people, in the legislative branch of the Government. 5. Show, that the Whigs have occupied this position, all along, and still occupy it; and that Whig measures are for the *whole* people, against the claims of officeholders and public agents. 6. Show, that the genius, doctrines, and practice of Locofocoism are alike hostile to liberty and democracy. All these things are manifest, and the facts need only be cited, to be felt.

IMPORTANCE OF SYMBOLS

Whig democracy prevailed in 1840, in our opinion, only because it was *believed* to be *true* democracy. We are also persuaded, it can only prevail now and ultimately *for the same reason.* We would not lay aside the *"Log Cabin,"* nor *"Hard Cider,"* for they are the appropriate symbols of democracy; nor even the *"Coon,"* for people like to laugh; nor *songs,* for a great statesman once said truly: "Give me the making of the *ballads* of a nation, and I don't care who makes its laws." Let it not, however, be supposed we recommend *drinking.* We only speak of "Hard Cider" as a *symbol.* Doubtless, there will be many new and appropriate devices. The Poetry of symbols is the natural language of the heart—the first and everstanding altar of enthusiasm.

MR. CLAY AS THE CANDIDATE FOR THE PRESIDENCY

It is fortunate for the Whig democracy of the country that the democracy of their candidate for the Presidency is so legible and apparent in the chapter of his public life. It may surprise some of the Whigs, but it will be a *poser* to the Locofocos to find that nowhere in the republic can be found, among our public men, an *American democrat* from the stump, so consistent, so firm, so unchangeable, so uniform, amid all the fluctuations of parties, that have characterized our history. THERE HE IS, the SAME under Jefferson, Madison, Monroe, J.Q. Adams, Jackson, Van Buren, Tyler—always and invariably the uncompromising Advocate of democracy—of the people's rights, against the encroachments of Executive power; always defending American interests against foreign interests; always advocating protection for American labor and industry; always toiling for the welfare and glory of his own country; always sympathizing, not only with American democracy, but with democracy in every part of the globe, where the people were oppressed, or struggling for freedom; always the defender of the democracy of the Constitution, as the organ and instrument of the democracy of the country; always taking in charge the interests of the masses, not only for the equity of the principle, but as the surest way of promoting the general welfare; the same in defeat as in success, in adversity as in prosperity, under the dark clouds of calumny as in the bright sun of popular favor; never disheartened, never weary, never flagging; but ever prompting and cheering the nation onward to honorable fame and great achievement.

The Locofocos know full well, that they can not impeach the democracy of Henry Clay, nor blast the reputation he has won in the service of his country, and there is nothing they fear so much as the word, democracy, in such an application. Their trade in detraction, vilification, and slander, will avail them little on such a mark. Their only task is now to hold on tight the garment which they stole. We shall see, ere long, whether they do not stand shivering in the cold, or burning in the sun, for lack of a covering.

SUM OF THE MATTER

The result of the whole is—1. That Locofocoism is a *new* system of party tactics, never before known to the country, having no politics in particular, except such as lead to power and the spoils of office. 2. That the leaders only are benefited, while the people are made tools of, and necessarily injured. 3. That it is chiefly indebted for its success to the assumption of a false name for itself, and to bestowing a false one on its opponents. 4. That it still *"relies"* on the continuance of this fraud for future success.

That it is a *new system* will be apparent to the slightest reflection on its origin, rise, and singular developments. That it has no principle, but the profit of the Oligarchs, is demonstrated by the facts of our history since its advent. That the people are injured, behold the devastations and overthrow of our national prosperity under its rule. That its success is attributable to the cause we have assigned, observe the facts we have recited. And that they still rely on this, take their own word for it.

THE WAY TO DO IT

ONE thing, *all*, doubtless, will agree in, *to wit*, that to have a good crop in the autumn of 1844, the seed can not be put in the ground *too soon*. It is surprising that the importance of *early* efforts to inform the people is not more deeply, more *practically* felt by those whose *appropriate* business it is to put the means in their hands. The Locofocos have nothing to gain, but everything to lose, by debate before the people. In every important position they occupy, they are forced to *defend*, and they are exceedingly vulnerable, while the Whigs occupy precisely the position they did in 1840, viz, *carrying the war into Africa*. All the *facts and principles* which gave the Whigs triumph then, are now more clearly brought out, more impressively stated, and are in all respects more available for effect. It only requires that they should be thrown into the *lap*, and put under the *nose* of the people. Let the Locos *fire back*. It is only the fire of a retreating, discomfited foe. Their last rally is a *forlorn hope*. Give the people *ammunition*, and let the word go round,—"Pick your flints, and try it again." *Remember*—all they want is *ammunition, in good time.* "WHIGS!"— cried he, whose voice for forty years had been heard from the high places of the land, now speaking to his neighbors, near his own hearth, the 9th of June, 1842—"WHIGS!—AROUSE!—AWAKE!—SHAKE OFF THE DEW-DROPS THAT GLITTER ON YOUR GARMENTS, AND ONCE MORE MARCH TO BATTLE AND TO VICTORY."

5
THE FAMILY, THE NATION, AND THE CHURCH

Daniel D. Barnard
THE SOCIAL SYSTEM

A recurring theme in Whig rhetoric was the organic unity of society. Where-as the Jacksonians often spoke of the conflicting interests of "producers" and "nonproducers," the "house of have" and the "house of want," the Whigs were usually concerned with muting social conflict. The interdependence of different classes, geographical regions, and interest groups within the nation was an article of Whig faith. Many Whig economic, political, and cultural positions can be interpreted as efforts to create national unity and preserve social harmony. The following address, delivered before the faculty and alumni of Trinity College, Hartford, provides an excellent example of this kind of thinking.

Daniel D. Barnard (1796–1861) was a lawyer and journalist who served several terms as Whig congressman from New York State. He wrote on the European revolutions of 1830 and 1848 and later became United States minister to Prussia.

The present is a period of great restlessness and agitation among the popular elements of the world. The established order of things is almost every where being questioned, disturbed, and, in many cases, subverted. There is a great demand for rights, and for the redress of wrongs—which is all very well, only one would like to be able to discover, along with these, some corresponding inquiry after duties and obligations. While every body is thinking of rights and nobody is thinking of duties, it is not likely that any very valuable discoveries will be made or improvements effected. Statesmanship, or what goes by that name, is very much employed of late in teaching mankind that

SOURCE. Daniel D. Barnard, *The Social System. An Address Pronounced Before the House of Convocation of Trinity College* (Hartford, Conn., 1848).

political government, even in the mildest and purest form yet devised, instead of being something ordained of God, if necessary at all is a necessary evil, and is little else any where than a stupendous fraud on human rights and human liberty, devised and practised by cunning and wicked men for their own purposes of oppression and profit. Philanthropy, becoming speculative and philosophical, seems to discover no way of righting the wronged, redressing the grievances and remedying the miseries of mankind, but by turning society the bottom side up, and the upside down. Even in religion, there are so many short and easy methods to the conversion of the world, and men love independence so much better than obedience, that any way seems better to multitudes of men than the appointed way; this becomes a narrow road which shows only here and there a traveller. Popular revolutions are now-a-days effected with strange facility— happily with comparatively little bloodshed, even in countries little given to change; and in this country, we have discovered a method of revolutionizing a state or government, with about as little trouble as a reverse motion is given to the engine of a locomotive, or a steamer. We can go forward, or back, or turn on our course by a sharp angle, without seeming to derange the political machinery in any sensible degree. All this we do in the name of reform and of progress. Men are becoming wise above what is written, whether on profane or sacred pages. Government and law are allowed to have very little stability, and therefore command very little respect. And as for the functionaries of government, and the ministers of the law, they are apt to be regarded, and too often, personally considered, seem only worthy to be regarded, not as governers and rulers set up, according to divine authority, "for the punishment of evil-doers and the praise of those that do well"—not as representing the majesty of the law or of the state—but as servile placemen, who perhaps have forfeited their honor in gaining their places, and who represent nothing—but a job.

Perhaps the severest trial to which the virtue of any people can be subjected, is when every man has a share in the government; for when every one governs, few indeed are willing to submit to be governed; when every one commands, nobody likes to obey. Yet the habit and practice of obedience is indispensable to the moral health of every people; and there can be no habits of obedience, when there is no habitual reverence or respect for the laws, or for the public authorities. No community can very long govern itself by popular forms, which discards or turns its back on the cardinal principle of loyalty and obedience as a religious sentiment and duty. When demagogues take the control of the people, and become their schoolmasters, they will very soon be educated out of every true notion of government and every true idea of liberty. . . .

It cannot be too often repeated, or too strongly insisted on, wherever the truth on this subject is meant to be sternly vindicated—and in this I do but respond to the sentiment of both the eloquent gentlemen who have preceded me in an address before this body—that there are three organizations in the world, of special and divine appointment; that of the Family, that of the State, and that of the Church. These are three distinct yet parallel and consistent forms of organic existence and order, which together, in their perfection and purity, and according to their universality, must give and secure to mankind all the comfort and happiness which they are capable of in a life of trial and discipline. The first of these social organizations, through which the human being is introduced into this mortal state, reaches back to that void region of nothingness out of which he is taken; the last, through which he may hope to be finally introduced into a new existence and a more perfect society, connects itself with that boundless future after which every rational mind lifts a hopeful aspiration.

If men cannot be made happy in this life, in and through these three organizations, they cannot be made happy at all. If they cannot be made happy in subjection to the fundamental and necessary principles involved in these three organizations, they cannot be made happy at all. And the great fact in regard to each and all of them is this; that there are laws, to be enforced and to be obeyed; there is authority on one side—authority of divine ordination—and there must be obedience on the other. Men can never be happy till these laws, and this authority, are reverenced, submitted to, and obeyed.

There have been a great many devices first and last in the world for escaping from the restraints of necessary law and authority. Demagogues and disorganizers must be expected to go wrong in this matter of course. They go wrong of purpose, or they follow a will and way of their own, no matter whether it be right or wrong. But there are reformers, who do as much mischief in their way as the others, who yet probably mean well, and really desire to serve the interests of mankind in the best manner. And there are philanthropists who devote their lives to doing good—and it is really wonderful how much good some of them seem to do, considering the perverse and wrong way in which they set about it. If these reformers and philanthropists had always kept in mind and in view, the necessary existence and sacred character of the three organizations, or forms of social life, to which I have referred, with some proper appreciation of their claims on the reverence and obedience of all men; if their plans had been formed with reference to them; if they had acted, or professed to act, in and through them, and by means and agencies strictly auxiliary to them; it cannot be doubted that the cause of humanity and civilization would have been much better served by them than it has been. Indeed, the cause of humanity and civilization—the permanent bettering of the social condition of mankind—has never been promoted at all, by any means or agency whatever which was essentially at war with these social forms, or which was designed to operate, and did operate, independently of them. . . .

The social system of the country is not a thing about which we, or any body who lives under it, may be indifferent—unless we are indifferent to life, and nearly all that renders life worth having. It touches every one of us very nearly; it connects itself intimately with our life, in all its relations, with what we are, and what we have, and what we enjoy, or may hope to enjoy. It connects itself intimately with our intellectual life, our moral, religious, and social life. None of these could be what they are without it. It guards our infancy, it nourishes our manhood, it comforts our age—in so far as these are guarded, and nourished, and comforted at all in the social state—and when it can no longer give us present enjoyments, or we can no longer taste or relish them, it comes to us with hopes and promises that light up the darkness of the future, and enable us to see our children, and those who shall stand in our places, with the uncounted hosts to which their numbers shall be swelled in successive generations, fortunate and happy as we have been, and perhaps far more fortunate and happy than we have been.

The first thing to be remarked in this connection is the necessary existence in every country of a social system of some sort. Man is essentially a social being. This is his state of nature. He is under a positive necessity to live in society, and form social relations with his fellows; and it is not a mere instinct with him to live in society, as it is with many creatures lower down in the scale of animal life; it is a real necessity. He cannot live at all, except in the social state—I mean he cannot live *as* man, he cannot be man, except in the social state. He may exist in solitude, but undisputed facts have shown that he ceases to be human, and becomes the most abject and miserable of brutes. His structure and constitution make it just as certain that he was formed to live in society, as the structure and constitution of fishes that they were made to live in the water, or those of birds that they were made to live in the air. His faculties cannot grow, they cannot be developed, in any other state, any more than fishes could grow in the air, or birds grow under the water. His faculties are adapted to the Social state—all of them, moral, and religious, and intellectual, and mechanical; there they have their aliment, and find employment and exercise, and get their growth and their strength. . . . He is born into society, and his teachers are always near him, and if they were not, he would know nothing, and he would be nothing, but a very miserable and brutish animal. On the mother's knee, in the bosom of the family, he has his first lessons, reaching the heart, and the fancy, and the mind, through the electric chain of human sympathies which binds heart to heart, and fancy to fancy, and mind to mind. And so the eduction of his powers and feelings goes on, through all the stages of his mortal being, and he is man, with the faculties and senses, the sense and sensibilities of man. . . . Man in solitude could not even have the faculty of speech; and as he could not converse, he could not think or reason; he could not have reflection, or sympathy, or sense, or affection. And what sort of a human being would that be?

Man is, then, essentially a social being; and wherever men are found on this earth, they are found in society, and with some sort of social organization. They live together in the social state; and this social state implies organization and regulation, it implies polity and government. Men cannot live together without regulation, without rule, without authority. And this is just as much a law of their nature, and a law of necessity, as that they should live in society at all. There is a popular phrase, often employed and applied to the human being —namely—"living in a state of nature"; and by which it is meant to express, or assume, what cannot possibly be true, either first, that man as man, may live and grow up in solitude, without conneccion or association in any way with his fellows; or, next, that men may aggregate, and so live together in herds, as wild horses do on the great prairies, without any principle of association or regulation, and with a complete personal independence in each individual—in short, that men may live together, without living together in society, without living in the social state. But this is impossible; the constitution of his nature does not admit of any thing of the sort. Men must not only live together side by side, but they must live together in relationship. Their natures are expressly adapted to their living together in relationship. All their great interests in life are interests of mutual or reciprocal relationship, and about these their best and highest faculties and affections are employed and exercised. Without them, indeed, their higher faculties and affections would not be developed at all. The relations of men to each other in society, especially where a high state of civilization has been attained, are almost infinite, and all these bring with them reciprocal obligations and duties, and these obligations and duties bring with them in their turn, the necessity of regulation, of rule, of authority, of government. There has been no society, no aggregation of men on the earth—History does not inform us of any—so rude and savage, as to have been without some sort of organization, some sort of rule and government. All have had their laws, and some authority by which those laws are enforced. . . .

Of necessity, then, according to the constitution of human nature, and by the appointment of God, men live together in society, in the social state, and under some sort of social organization, and civil polity. Every people must have a social system, of one kind or another; it may be very complete, or it may be very imperfect. If it be not one thing, it must be another. If it do not indicate a high state of civilization, it will indicate a moderate degree, or a low degree of civilization, or no civilization at all. The social system of any country, as it is found embodied in its political forms, may be properly regarded as expressing the state of civilization to which that country has attained. This is a point of principal interest belonging to the political organization; and another is this; that it forms and constitutes a guaranty for the conservation and maintenance of its civilization up to the point to which it has already been carried. If besides this, the political organization be such as to foster and favor a spirit of improvement and progress in the line of genuine civilization, and so expansive and elastic withal as to comprehend and secure every advance that is made, every new point of good and excellence that may be attained, to the entire avoidance of all necessity or excuse for violent changes and revolutions, whether bloody or bloodless; if such be the political organization of any country, happy and blessed are the people that are in such a case. . . .

Taking, in the first place, altogether an outside view of our political organization, we notice here a nation, properly so called, and a national government, or central governing power. And do not let us make the mistake of supposing that this is too commonplace a fact, to be of any account or consequence. We could not well be a civilized people without this strictly national organization and government. European civilization exists under this form of political organization—about all there is of it; and it is under this form that civilization has made the highest advance thus far in the history of the world.

And let it here be observed, that it took Europe a thousand years to reach this advanced political condition. From the fall of the Roman empire in the fifth, to the middle of the fifteenth century, there was properly no such thing as a nation in Europe; there was no nationality, in the true, modern sense of the word. . . . The idea of a modern nation is this: That it is composed of one homogenous people, forming one body, with a certain distinctive character, and having a certain principle of unity; occupying a fixed residence and home, that is, having a country to which fixed limits are assigned; and subject, as a nation, and in its unity as such, to one central government. There must be a people, forming a body politic, having a public sentiment, and will, and wisdom of its own, such as these may be; and there must be a government representing the nation, as the Patriarch represents the Family, or the Tribe, and presiding and ruling over it. Such is a modern nation with its government. It is a political family; and it was the marshalling of mankind into great political families, each having its own proper representative and governing head, and in each of which a certain character and principle of unity prevails, which marked the era and commencement of modern civilization in Europe. . . .

The political power of Europe for about four centuries, counting from the overthrow of the Western Empire of Rome, was essentially barbarian. Even the Church, as it existed among the German hordes of the period, when rude and ignorant men intruded into her sacred offices, and priests and even bishops, like Salone and Sagittarius, became chiefs of marauding bands, and wandered over the country, within their own bishoprics, pillaging and ravaging as they went—even the Church was at least half barbarian. This was the primitive state of modern Europe, with some partial relief from this general condition, in particular quarters.

The feudal system, rising out of the bosom of barbarian society, introduced a change, in some respects salutary, but while it lasted in its vigor, rendering all attempts, or tendencies, towards national formation, and the centralization of power, wholly unavailing and abortive. Causes, however, were at work, and events came on, which favored the consolidation of states and empires. When the Crusades were ended, the power of feudalism, as a political system, was very much broken. The independent jurisdiction and fierce authority of multitudes of baronial chiefs had very much given way. The people began to rise into importance and consideration on the one hand, and kings and sovereigns on the other. Authority, control, the power of government, national sovereignty, was beginning to be centralized and exist in fewer hands. And finally it resulted, as I have said already, that there arose in Europe real nations, and real national governments. Kings began to rule as they had not ruled before; for it is to be remarked that monarchy was the almost universal form which government assumed whenever, and wherever, the Germanic and Slavonian population became really nationalized. At first, however, this monarchy was something very different from what it afterwards became, or attempted to make itself. It was then representative. The great fundamental principle of national or popular consent was recognized as the foundation of rightful authority, exercised under existing forms. Monarchy, as a particular form of government, was the expression and embodiment of the collective will and aggregate wisdom of the nation. It was a new doctrine, that which was afterwards set up, that the Sovereign represented nothing but his own will, and that he held his power, not by any consent of the nation to the monarchy, as a particular form of government, but by an absolute and a divine right personal to himself. This was a great error which has not been corrected in all cases, without popular revolutions. And though examples of absolutism in government still remain in Europe, yet it may be safely affirmed that the only kind of monarchy recognized at this day, as legitimate, by enlightened public opinion, in any part of Europe, is that which makes the sovereign only the chief magistrate of the nation, the center and bond of society, the chief conservator of the public peace and of public order, and the chief administrator of the general justice of the realm; representing in his person, the majesty of the State, and the will and wisdom of the body of the nation, as expressed in the particular form of government which it has chosen, or by which it abides, and of which the office of the sovereign is only an incident.

The true condition, then, of civilization in Europe, at the present day, as expressed in the forms of political organization, is undoubtedly this: it rests on the general fact that the population has come to be arranged into distinct nations, or national families, with a centralized power constituting in each the national government; and it may be remarked, that in these nations respectively, civilization is more or less advanced, other things being equal, as the principle of unity has more or less prevailed in the nation, and that of representation in the centralized and governing power.

And now to come back to the more immediate consideration of our own political organization. We have here a nation, and a national government; we have this form of civilization; and so far as this is concerned, without any further comparison of political or social systems, we stand on the same line of advance with the leading civilized nations of the old world. Now, there are two leading points to be considered in order to determine whether the existing condition of our civilization, so far as it depends on political organization, is likely to be maintained and preserved, and what promise there is that any advance or progress will be made. These points have reference, first, to the principle of unity in respect to the nation—how that principle is provided for and secured in its political forms, and how, if at all, it is likely to be violated and sacrificed in the progress of events; and next, to the principle of representation in respect to the government—how that principle is provided for and secured, and how, if at all, it is likely to be violated and sacrificed. . . .

If we go back to that period of most uncommon interest when this nation was formed, when this people became a nation, and provided a national government for itself, we cannot fail to be struck with the remarkable completeness and perfectness of our political organization in both the important particulars to which I have adverted. Representation in government was a thing the people had long been familiar with, and if a general government were to be established at all, it could not be bottomed on any other principle. But there was a desperate struggle against forming a Union; this was the point of difficulty. There could not be a nation without it; and there was in some of the States, in the smallest as well as others, the same reluctance and resistance to the plan, arising from the same desire and pride of wielding an independent though petty jurisdiction, and a nominal sovereignty, which had operated in Europe for centuries to keep up the existence of a thousand miserable, independent local jurisdictions and sovereignties, and prevent their fusion, or consolidation into nations. But when the Union was carried, when the states had agreed to consolidate and form a nation, it was seen and felt at once that the true elements of a nation were there, and the true principles of national unity to combine and bind them in one body.

In regard to this principle of unity: The people of the several States had been colonists together under the same imperial and distant power. They had struggled together against the exactions of that power, and what they felt to be evils of their political condition. They had gone through a long, exhausting, and bloody war together, for their common relief and emancipation, which they had secured by common and heroic sacrifices. They were a homogeneous people, having had nearly a common origin; they spoke a common language, and had a common literature; their moral and intellectual training had been very much the same; the principal elements of personal character were very much the same in the several states; and in reference to the leading affairs and concerns of human life, they entertained views, and sentiments, and feelings, in common, at least quite as nearly so as the like thing had ever been witnessed in any example, or case, of a great community, at all distinguished for intelligence, in any quarter, or any age of the world; and, finally, though they occupied a country, even then, of very liberal extent, which brought the very extremes of climate within its boundaries, and gave great variety to their industry and their productions, there was a manifest and intelligent bond of union in all the leading articles and particulars of their economical interests and business affairs. . . .

And in respect to this national unity in the American people —at least looking at them as they stood when first the Old Thirteen came together—I know of nothing to compare with it in any considerable nation of Europe. Though Castile and Aragon in Spain had formed one people politically for more than four hundred years before this Union was established, yet there is not that unity today between them which existed between Massachusetts and Virginia in the first month or year of their coming together. Normandy and Burgundy and Brittany in France have not yet united, and probably never can unite as kindly. It is only that part of the British Isles to which the term England is properly applied, which constitutes a nation in true unity under the reign of the British Queen. Wales is Wales, and Scotland is Scotland still. Ireland is governed more like a subjugated province than an integral part of the empire.

And there is another important particular in which the empire of the European nations, or of many of them, fails of that unity which the American nation had as it was originally formed under the Constitution. Their governments are not merely national; they are imperial, and rule over provinces and detached or distinct districts, as Rome did, till her provinces turned round and tyrannized over her. They have their colonies, as England has in the most distant and diverse quarters of the globe—a source, no doubt, of great apparent political strength and consideration in the scale and family of nations, but a source also of great moral weakness at home. England, the home country and nation, would be a better governed, a freer and happier, and a more civilized country today, if she had never had a colony to look after and govern. . . . When a country has as much breadth of territory, and embraces as much variety in its population, as can be formed into one nation, consistently with the due preservation of the great principle of national unity, then there is enough for any one government to do to take care of the public interests of that nation. And whatsoever more it has to do, cometh of evil, tends to evil, and is evil.

In regard to the principle of representation to which I have referred;

I must now, after the time I have already occupied, pass this topic over, with only some very general remarks.

The true idea of the representative principle I take to be this; that government, instead of ruling by an absolute, prescriptive or personal right, rules under a responsible trust, and exercises only the powers committed to it. Government is a trust, to be executed according to the intent and purpose designed to be answered by it, and by reference to the will of those who have created and established it. Thus, on the one hand, it is the will of God that government should exert and possess all necessary powers, and that it should be exercised for the highest common good of those who are the subjects of it. On the other hand, the nation itself decides, or it may do so, on the form of government it will have, the kind of Constitution it prefers, and how the functionaries shall be chosen or designated, and under what restriction, or distribution and limitation of powers they shall act. . . .

It may often happen, even when the government is administered most conscientiously and wisely, that it may, for the time, be little in accord with the prevailing feelings and wishes of the people. Of course, in such a case, they will condemn the administration and seek to bring about a change. This they may do under the right of election. The true use of the elective system is to enable the people to get rid of bad men and a bad administration; but, of course, it is just as potent an engine when they choose to employ it against good men, and a good administration. By the proper use of this power, the representative principle may be preserved and maintained; but with equal facility this very power may be employed to destroy the principle of representation, simply by converting the right of election into the right of administration and government. Election is itself a trust of a very high character. The elector does not exercise his franchise for himself, but for the whole body politic. Properly employed, election would place the administration habitually in the hands of the most worthy—τωυ αριστωυ—it would make the government an aristocracy—not in the sense so properly condemned in our day—but in the true, original, Greek signification of the term—a government of the most worthy—such a government as the country, in fact, once had, if never but once; I mean in the time of the first Congress and of the first President of the United States. But election may also be used to place the worst men in power; to create either a tyranny—the worst, perhaps, with which any country can be visited—the tyranny of petty demagogues, introduced into power, and supported in their pretensions and career, by an inflamed and unreasoning populace; or, a worse state of things still, a rule of mingled anarchy and malignity, under an unrestrained ochlocratic domination.

Let me be allowed to say, that it seems to me the exercise of this eminent right of election by the people may well be regarded as a trial, of no ordinary severity, to which they are subjected. Certainly it may be made, and ought to be made, one of the highest and most effective means that could possibly be employed, for their discipline and culti-vation, and for their advancement in intelligence and virtue. By the use of this power, they may heap blessings and benefits on their own heads; by the abuse of it, they may destroy themselves. It is a means of high political and moral discipline, which they have voluntarily taken into their own hands, but which they may wrest to their ruin if they will. . . . The point for those who take any part in forming the character and leading the opinions of the people to consider is, what they can do to keep the people true to themselves, and up to the high duties and responsibilities of their position. One thing we may count on as pretty certain, if the Leaders, Lawgivers and Instructors of the people—if Moses and Joshua—be not faithful to their trust, the people will not be likely to get further in their way towards the land of political promise, even after having once got quite clear of the wilder-ness, than to stand on the eminence that overlooks it. . . .

But I turn now to say a word or two on those other organizations, or associations, which I have already more than once referred to. Along with the State, we must have the Family, and the Church.

And first, in regard to the Family. There is, perhaps, no country in the world, thus far, where the sacredness and purity of the Family relations have been more scrupulously preserved, than in our own. Let us hope that we are not soon to degenerate from this high position. At the same time it is not to be disguised that there are theories of social reform industriously urged on the humbler classes of society, and with no inconsiderable effect, which are designed, or at least calculat-ed, to strike a fatal blow at the family relations. Under the plausible promise of improving the condition of labor, associations are recom-mended which are at war with the sacred institution of the family, and indeed with the whole structure of society, and through which, if they can have any success, a mischief will be done too serious and awful to be contemplated without horror.

But this is not all. If the Family relations are to be maintained at all in their purity, and so as to secure and promote social happiness, they must be maintained on the basis on which they were originally placed by their divine author. The first great principle to be preserved is the essential unity of the two persons who compose the one head of the

Family. "They twain shall be one flesh." The union is a mystic one, properly existing only under the most solemn religious sanctions, and with which profane hands should scarcely intermeddle. Happily for our country, as well as for that from which we have chiefly derived our political and legal institutions, the system of the Common Law, which generally prevails with us, accords mainly with the religious view and character of the conjugal relation, and of its marital rights. Generally, too, it may be said that our legislation on this subject—at least until within a recent period—has not widely departed from the notion and spirit of the original law of this relation. Unhappily, however, as it seems to me, a disposition has prevailed of late in some quarters of the country, to bring this sacred relation under the rules of the Civil Law—a system, so far as it is applied to the domestic relations, as much below that of the Common Law, as the heathen manners and philosophy in which it originated were below the sublime and elevated doctrines and precepts of Christianity. Just in proportion as this sacred and religious relation is brought down, by law, to the low level of a mere civil contract, whether by slovenly and unseemly provisions, made for the solemnization of marriage, or otherwise; and just in proportion as the law shall interpose to separate the temporal estates and interests of the parties, to place them in antagonist attitudes to each other, to afford them facilities for causes of difference, and for holding each other to mutual accountability in the courts, and, above all, to multiply grounds of separation; just in proportion as these things are done, will the religious tie and sanction which give this relation its mystic unity be weakened, its purity be degraded, and its sacredness profaned.

And now in regard to the Church, as one of the three associations of perpetual necessity—this being the most sacred of all—which lie at the foundation of the social system. . . . Out of all doubt, the moral training of mankind—since this cannot be separated from religion—is committed to the Church. The law of justice, the law of kindness, the law of charity, the law of brotherly love—these are never taught and enforced effectually on men any where but in the Church. True Liberty, true Equality, true Fraternity—these are taught no where but in the Church. Political leaders and social reformers, who never look to Christianity and the Church for the meaning of these terms and the doctrines properly involved in them, are only blind guides to lead the people to their destruction. It is in the Church that the true nature of the Family, and of the domestic relations, and the duties involved in them, are taught and enforced, and no where else. And here, and no where else, are taught the true character of political government, its divine authority and sanctions, and the religious duty of reverence and obedience on the part of all its subjects. Here, too, and no where else, may be learned the true nature of the relations which men sustain towards each other in the varied business and multiplied operations and affairs of active life, and the duties and demeanor proper to every station and degree of human existence. And here, and here only—in the principles and doctrines of Christianity, maintained and enforced in the Church, sternly inculcating the faith once for all delivered to it—will be found, according to my humble but undoubting convictions, the true method of solving all those appalling difficulties which now so disturb and distract communities and nations under the agitations set on foot by ignorant or unprincipled men, growing out of the relations between property and labor, and between the rich and the poor.

When every man shall be of the exact stature of every other man, and every soul the exact pattern of every other soul; when infants shall no longer be born into the world, but full grown men and women; when time and chance shall happen in exactly the same measure, to all; when none shall be younger or older, feebler or stronger, simpler or wiser, than any and every body else; then I suppose we may expect to see that precise equality of condition—that mathematical dead level in society—which some modern philosophers seem to dream of as a state of human perfection and felicity. So long, however, as men shall continue to be born, and live, and die, after the present fashion—so long as the Sermon on the Mount does not become obsolete, and wholly inapplicable, in every lesson and precept, to men in the social state—I suppose we must expect to see great diversities, oftentimes painful ones, in their condition and stations in society; we shall still have men of property and men of toil, masters and servants, employers and employed, rich and poor. And so long as this shall be the state of human society, I believe it will be found, after all struggles to escape from it are over, that there is only one effectual method of bringing about a real and lasting improvement in the social condition of men, and that is by bringing them together in one brotherhood of love in the bosom of the Church, where all alike, of every grade and condition, shall become the teachable and willing subjects of its doctrines and its discipline. The poor will never be provided for as they ought to be, or cared for as they ought to be, till the time shall come, as come it will, one day, when in every parish they shall be the voluntary charge of the local Christian fellowship of which they form a part. The great economical and social questions between Capital and Labor, which are now fast separating into hostile classes those who ought to be friends, as being mutually dependent on each other, though in different degrees, and between whom unwise men and bad men, are every where busy sowing dissension and bitter enmity, will never be satisfactorily adjusted and settled until the parties shall be brought together in a school and fellowship which shall make them the brethern of one sacred household, and where they shall be mutually as willing and anxious to understand and practice their reciprocal duties towards each other, as they are now to understand and insist on their respective rights. When they shall come to meet, as brothers, around a common altar of worship, in the communion of the Catholic Church, then, and not sooner, will they learn to do that willing justice to each other, without strife or envyings, which no laws, and no social organizations, under mere civil authority, can ever teach, secure or enforce. I am not preaching a sermon—that is not my calling; but I am endeavoring to state and insist on an economical truth. I am looking after the means of improving the social condition of mankind, and I happen to find them just where the Church finds and offers the means of their salvation.

The question, after all, is, in what is our hope? How shall the advantages of our social position be best secured, the hazards to which we are exposed avoided, and our progress in true felicity advanced? Others may rest their hopes in other things—in a thousand new devices which ingenious men are always ready to invent for the sovereign cure of all political and social ills. For myself I choose to trust first of all to those appointments and associations which were ordained of old, by a better wisdom than that of men; and then to agencies subordinate and auxiliary to them. Society must rest on the Family, on the State, and on the Church, as organizations of divine ordination. The Family must be held sacred; Government must be respected and obeyed, and the Church loved and venerated as a heaven-born mother.

Part Three
EDUCATION AND CULTURE

1

THE EDUCATED PERSON IN AMERICA

Nicholas Biddle
PRINCETON COMMENCEMENT ADDRESS

Nicholas Biddle (1786–1844) was the president of the Bank of the United States from 1822 to 1839, and as such became a major antagonist of Andrew Jackson. Biddle's conduct of his side of the "Bank War" still remains controversial. Before long he was operating his institution—and thereby manipulating the national economy—in close consultation with Clay and Webster as part of a determined effort to drive the Jacksonians out of power. But Biddle's financial and political strategies failed. The BUS lost its federal charter (in 1836) and, though it continued in existence for a few years under a Pennsylvania state charter, eventually went bankrupt.

In this selection we find Biddle playing a different role. The financier-politician was also a man of literary tastes. He had studied classics and French at the University of Pennsylvania during a precocious childhood and tried his hand at poetry and literary criticism as well as at diplomacy and law before turning to business. Here, he is addressing the graduating class at Princeton on the function of the "man of letters" in American society. Biddle's aspirations for a group who would offer the country guidance in cultural affairs seem somewhat analogous to his belief in centralized economic direction. His allusions to the historic dangers of demagogy have veiled, but unmistakable, implications for the politics of his own day. The reader may be interested in comparing Biddle's address with the famous "American Scholar" oration of Ralph Waldo Emerson, delivered two years later.

You have this day finished your education—you must now begin your studies. This education will have been unavailing, if it has not taught that although much is done, much remains to be done. The taste for letters is yours, the capacity to acquire knowledge is yours—and your minds, prepared by discipline and instruction, have received the seeds

SOURCE. Nicholas Biddle, *An Address Delivered Before the Alumni Association of Nassau Hall, on the Day of the Annual Commencement of the College of New Jersey, September 30, 1835* (Princeton, 1835).

of all useful learning. But the harvest they may yield depends wholly on yourselves. If these rich possessions be neglected, they will run to waste and destruction, leaving you the melancholy examples of an abortive effort at improvement. But care and cultivation will add largely to your present acquirements, and conduct you to any honors or distinctions to which you may aspire. To this you are often exhorted by those preceptors whose own success is the best testimony of the value of their instructions—but I cannot do you a greater service than by adding my own experience to their assurance, that liberal studies will be the safest guides and the truest friends in every condition, private or public, to which you may be destined.

You come on the stage of life at a peculiar period. For more than half a century the world has been shaken by a great struggle between new ideas and old institutions. The mass of mankind have outgrown the restraints of their infancy, and are striving to adapt their governments to their opinions, while the great problem on the part of existing authorities is how to yield gracefully, and seem to concede what may else be extorted. Whatever may be the result, the contest itself has developed an intense, and sometimes a distempered, energy in the passions of men—and forced a wider diffusion of knowledge—a more universal education—a more alert and excited feeling among all conditions. Such a community requires in its leaders a corresponding power of intellect. They will not submit their rights, or liberties, or complicated interests to incompetent hands—and although sometimes misled by passion, their purpose is to give power to those only who have capacity to employ it usefully and safely. From you, therefore, destined as you naturally are to be prominent in your native communities, more is expected—more will be exacted—and your only hope of distinction is, to be in advance of those whom you aspire to lead. You must go on, or you must go down; and you can go on only by diligent perseverance in your studies, so as to withstand the heated competition around you. They are more valuable now, from their power to counteract the influence of mere physical wants, which is the tendency of our age. The wonders of mechanical improvement have so surprised the world, and so multiplied its physical pleasures, that we sometimes incline to exaggerate their value. The personal comforts which they furnish, have tended to unspiritualize the understanding, and make us prone to disparage more intellectual pursuits, which yield no such luxurious enjoyments. But so long as the heart and the imagination most influence human actions—so long as mind predominates over matter—that is, while our race endures, the nature of man—his passions, his history, and his destiny will ever be the noblest study of a human being. In every walk of life you will find their advantages. You can engage in no pursuit where they will not ensure a superiority over less instructed competitors. In those deemed exclusively mechanical, they excite to experiment, they suggest improvements, they render labor more intelligent, and, therefore, more productive. Even the most monotonous routine of mechanical life leaves many hours to the dominion of solitary reflection, which early instruction might kindle into usefulness. They are more necessary in our country, because labor has attached to it here two peculiarities, almost unknown elsewhere—power and leisure—political power, which education can alone render valuable—and leisure, the natural result of the general prosperity—but the most dangerous gift to an uncultivated mind.

There are some who fear that these studies may inspire a distaste for industry, and that the fields and workshops may be abandoned, because they who work can also read. But men need not hate labor because they love study—nor look above their profession, because they can look beyond it. The industry of any community may be safely trusted to the actual wants which make it necessary, and the spirit of accumulation which makes it afterwards agreeable—and the only effect will be, not to make men work less, but to make that work more skilful. Pass through the other occupations of life, and cultivation maintains its ascendancy. Men are commonly more intelligent in their affairs, generally more successful, always more respected, for habits of taste and literary cultivation. As you ascend in the scale of life, their efficacy is still more striking. In the sacred calling, among those who are equal in the essentials of Christian virtue, how much more of honor and of usefulness is the portion of that scholar whose learning enables him to trace back to its source the stream of revelation, separating from its pure waters the turbid infusion which the imperfection of human language, or the misguided zeal of fanatics may have mingled with it. In the healing art, what resources for alleviating human suffering and prolonging the existence of those we love, may be employed by him who renders every age and every climate tributary to his improvement. In the kindred profession of the law, which embraces the whole circle of human affairs, the highest honors are reserved, not for him who is content with the ordinary routine of litigation, but for the riper scholar who seeks in every science—in all liberal arts, and throughout the whole domain of letters, whatever may adorn or dignify his noble occupation. But it is on the wider field of usefulness, for which every American should be prepared, that these studies are of the highest value. You are all destined for public life. Many of you will, I trust, be conspicuous there. I deem it right, then, earnestly to impress on you the influence of liberal studies on public duties, by explaining my own conviction, that inattention to them is a prevailing defect among us—that one of the greatest dangers to our institutions arises from the want of them—and that, without them, no public man can ever acquire extended usefulness or durable fame.

In our country, too many young men rush into the arena of public life without adequate preparation. They go abroad because their home is cheerless. They fill their minds with the vulgar excitement of what they call politics, for the want of more genial stimulants within. Unable to sustain the rivalry of more disciplined intellects, they soon retire in disgust and mortification, or what is far worse, persevere after distinctions which they can now obtain only by artifice. They accordingly take refuge in leagues and factions—they rejoice in stratagems —they glory in combinations—weapons all these, by which mediocrity revenges itself on the uncalculating manliness of genius—and mines its way to power. Their knowledge of themselves inspires a low estimate of others. They distrust the judgment and the intelligence of the community, on whose passions alone they rely for advancement—and their only study is to watch the shifting currents of popular prejudice, and be ready at a moment's warning to follow them. For this purpose, their theory is, to have no principles and to give no opinions, never to do any thing so marked as to be inconsistent with doing the direct reverse—and never to say any thing not capable of contradictory explanations. They are thus disencumbered for the race—and as the ancient mathematician could have moved the world if he had had a place to stand on, they are sure of success if they have only room to turn. Accordingly, they worship cunning, which is only the counterfeit of wisdom, and deem themselves sagacious only because they are selfish. They believe that all generous sentiments of love of country, for which they feel no sympathy in their own breasts, are hollow pretences in others—that public life is a game in which success depends on dexterity—and that all government is a mere struggle for place. They thus disarm ambition of its only fascination, the desire of authority in order to benefit the country; since they do not seek places to obtain power, but power to obtain places. Such persons may rise to great official stations—for high offices are like the tops of the pyramids, which reptiles can reach as well as eagles. But though they may gain places, they never can gain honors—they may be politicians—they never can become statesmen. The mystery of their success lies in their adroit management of our own weakness —just as the credulity of his audience makes half the juggler's skill. Personally and singly, objects of indifference, our collected merits are devoutly adored when we acquire the name of "the people." Our sovereignty, our virtues, our talents, are the daily themes of eulogy: they assure us that we are the best and wisest of the human race—that their highest glory is to be the instruments of our pleasure, and that they will never act nor think nor speak but as we direct them. If we name them to executive stations, they promise to execute only what we desire—if we send them to deliberative bodies, they engage never to deliberate, but be guided solely by the light of our intuitive wisdom. Startled at first by language, which, when addressed to other sovereigns, we are accustomed to ridicule for its abject sycophancy, constant repetition makes it less incredible. By degrees, although we may not believe all the praise, we cannot doubt the praiser, till at last we become so spoiled by adulation, that truth is unwelcome. If it comes from a stranger, it must be prejudice—if from a native, scarce less than treason; and when some unhappy traveller ventures to smile at follies which we will not see or dare not acknowledge, instead of disregarding it, or being amused by it, or profiting by it, we resent it as an indignity to our sovereign perfections. This childish sensitiveness would be only ludicrous if it did not expose us to the seduction of those who flatter us only till they are able to betray us—as men praise what they mean to sell—treating us like pagan idols, caressed till we have granted away our power—and then scourged for our impotence. Their pursuit of place has alienated them from the walks of honest industry—their anxiety for the public fortunes has dissipated their own. With nothing left either in their minds or means to retreat upon; having no self-esteem, and losing that of others, when they cease to possess authority, they acquire a servile love of sunshine—a dread of being what is called unpopular, that makes them the ready instruments of any chief who promises to be the strongest. They degenerate at last into mere demagogues, wandering about the political common, without a principle or a dollar, and anxious to dispose to the highest bidder of their only remaining possession, their popularity. If successful, they grow giddy with the frequent turns by which they rose, and wither into obscurity. If they miscalculate—if they fall into that fatal error—a minority—retirement, which is synonymous with disgrace, awaits them, while their more fortunate rivals, after flourishing for a season in a gaudy and feverish notoriety, are eclipsed by some fresher demagogue, some more popular man of the people. Such is the melancholy history of many persons, victims of an abortive ambition, whom more cultivation might have rendered useful and honorable citizens.

Above this crowd and beyond them all stands that character which I trust many of you will become—a real American statesman.

For the high and holy duty of serving his country, he begins by deep and solitary studies of its constitution and laws, and all its great interests. These studies are extended over the whole circumference of knowledge—all the depths and shoals of the human passions are sounded to acquire the mastery over them. The solid structure is then strengthened and embellished by familiarity with ancient and modern languages—with history, which supplies the treasures of old experience—with eloquence, which gives them attraction—and with the whole of that wide miscellaneous literature, which spreads over them all a perpetual freshness and variety. These acquirements are sometimes reproached by the ignorant as being pedantry. They would be pedantic if they intruded into public affairs inappropriately, but in subordination to the settled habits of the individual, they add grace to the strength of his general character, as the foliage ornaments the fruit that ripens beneath it. They are again denounced as weakening the force of native talent, and contrasted disparagingly with what are called rough and strong minded men. But roughness is no necessary attendant on strength; the true steel is not weakened by the highest polish—just as the scimitar of Damascus, more flexible in the hands of its master, inflicts a keener wound than the coarsest blade. So far from impairing the native strength of the mind, at every moment this knowledge is available. In the play of human interests and passions, the same causes ever influence the same results; what has been, will again be, and there is no contingency of affairs on which the history of the past may not shed its warning light on the future. The modern languages bring him into immediate contact with the living science and the gifted minds of his remote contemporaries. All the forms of literature, which are but the varied modifications in which the human intellect develops itself, contribute to reveal to him its structure and its passions—and these endowments can be displayed in a statesman's career only by eloquence—itself a master power, attained only by cultivation, and never more requiring it than now, when its influence is endangered by its abuse. Our institutions require and create a multitude of public speakers and writers—but, without culture, their very numbers impede their excellence—as the wild richness of the soil throws out an unweeded and rank luxuriance. Accordingly, in all that we say or write about public affairs, a crude abundance is the disease of our American style. On the commonest topic of business, a speech swells into a declamation—an official statement grows to a dissertation. A discourse about any thing must contain every thing. We will take nothing for granted. We must commence at the very commencement. An ejectment for ten acres, reproduces the whole discovery of America—a discussion about a tariff or a turnpike, summons from their remotest caves the adverse blasts of windy rhetoric—and on those great Serbonian bogs, known in political geography as constitutional questions, our ambitious fluency often begins with the general deluge, and ends with its own. It is thus that even the good sense and reason of some become wearisome, while the undisciplined fancy of others wanders into all the extravagances and the gaudy phraseology which distinguish our western orientalism. The result is that our public affairs are in danger of becoming wholly unintelligible—concealed rather than explained, as they often are, in long harangues which few who can escape will hear, and in massive documents which all who see will shun. For this idle waste of words—at once a political evil and a social wrong—the only remedy is study. The last degree of refinement is simplicity; the highest eloquence is the plainest; the most effective style is the pure, severe and vigorous manner, of which the great masters are the best teachers.

But the endearing charm of letters in a statesman is the calmness and dignity which they diffuse over his whole thoughts and character. He feels that there are higher pursuits than the struggles for place. He knows that he has other enjoyments. They assist his public duties —they recruit his exhausted powers, and they fill, with a calm and genuine satisfaction, those hours of repose so irksome to the mere man of politics. Above all, and what is worth all, they make him more thoroughly and perfectly independent. It is this spirit of personal independence which is the great safeguard of our institutions. It seems to be the law of our physical and of our moral nature, that every thing should perish in its own excesses. The peculiar merit of free institutions is, that they embody and enforce the public sentiment— the abuse which has destroyed them is, that they execute prematurely, the crude opinions of masses of men without adequate reflection, and before the passions which excited them can subside. Opinions now are so easily accumulated in masses, and their action is so immediate, that unless their first impulses are resisted, they will not brook even the restraints which, in cooler moments, they have imposed on themselves, but break over the barriers of their own laws. Their impatience is quickened by the constant adulation from the competitors for their favor, till, at last, men become unwilling to hazard offence by speaking wholesome truth. It is thus that the caprice of a single individual, some wild phantasy, perhaps, of some unworthy person, easily corrected, or, if there were need, easily subdued at first—when propagated over numerous minds, not more intelligent than the first, becomes, at length, commanding—and superior intellects are overawed by the imposing presence of a wide-spread folly, as the noxious vapor of the lowest marsh may poison, by contagion, a thousand free hills. That is our first danger. The second and far greater peril is when these excited masses are wielded by temporary favorites, who lead them against the constitution and the laws. For both these dangers, the only security for freedom is found in the personal independence of public men. This independence is not a mere abundance of fortune, which makes place unnecessary—for wealth is no security for personal uprightness—but it is the independence of mind, the result of talents and education, which makes the possessor conscious that he relies on himself alone—that he seeks no station by unworthy means—will receive none with humiliation —will retain none with dishonor. They take their stand accordingly. Their true position is that where they can best defend the country equally from this inflamed populace and their unworthy leaders—on the one hand, resisting this fatal weakness—the fear of losing popular favor—and, on the other, disdaining all humiliating compliances with men in power.

Of the ancient and modern world, the best model of the union of the man of letters and the statesman was he, with whose writings your studies have made you familiar—Cicero. The most diligent researches, the most various acquirements, prepared him for the active career of public life, which he mingled with laborious studies, so as never, for a moment, to diminish the vigor of his public character. How often, and how well he served his country all history attests. When the arts and the arms of Cataline had nearly destroyed the freedom of Rome, it was this great man of letters who threw himself into the midst of that band of desperate conspirators, and by his single intrepidity and eloquence rescued the republic.

When that more noble and dangerous criminal, Caesar, broke down the public liberty, after vainly striving to resist the tide of infatuation, Cicero retired to his farm, where he composed those deep philosophical works which have been the admiration of all succeeding time. But they could not avert his heart from his country—and on that day—on that very hour when the dagger of Casca avenged the freedom of Rome, he was in the Senate, and the first words of Brutus on raising his bloody steel were to call on Cicero—the noblest homage, this, which patriotism ever paid to letters.

Let it not diminish your admiration that Cicero was proscribed and put to death. They who live for their country must be prepared to die for it. For the same reason, hatred to those who enslaved his country, his great predecessor, Demosthenes, shared a similar fate. But both died in their country's service—and their great memories shall endure for ever, long after the loftiest structures of the proudest sovereigns. There were kings in Egypt who piled up enormous monuments with the vain hope of immortality. Their follies have survived their history. No man can tell who built the pyramids. But the names of these great martyrs of human liberty have been in all succeeding time the trumpet call to freedom. Each word which they have spoken is treasured, and has served to rally nations against their oppressors.

Trained by these studies and animated by the habitual contemplation of the examples of those who have gone before you, as a true American statesman, you may lay your hand on your country's altar. From that hour—swerved by no sinister purpose, swayed by no selfish motive—your whole heart must be devoted to her happiness and her glory. No country could be worthier of a statesman's care. On none has nature lavished more of the materials of happiness and of greatness—as fatal if they are misdirected, as they must be glorious when rightly used. On the American statesman, then, devolves the solemn charge of sustaining its institutions against temporary excesses, either of the people or their rulers—and protecting them from their greatest foes—which will always lie in their own bosom. You can accomplish this only by persevering in your own independence—by doing your duty fearlessly to the country. If you fail to please her, do not the less serve her, for she is not the less your country. Never flatter the people—leave that to those who mean to betray them. Remember that the man who gave the most luxurious entertainments to the Roman people was the same who immediately after destroyed their freedom. That was Julius Caesar. Remember that the most bloody tyrant of our age was the meanest in his courtship to the mob, and scarcely ever spoke without invoking for his atrocities what he called "the poor people." That man was Robespierre. Never let any action of your life be influenced by the desire of obtaining popular applause at the expense of your own sincere and manly convictions. No favor from any sovereign—a single individual, or thirteen millions, can console you for the loss of your own esteem. If they are offended, trust to their returning reason to do you justice, and should that hope fail, where you cannot serve with honor, you can retire with dignity. You did not seek power—and you can readily leave it, since you are qualified for retirement, and since you carry into it the proud consolation of having done your duty.

But should you ever be called to act the stern, yet glorious part which these patriot statesmen performed, you will not fail in the requisite energy. It may be, that, not as of old, another robust barbarian from Thrace, like Maximin—not a new gladiator slave, like Spartacus—but some frontier Cataline may come up with the insolent ambition to command you and your children. More dangerous still, the people may be bartered away as other sovereigns have been, by faithless favorites, just as the very guards at Rome sold the empire at open auction to the highest bidder, Julian. The same arts which succeeded of old may not be unavailing here—a conspiracy of profligate men, pandering to the passions of the people, may inflame them to their ruin—and the country, betrayed into the hands of its worst citizens, may be enslaved with all the appearances of freedom. Should that day come, remember never to capitulate—never to compromise—never to yield to the country's enemies. Remember that crime is not the less guilty—it is only the more dangerous by success. If you should see the cause betrayed by those who ought to defend it, be you only the more faithful. Never desert the country—never despond over its fortunes. Confront its betrayers, as madmen are made to quail beneath the stern gaze of fearless reason. They will denounce you. Disregard their outcries—it is only the scream of the vultures whom you scare from their prey. They will seek to destroy you. Rejoice that your country's enemies are yours. You can never fall more worthily than in defending her from her own degenerate children. If overborne by this tumult, and the cause seems hopeless, continue self-sustained and self-possessed. Retire to your fields, but look beyond them. Nourish your spirits with meditation on the mighty dead who have saved their country. From your own quiet elevation, watch calmly this servile route as its triumph sweeps before you. The avenging hour will at last come. It cannot be that our free nation can long endure the vulgar dominion of ignorance and profligacy. You will live to see the laws re-established—these banditti will be scourged back to their caverns—the penitentiary will reclaim its fugitives in office, and the only remembrance which history will preserve of them, is the energy with which you resisted and defeated them.

My last words then to you, my young friends, are to pursue the studies which you have successfully begun. You may always confide in them as the ornaments of prosperity—the consolation of adverse fortune—your support in public life—your refuge in retirement—giving to the private citizen his most refined enjoyments, and to the statesman, independence and distinction.

2
RELIGIOUS IDEOLOGY
AND POLITICAL FREEDOM

Lyman Beecher
A PLEA FOR THE WEST

Lyman Beecher (1775–1863) represents the religious dimension of Whiggery. The son of a blacksmith, Beecher made himself one of the country's leading preachers and fathered one of our greatest literary families; its best remembered member is the novelist Harriet Beecher Stowe. A combative man, Beecher found himself continually caught up in controversy. In theology he was a Calvinist of the "new school" and was tried for heresy by more conservative churchmen. (He won acquittal.) He engaged in many crusades against what he took to be evils—among them intemperance, Unitarianism, and slavery. His years as president of Lane Seminary in Ohio were among the stormiest of all; a rebellion by disaffected students against the trustees led to the founding of Oberlin College.

This statement shows Beecher in a characteristic mood, calling for help in establishing Protestant colleges on the frontier to counteract the influence of the colleges Catholics were starting. He delivered the address in various cities as he toured the country in search of funds. There was a strong streak of nativism and anti-Catholicism among many Whigs; occasionally these feelings provoked mob violence. Here, however, Beecher is trying to appeal to reason rather than prejudice. As to how well he succeeded, readers are likely to differ.

It was the opinion of [Jonathan] Edwards that the millenium would commence in America. When I first encountered this opinion, I thought it chimerical; but all providential developments since, and all the existing signs of the times, lend corroboration to it. But if it is by the march of revolution and civil liberty that the way of the Lord is to be prepared, where shall the central energy be found, and from what nation shall the renovating power go forth? What nation is blessed

SOURCE. Lyman Beecher, *A Plea for the West* (Cincinnati, 1835).

133

with such experimental knowledge of free institutions, with such facilities and resources of communication, obstructed by so few obstacles, as our own? There is not a nation upon earth which, in fifty years, can by all possible reformation place itself in circumstances so favorable as our own for the free unembarrassed application of physical effort and pecuniary and moral power to evangelize the world.

But if this nation is, in the providence of God, destined to lead the way in the moral and political emancipation of the world, it is time she understood her high calling, and were harnessed for the work. For mighty causes, like floods from distant mountains, are rushing with accumulating power to their consummation of good or evil, and soon our character and destiny will be stereotyped forever.

It is equally plain that the religious and political destiny of our nation is to be decided in the West. There is the territory, and there soon will be the population, the wealth, and the political power. The Atlantic commerce and manufactures may confer always some peculiar advantage on the East. But the West is destined to be the great central power of the nation, and under heaven, must affect powerfully the cause of free institutions and the liberty of the world.

The West is a young empire of mind and power and wealth and free institutions, rushing up to a giant manhood, with a rapidity and a power never before witnessed below the sun. And if she carries with her the elements of her preservation, the experiment will be glorious—the joy of the nation—the joy of the whole earth, as she rises in the majesty of her intelligence, benevolence, and enterprise, for the emancipation of the world.

It is equally clear that the conflict which is to decide the destiny of the West will be a conflict of institutions for the education of her sons, for purposes of superstition or evangelical light; of despotism, or liberty. . . .

By whom shall the work of rearing the literary and religious institutions of the West be done?

Not by the West alone.

The West is able to do this great work for herself—and would do it, provided the exigencies of her condition allowed to her the requisite time. The subject of education is no where more appreciated; and no people in the same time ever performed so great a work as has already been performed in the West. Such an extent of forest never fell before the arm of man in forty years, and gave place, as by enchantment, to such an empire of cities, and towns, and villages, and agriculture, and merchandise, and manufactures, and roads, and rapid navigation, and schools, and colleges, and libraries, and literary enterprise, with such a number of pastors and churches, and such a relative amount of religious influence, as has been produced by the spontaneous effort of the religious denominations of the West. The later peopled states of New England did by no means come as rapidly to the same state of relative intellectual and moral culture as many portions of the West have already arrived at, in the short period of forty, thirty, and even twenty years.

But this work of self-supply is not completed, and by no human possibility could have been completed by the West, in her past condition.

No people ever did, in the first generation, fell the forest, and construct the roads, and rear the dwellings and public edifices, and provide the competent supply of schools and literary institutions. New England did not. Her colleges were endowed extensively by foreign munificence, and her churches of the first generation were supplied chiefly from the mother country; and yet the colonists of New England were few in number, compact in territory, homogeneous in origin, language, manners, and doctrines; and were coerced to unity by common perils and necessities; and could be acted upon by immediate legislation; and could wait also for their institutions to grow with their growth and strengthen with their strength. But the population of the great West is not so, but is assembled from all the states of the Union, and from all the nations of Europe, and is rushing in like the waters of the flood, demanding for its moral preservation the immediate and universal action of those institutions which discipline the mind, and arm the conscience and the heart. And so various are the opinions and habits, and so recent and imperfect is the acquaintance, and so sparse are the settlements of the West, that no homogeneous public sentiment can be formed to legislate immediately into being the requisite institutions. And yet they are all needed immediately, in their utmost perfection and power. A nation is being "born in a day," and all the nurture of schools and literary institutions is needed, constantly and universally, to rear it up to a glorious and unperverted manhood. . . .

But how shall the requisite supply of teachers for the sons and daughters of the West be raised up? It can be accomplished by the instrumentality of a learned and pious ministry, educated at the West. . . .

We must educate! We must educate! or we must perish by our own prosperity. If we do not, short from the cradle to the grave will be our race. If in our haste to be rich and mighty, we outrun our literary and religious institutions, they will never overtake us; or only come up after the battle of liberty is fought and lost. . . .

There is no danger that our agriculture and arts will not prosper: the danger is, that our intelligence and virtue will falter and fall back into a dark minded, vicious populace—a poor, uneducated, reckless mass of infuriated animalism, to rush on resistless as the tornado, or to burn as if set on fire of hell.

Until Europe, by universal education, is delivered from such masses of feudal ignorance and servitude, she sits upon a volcano, and despotism and revolution will arbitrate her destiny. . . .

The great experiment is now making, and from its extent and rapid filling up is making in the West, whether the perpetuity of our republican institutions can be reconciled with universal suffrage. Without the education of the head and heart of the nation, they cannot be; and the question to be decided is, can the nation, or the vast balance power of it, be so imbued with intelligence and virtue as to bring out, in laws and their administration, a perpetual self-preserving energy? We know that the work is a vast one, and of great difficulty; and yet we believe it can be done. . . .

But whatever we do, it must be done quickly; for there is a tide in human things which waits not—moments on which the destiny of a nation balances, when the light dust may turn the right way or the wrong. And such is the condition of our nation now. Mighty influences are bearing on us in high conflict, for good or for evil—for an immortality of woe or blessedness; and a slight effort now may secure what ages of repentance cannot recover when lost, and soon the moment of our practical preservation may have passed away. . . .

According to the most accurate estimation which can be obtained, there are in the United States about a million and a half of children without the means of education, and about an equal number of adults, either foreigners or native Americans, that are uneducated. These large masses of unenlightened mind lie in almost every portion of this nation, and frightful statistics have been officially given by legislative investigation in several of our states. In one of the smaller eastern states there are thirty thousand adults that cannot read or write. In one of the largest there are *four hundred thousand* adults and children who have had no instruction, and no means provided. In one of the western states, two-thirds of all the children in the state are destitute of any provision for education. These are the states who have taken the lead in making legislative investigations. Equally appalling developments await many of the other states so soon as they have public spirit enough to take the same method for information. Every where, and in all ages, such masses of ignorance are the material of all others most dangerous to liberty; for, as a general fact, *uneducated mind is educated vice.* But the safety of our republic depends upon the intelligence, and moral principle, and patriotism, and property of the nation. These, whatever topical inflammation may break out and push on to desperate measures, will by a common instinct of self-preservation recoil when the precipice appears, and will unite in measures of common safety. But if in this moment of recoil there be a populace behind—a million of voters without intelligence, or conscience, or patriotism, or property, and driven on by demagogues to forbid recoil and push us over, in a moment all may be lost. Half a million of unprincipled, reckless voters, in the hands of demagogues, may, in our balanced elections, overrule all the property, and wisdom, and moral principle of the nation.

This danger from uneducated mind is augmenting daily by the rapid influx of foreign emigrants, unacquainted with our institutions, unaccustomed to self-government, inaccessible to education, and easily accessible to prepossession, and inveterate credulity, and intrigue, and easily embodied and wielded by sinister design. In the beginning this eruption of revolutionary Europe was not anticipated, and we opened our doors wide to the influx and naturalization of foreigners. But it is becoming a terrific inundation; it has increased upon our native population from five to thirty-seven per cent, and is every year advancing. It seeks, of course, to settle down upon the unoccupied territory of the West, and may at no distant day equal, and even outnumber the native population. What is to be done to educate the millions which in twenty years Europe will pour out upon us?

But what if this emigration, self-moved and slow in the beginning, is now rolling its broad tide at the bidding of the powers of Europe hostile to free institutions, and associated in holy alliance to arrest and put them down? Is this a vain fear? Are not the continental powers alarmed at the march of liberal opinions, and associated to put them down? and are they not, with the sickness of hope deferred, waiting for our downfall? It is the light of our republican prosperity, gleaming in upon their dark prison house, which is inspiring hope, and converting chains into arms. It is the power of mind, roused by our example from the sleep of ages and the apathy of despair, which is sending earthquake under the foundations of their thrones; and they have no hope of rest and primeval darkness, but by the extinction of our light. By fleets and armies they cannot do it. But do they, therefore, sleep on their heaving earth and tottering thrones? Has

Metternich yet to form an acquaintance with history? Does he dream that there is but one way to overturn republics, and that by the sword? Has he yet to learn how Philip, by dividing her councils, conquered Greece? and how, by intestine divisions, Rome fell? If the potentates of Europe have no design upon our liberties, what means the paying of the passage and emptying out upon our shores such floods of pauper emigrants—the contents of the poor house and the sweepings of the streets?—multiplying tumults and violence, filling our prisons, and crowding our poor houses, and quadrupling our taxation, and sending annually accumulating thousands to the polls to lay their inexperienced hand upon the helm of our power? Does Metternich imagine that there is no party spirit in our land, whose feverish urgency would facilitate their naturalization and hasten them to the ballot box?—and no demagogues, who for a little brief authority, however gained, would sell their country to an everlasting bondage? A foreign influence acting efficaciously on the councils of a republic, has always been regarded and always proved itself to be among the most fatal to liberty. But in no form can it assume such power as in the form of a consolidated mass of alien votes, to balance in contested elections the suffrage of the nation; rendering foreigners the most favored and most courted people, and giving an easy predominance to foreign influence in our national councils. That wily politician does not sleep over our prosperity, or despair of our overthrow. But he exults full of hope that we sleep while he is sowing with broad cast among us the elements of future strife, and preparing our ruin by the only means by which republics have ever fallen.

It is the testimony of American travelers that the territorial, civil and ecclesiastical statistics of our country, and the action and bearing of political causes upon our institutions, are more familiar at Rome and Vienna, than with us; and that tracts and maps are in circulation, explanatory of the capacious West, and pointing out the most fertile soils and most favored locations, and inviting to emigration. These means of a stimulated expatriation are corroborated by the copious and rapidly increasing correspondence of those who have already arrived, and the increasing facilities of transportation.

But if, upon examination, it should appear that three-fourths of the foreign emigrants whose accumulating tide is rolling in upon us, are, through the medium of their religion and priesthood, as entirely accessible to the control of the potentates of Europe as if they were an army of soldiers, enlisted and officered, and spreading over the land; then, indeed, should we have just occasion to apprehend danger to our liberties. It would be the union of church and state in the midst of us. . . .

But before I proceed, to prevent misapprehension, I would say that I have no fear of the Catholics, considered simply as a religious denomination, and unallied to the church and state establishments of the European governments hostile to republican institutions.

Let the Catholics mingle with us as Americans, and come with their children under the full action of our common schools and republican institutions, and the various powers of assimilation, and we are prepared cheerfully to abide the consequences. If in these circumstances the protestant religion cannot stand before the Catholic, let it go down, and we will sound no alarm, and ask no aid, and make no complaint. It is no ecclesiastical quarrel to which we would call the attention of the American nation.

Nor would I consent that the civil and religious rights of the Catholics should be abridged or violated. As naturalized citizens, to all that we enjoy we bid them welcome, and would have their property and rights protected with the same impartiality and efficacy that the property and rights of every other denomination are protected; and we should abhor the interposition of lawless violence to injure the property or control the rights of Catholics as vehemently as if it were directed against protestants and their religion. For when the day comes that lawless force prevails, argument and free inquiry are ended, and law and courts are impotent and useless, and liberty is extinct, and anarchy by its terrors will compel men to call in the protection of despotic power to save them from the pursuing hell. The late violence done to Catholic property at Charlestown[1] is regarded with regret and abhorrence by protestants and patriots throughout the land, though the excitement which produced it had no relation whatever to religious opinions, and no connection with any religious denomination of Christians.

We are equally opposed to any attempt to cast odium upon Catholics of the present generation for any maxims, doctrines or practices of past ages, which are now by the competent authority of the pope or a general council disavowed. But for all the political bearings of their unchangeable and infallible creed, and for all the deeds of persecution and blood, justified by their principles and perpetrated by Catholic powers, and not disavowed by his holiness or by a council, the Catholic church is accountable, whatever may be the personal opinion of particular individuals or particular departments of that great community.

In our animadversions, however, even on these things, a declamatory, virulent, contemptuous, sarcastic, taunting, denunciatory style is

[1] A Protestant mob burned down the Ursuline convent there in 1834. Ed.

as unchristian as it is in bad taste and indiscreet. The invidious technics of the old controversy have gone into oblivion, and it is impossible to bring back the image and body of the times gone by as they stood in dreadful reality around our persecuted fathers; and however the urgency of oppression in a rough age may palliate the use of such terms by them, sound argument with meek firmness had been better even then: and it is one of the most hopeful signs of the present times, that public sentiment demands such courtesy of all religious controvertists now, and will not endure a dialect of rudeness, ill-temper and violence. If the reaction upon Catholics for the use of such language is not as stern and powerful as on protestants, it is only because as strangers and a minority, more aggressive language will be tolerated in them than the protestant majority will be permitted to hurl back; while even they, in the use of invidious terms, and the manifestation of a virulent, discourteous and contemptuous spirit, are fast using up both the sympathy and the patience of the community in their behalf.

Besides, the Catholics in great numbers are with us, and their increase by emigration, if it can be regulated, can never be wholly prevented. Our rich unoccupied territory, our national works, and their poverty and oppression at home, will as certainly bring over adventurers as a vacuum will call in the circumjacent atmosphere; and it is impossible to avert the danger from so much exile population but by a friendly approximation, and the ubiquity and powerful illumination of our institutions, and the overcoming influence of Christian enterprise and Christian love. It is not the striking of the fist which will disarm them, but words and acts of kindness and the warm beating of our heart; while contemptuous treatment will augment their hatred of protestants, and rivet their prejudice, and deliver them over double bound to the power of their priesthood, already too great for their happiness and our safety.

In this view of the subject, I cannot but regret the manner in which the controversy between the Catholics and protestants has in various instances been conducted, in which the style and temper, as the means of doing good, were the very worst that could have been chosen, and the very best as the means of aiding the cause they were intended to oppose. Important facts and powerful arguments have been given, but so mingled with invective and taunt, and sarcasm, and reviling, as to injure the cause as much by the disgust occasioned, as it was aided by the power of argument.

It is to the political claims and character of the Catholic religion, and its church and state alliance with the political and ecclesiastical governments of Europe hostile to liberty, and the tendency upon our republican institutions of flooding the nation suddenly with emigrants of this description, on whom for many years European influence may be exerted with such ease, and certainty, and power, that we call the attention of the people of this nation. Did the Catholics regard themselves only as one of many denominations of Christians, entitled only to equal rights and privileges, there would be no such cause for apprehension while they peaceably sustained themselves by their own arguments and well doing. But if Catholics are taught to believe that their church is the only church of Christ, out of whose inclosure none can be saved—that none may read the Bible but by permission of the priesthood, and no one be permitted to understand it and worship God according to the dictates of his own conscience—that heresy is a capital offence not to be tolerated, but punished by the civil power with disfranchisement, death and confiscation of goods—that the pope and the councils of the church are infallible, and her rights of ecclesiastical jurisdiction universal, and as far as possible and expedient may be of right, and ought to be as a matter of duty, enforced by the civil power—that to the pope belongs the right of interference with the political concerns of nations, enforced by his authority over the consciences of Catholics, and his power to corroborate or cancel their oath of allegiance, and to sway them to obedience or insurrection by the power of life or death eternal; if such, I say, are the maxims avowed by her pontiffs, sanctioned by her councils, stereotyped on her ancient records, advocated by her most approved authors, illustrated in all ages by her history, and still unrepealed, and still acted upon in the armed prohibition of free inquiry and religious liberty, and the punishment of heresy wherever her power remains unbroken; if these things are so, is it invidious and is it superfluous to call the attention of the nation to the bearing of such a denomination upon our civil and religious institutions and equal rights? It is the right of self-preservation, and the denial of it is treason or the infatuation of folly. . . .

But it is a contest, it is said, about religion—and religion and politics have no sort of connection. Let the religionists fight their own battles; only keep the church and state apart, and there is no danger.

It is a union of church and state which we fear, and to prevent which we lift up our voice: a union which never existed without corrupting the church and enslaving the people, by making the ministry independent of them and dependent on the state, and to a great extent a sinecure aristocracy of indolence and secular ambition, auxiliary to the throne and inimical to liberty. No treason against our free institutions would be more fatal than a union of church and state; none, when perceived, would bring on itself a more overwhelming public indignation, and which all protestant denominations would resist with more loathing and abhorrence. . . .

"But why so much excitement about the Catholic religion? Is not one religion just as good as another?"

There are some who think that Calvinism is not quite as good a religion as some others. I have heard it denounced as a severe, unsocial, self-righteous, uncharitable, exclusive, persecuting system —dealing damnation round the land—compassing sea and land to make proselytes, and forming conspiracies to overturn the liberties of the nation by an unhallowed union of church and state. There have been those, too, who have thought it neither meddlesome nor persecution to investigate the facts in the case, and scan the republican tendencies of the Calvinistic system. Though it has always been on the side of liberty in its struggles against arbitrary power; though, through the puritans, it breathed into the British constitution its most invaluable principles, and laid the foundations of the republican institutions of our nation, and felled the forests, and fought the colonial battles with Canadian Indians and French Catholics, when often our destiny balanced on a pivot and hung upon a hair; and though it wept, and prayed, and fasted, and fought, and suffered through the revolutionary struggle, when there was almost no other creed but the Calvinistic in the land; still it is the opinion of many, that its well doings of the past should not invest the system with implicit confidence, or supersede the scrutiny of its republican tendencies. They do not think themselves required to let Calvinists alone; and why should they? We do not ask to be let alone, nor cry persecution when our creed or conduct is analyzed. We are not annoyed by scrutiny; we seek no concealment. We court investigation of our past history, and of all the tendencies of the doctrines and doings of the friends of the reformation; and why should the Catholic religion be exempted from scrutiny? Has it disclosed more vigorous republican tendencies? Has it done more to enlighten the intellect, to purify the morals, and sanctify the hearts of men, and fit them for self-government? Has it fought more frequently or successfully the battles of liberty against despotism? or done more to enlighten the intellect, purify the morals, and sanctify the heart of the world, and prepare it for universal liberty?

I protest against that unlimited abuse with which it is thought quite proper to round off declamatory periods against the religion of those who fought the battles of the reformation and the battles of the revolution, and that sensitiveness and liberality which would shield from animadversion and spread the mantle of charity over a religion which never prospered but in alliance with despotic governments, has always been and still is the inflexible enemy of liberty of conscience and free inquiry, and at this moment is the mainstay of the battle against republican institutions. A despotic government and despotic religion may not be able to endure free inquiry, but a republic and religious liberty cannot exist without it. Where force is withdrawn, and millions are associated for self-government, the complex mass of opinions and interests can be reduced to system and order only by the collision and resolution of intellectual and moral forces. To lay the ban of a fastidious charity on religious free inquiry, would terminate in unthinking apathy and the intellectual stagnation of the dark ages. Whatever European nations may do, our nation must read and think from length to breadth, from top to bottom. It is a perilous experiment we have adventured upon; but it is begun, and we cannot go back. For mind has felt its own power, and is girding itself for efforts never yet made, and with means and motives never before possessed, and on such a field as before was never opened, and it is only the mighty salutary action of mind which can carry us through.

It is an anti-republican charity, then, which would shield the Catholics, or any other religious denomination, from the animadversion of impartial criticism. Denominations, as really as books, are public property, and demand and are benefited by criticism. And if ever the Catholic religion is liberalized and assimilated to our institutions, it must be done, not by a sickly sentimentalism screening it from animadversion, but by subjecting it to the tug of controversy, and turning upon it the searching inspection of the public eye, and compelling it, like all other religions among us, to pass the ordeal of an enlightened public sentiment.

"But are not the Catholics sincere?—why not, then, let them alone?" That they are sincere in their faith there can be no doubt. But what the republican tendency of their faith is, depends on what they believe, and not on the simple fact that they do believe it. If they believe in the rights and duties of universal education, of free inquiry, of reading and understanding the Bible, and in the liberty and equality of all religious denominations, and that they and we are accountable only to God and the laws of the land, it is well. But if they believe that the pope and the church are infallible, that his ecclesiastical jurisdiction is universal, that he and the priests have the power of eternal life or death, in the bestowment or refusal of pardon as they obey or disobey them, that no man may read the Bible without the permission of the priesthood, or understand it but as they interpret, and that every Catholic is bound to believe implicitly as the church believes, and that all non-Catholics are heretics, and *heresy* a capital offence, and the extermination of heretics by force duty; then the more anti-republican the elements of their faith are, the more terrific is their sincerity, which on the peril of their soul would make them the instruments of a foreign policy in overturning our institutions for the establishment of those of their own church. . . .

"But have not the Catholics just as good a right to their religion as other denominations have to theirs?" I have said so. I not only admit their equal rights, but insist upon them; and am prepared to defend their rights as I am those of my own and other protestant denominations. The Catholics have a perfect right to proselyte the nation to their faith if they are able to do it. But I too have the right of preventing it if I am able. They have a right freely to propagate their opinions and arguments; and I too have a right to apprise the nation of their political bearings on our republican institutions. . . .

But it is said the Catholic religion is not what it used to be, the claims and dogmas, and bigotry, and persecuting maxims, and superstitions of the Catholic church have passed away. She has felt the spirit of the age, and yielded to its demands, and henceforth, and especially in this country, we have to anticipate only a revised and corrected edition of the Catholic church.

As republicans and christians, we certainly hail the day when the Catholic church shall be reformed, and we are not reluctant to believe, on proper evidence, that the Catholics of this country perceive and renounce the past unscriptural and anti-republican claims, maxims, and deeds of the church of Rome. We only desire that their professions and disclaimers should not be received in evidence that the Roman church is reformed, till the same authority which enacted her erroneous maxims and authorized the unchristian conduct, has conceded her fallibility and repealed the criminal decisions of her popes and councils, and professed repentance for her evil deeds, and made proclamation that she admits her members to the rights of conscience, and free inquiry, and civil liberty; but so long as the infallibility of the church is claimed, and all her maxims remain unrepealed, and are rigidly enforced wherever the march of liberal opinions has not compelled a relaxation. Such disclaimers can be regarded only as evidence of what necessity extorts and expediency dictates, and the accommodating policy of the church has always permitted to her loyal sons. . . .

To the question, "What is to be done?" I would say a few things to obviate misapprehension, and indicate what would seem to be the plain practical course.

In the first place, while the language of indiscriminate discourtesy towards immigrants, calculated to wound their feelings, and cast odium on respectable and industrious foreigners, is carefully to be avoided; an immediate and energetic supervision of our government is demanded to check the influx of immigrant paupers, thrown upon our shores by the governments of Europe, corrupting our morals, quadrupling our taxation, and endangering the peace of our cities, and of our nation.

It is equally plain, also, that while we admit the population of Europe to a participation in the blessings of our institutions and ample territory, it is both our right and duty so to regulate the influx and the conditions of naturalization that the increase shall not outrun the possibility of intellectual and moral culture, and the unregulated action of the European population bring down destruction on ourselves and them. In what manner the means of self-preservation shall be applied, it does not belong to my province to say. Doubtless a perfect remedy may be difficult, perhaps impossible; but should we therefore look upon the appalling scene in pale amazement and trembling impotency? . . .

We entered upon the experiment of self-government, when a homogenous people, with diffidence, and multiplied checks, and balances in our constitution, and have watched and encountered, with decision and care, the dangers developed in the progress of its administration; but why should there be such vigilance to guard our institutions from domestic perils, and such reckless improvidence in exposing them, unwatched, to the most powerful adverse influence which can be brought to bear upon them from abroad?

In respect to the Catholic religion, and its political bearings, there is an obvious and safe course. It is the medium between denunciation and implicit confidence, between persecution and indiscriminate charity. It includes a thorough knowledge of the principles, history, and present conduct of the papal church, where its power is unobstructed. . . .

If we do not provide the schools which are requisite for the cheap and effectual education of the children of the nation, it is perfectly certain that the Catholic powers of Europe intend to make up our deficiency, and there is no reason to doubt that they will do it, until by immigration and Catholic education we become to such an extent a

Catholic nation, that, with their peculiar power of acting as one body, they will become the predominant power of the nation, or if not predominant, sufficient to embarass our republican movements, by the easy access and powerful action of foreign influence and intrigue. We have no right to complain that the Catholics of this country, aided from Europe, should seek to accomplish a work which we neglect—and we do not complain either of his holiness of Rome or of his majesty of Austria, or his wily minister Metternich. They pursue the policy in supplying our deficiency of education, which, with their views of right and self-preservation, they ought to pursue, and the Catholics in this country have a perfect right to gather funds from Europe to purchase lands—rear cathedrals—multiply churches—and sustain immigrant ministers, and to sustain the unendowed bishoprics for fifty years to come, and establish nunneries, and support the sisterhood, and establish cheap and even gratuitous education amid all the destitute portions of our land. They have a right to do it, and according to their principles they ought to do it, and they are doing it, and they will do it, unless as a nation of republicans, jealous of our liberties, and prompt to sustain them by a thorough intellectual and religious culture as well as by the sword, we arise, all denominations and all political parties, to the work of national education. . . .

Americans, republicans, christians, can you, will you, for a moment, permit your free institutions, blood bought, to be placed in jeopardy, for want of the requisite intellectual and moral culture?

One thing more only demands attention, and that is the extension of such intellectual culture, and evangelical light to the Catholic population, as will supersede implicit confidence, and enable and incline them to read, and think, and act for themselves. They are not to be regarded as conspirators against our liberties, their system commits its designs and higher movements, like the control of an army, to a few governing minds, while the body of the people may be occupied in their execution, unconscious of their tendency. I am aware of the difficulty of access, but kindness and perseverance can accomplish any thing, and wherever the urgency of the necessity shall put in requisition the benevolent energy of this Christian nation—the work under the auspices of heaven will be done.

It is a cheering fact, also, that the nation is waking up—a blind and indiscriminate charity is giving place to sober observation, and a Christian feeling and language towards Catholics is taking the place of that which was petulant, and exceptionable. There is rapidly extending a just estimate of danger. Multitudes who till recently, regarded all notices of alarm as without foundation, are now beginning to view the subject correctly, both in respect to the reality of the danger, and the means which are necessary to avert it, and both the religious and the political papers are beginning to lay aside the language of asperity and to speak the words of truth and soberness. Under such auspices we commit the subject to the guardianship of heaven, and the intelligent instrumentality of our beloved country.

3

EDUCATION AS A MEANS
OF SOCIAL CONTROL

Horace Mann
THE NECESSITY OF EDUCATION IN A REPUBLICAN
GOVERNMENT

The name of Horace Mann (1796–1859) will always be prominent in the annals of American education. The work that made him famous was accomplished between 1837 and 1848 when, as secretary of the newly created Massachusetts Board of Education, he completely reorganized the public school system of the state and founded the first teachers' college in America. Mann's achievement became a model for educational administrators throughout the country. But Mann was also involved in many other activities, including temperance and the movement to provide hospitalization for the insane. He fought not only against slavery but against racial segregation as well. In 1848 he was elected to the House of Representatives to fill the vacancy created by John Quincy Adams' death. Later Mann became president of Antioch, one of the first coeducational colleges.

Like the two previous selections, this one discusses the function of educational institutions in society. But while Biddle and Beecher addressed themselves to higher learning, Mann is concerned with the common schools. He gave this lecture after his first year on the Board of Education. The fascinating mixture of a conservative rationale with liberal measures is typical of Whig reform.

I venture, my friends, at this time, to solicit your attention, while I attempt to lay before you some of the relations which we bear to the cause of Education, because we are the citizens of a Republic; and thence to deduce some of the reasons, which, under our political institutions, make the proper training of the rising generation the highest earthly duty of the risen.

SOURCE. Horace Mann, "The Necessity of Education in a Republican Government" (1838), *Life and Works of Horace Mann,* ed. Mary Mann (Cambridge, Mass., 1867), II, 143–188.

It is a truism, that free institutions multiply human energies. A chained body cannot do much harm; a chained mind can do as little. In a despotic government, the human faculties are benumbed and paralyzed; in a Republic, they glow with an intense life, and burst forth with uncontrollable impetuosity. In the former, they are circumscribed and straitened in their range of action; in the latter, they have "ample room and verge enough," and may rise to glory or plunge into ruin. . . .

Now it is undeniable that, with the possession of certain higher faculties—common to all mankind—whose proper cultivation will bear us upward to hitherto undiscovered regions of prosperity and glory, we possess, also, certain lower faculties or propensities—equally common—whose improper indulgence leads, inevitably, to tribulation, and anguish, and ruin. The propensities to which I refer seem indispensable to our temporal existence, and, if restricted within proper limits, they are promotive of our enjoyment; but, beyond those limits, they work dishonor and infatuation, madness and despair. As servants, they are indispensable; as masters, they torture as well as tyrannize. Now despotic and arbitrary governments have dwarfed and crippled the powers of doing evil as much as the powers of doing good; but a republican government, from the very fact of its freedom, unreins their speed, and lets loose their strength. It is justly alleged against despotisms that they fetter, mutilate, almost extinguish the noblest powers of the human soul; but there is a *per contra* to this, for which we have not given them credit; they circumscribe the ability to do the greatest evil, as well as to do the greatest good.

My proposition, therefore, is simply this: If republican institutions do wake up unexampled energies in the whole mass of a people, and give them implements of unexampled power wherewith to work out their will, then these same institutions ought also to confer upon that people unexampled wisdom and rectitude. If these institutions give greater scope and impulse to the lower order of faculties belonging to the human mind, then they must also give more authoritative control and more skilful guidance to the higher ones. If they multiply temptations, they must fortify against them. If they quicken the activity and enlarge the sphere of the appetites and passions, they must, at least in an equal ratio, establish the authority and extend the jurisdiction of reason and conscience. In a word, we must not add to the impulsive, without also adding to the regulating force.

If we maintain institutions, which bring us within the action of new and unheard-of powers, without taking any corresponding measures for the government of those powers, we shall perish by the very instruments prepared for our happiness.

The truth has been so often asserted, that there is no security for a republic but in morality and intelligence, that a repetition of it seems hardly in good taste. But all permanent blessings being founded on permanent truths, a continued observance of the truth is the condition of a continued enjoyment of the blessing. I know we are often admonished that, without intelligence and virtue as a chart and a compass to direct us in our untried political voyage, we shall perish in the first storm; but I venture to add that, without these qualities, we shall not wait for a storm—we cannot weather a calm. If the sea is as smooth as glass we shall founder, for we are in a stone boat. Unless these qualities pervade the general head and the general heart, not only will republican institutions vanish from amongst us, but the words *prosperity* and *happiness* will become obsolete. And all this may be affirmed, not from historical examples merely, but from the very constitution of our nature. We are created and brought into life with a set of innate, organic dispositions or propensities, which a free government rouses and invigorates, and which, if not bridled and tamed, by our actually seeing the eternal laws of justice, as plainly as we can see the sun in the heavens—and by our actually feeling the sovereign sentiment of duty, as plainly as we feel the earth beneath our feet—will hurry us forward into regions populous with every form of evil.

Divines, moralists, metaphysicians, almost without exception, regard the human being as exceedingly complex in his mental or spiritual constitution, as well as in his bodily organization; they regard him as having a plurality of tendencies and affections, though brought together and embodied in one person. Hence, in all discussions or disquisitions respecting human nature, they analyze or assort it into different classes of powers and faculties.

First, there is a conscience in every one of us, and a sense of responsibleness to God, which establish a moral relation between us and our Creator; and which, though we could call all the grandeur and the splendors of the universe our own, and were lulled and charmed by all its music and its beauty, will forever banish all true repose from our bosom, unless our nature and our lives are supposed to be in harmony with the divine will. The object of these faculties is their Infinite Creator; and they never can be supremely happy unless they are tuned to perfect concord with every note in the celestial anthems of love and praise.

Then there is a set of faculties that we denominate social or sympathetic, among the most conspicuous of which is benevolence or philanthropy—a sentiment which mysteriously makes our pulse throb, and our nerves shrink, at the pains or adversity of others, even though, at the same time, our own frame is whole, and our own fortunes gladdening. How beautiful and marvellous a thing it is, when imbosomed in a happy family, surrounded by friends and children—which even Paradise had not—that the history of idolatry in the far-off islands of the Pacific, or of the burning of Hindu widows on the other side of the globe, amongst a people whom we never saw and never shall see, should pierce our hearts like a knife! How glorious a quality of our nature it is, that the story of some old martyr or hero, who nobly upheld truth with life, though his dust has now been blown about by the winds for twenty centuries, should transport us with such feelings of admiration and ecstasy, that we long to have been he, and to have borne all his sufferings; and we find ourselves involuntarily sublimed by so noble a passion, that the most terrible form of death, if hallowed by a righteous cause, looks lovely as a bride to the bridegroom!

There are also the yearning, doting fondness of parents for children, of natural kindred for each other, and the passionate, yet pure affection of the sexes, which fit us for the duties and the endearments of domestic life. Even that vague general attachment to our fellow-beings, which binds men together in fraternal associations, is so strong, and is universally recognized as so natural, that we look upon hermits and solitaries as creatures half-mad or half-monstrous. The sphere of these sentiments or affections is around us and before us—family, neighborhood, country, kind, posterity.

And lastly, there is the strictly selfish part of our nature, which consists of a gang of animal appetites, a horde of bandit propensities, each one of which, by its own nature, is deaf to the voice of God, reckless of the welfare of men, blind, remorseless, atheistic; each one of the whole pack being supremely bent upon its own indulgence, and ready to barter earth and heaven to win it. We all have some pretty definite idea of beasts of prey and of birds of prey; but not among the whelps of the lion's lair, not among the young of the vulture's nest, are there any spoilers at all comparable to those that may be trained from the appetites and propensities which each human being brings with him into the world. I am sorry not to be able to speak of this part of our common nature in a more complimentary manner; but to utter what facts will not warrant, would be to exchange the records of truth for a song of Delilah. . . .

There are other original, innate propensities, which cannot properly be discussed on an occasion like this. Their action, within certain limits, is necessary to self-preservation, and to the preservation of the race; a description of their excesses would make every cheek pale and every heart faint. . . .

Let us now turn for a moment to see what means and stimulants our institutions have provided for the use of the mighty powers and passions they have unloosed. No apparatus so skilful was ever before devised. Instead of the slow and cumbrous machinery of former times, we have provided that which is quick-working and far-reaching, and which may be used for the destruction as easily as for the welfare of its possessors. Our institutions furnish as great facilities for wicked men, in all departments of wickedness, as phosphorus and lucifer matches furnish to the incendiary. What chemistry has done, in these prepara-tions, over the old art of rubbing two sticks together, for the wretch who would fire your dwelling, our social partnerships have done for flagitious and unprincipled men. Through the right, almost universal, of suffrage, we have established a community of power; and no propo-sition is more plain and self-evident, than that nothing but mere popular inclination lies between a community of power and a community in every thing else. And though, in the long run, and when other things are equal, a righteous cause always has a decisive advantage over an evil one, yet, in the first onset between right and wrong, bad men possess one advantage over the good. They have double resources—two armories. The arts of guilt are as welcome to them as the practices of justice. They can use poisoned weapons as well as those approved by the usages of war.

Again; has it been sufficiently considered, that all which has been said, and truly said, of the excellence of our institutions, if adminis-tered by an upright people, must be reversed and read backwards, if administered by a corrupt one? I am aware that some will be ready to say, "We have been unwise and infatuated to confide all the constitu-ents of our social and political welfare to such irresponsible keeping." But let me ask of such—of what avail is their lamentation? The irresistible movement in the diffusion of power is still progressive, not retrograde. Every year puts more of social strength into the hands of physical strength. The arithmetic of numbers is more and more excluding all estimate of moral forces, in the administration of government. And this, whether for good or for evil, will continue to be. Human beings cannot be remanded to the dungeons of imbecility, if they are to those of ignorance. The sun can as easily be turned backwards in its course, as one particle of that power, which has been conferred upon the millions, can be again monopolized by the few. To discuss the question, therefore, whether our institutions are not too free, is, for all practical purposes, as vain as it would be to discuss the question whether, on the whole, it was a wise arrangement on the part of Divine Providence, that the American continent should ever have been created, or that Columbus should have discovered it. And let me ask, further, have those who believe our institutions to be too free, and who, therefore, would go back to less liberal ones—have they settled the question, how far back they will go? Will they go back to the dark ages, and recall an eclipse which lasted centuries long? or will they ascend a little higher for their models, to a time when our ancestors wore undressed skins, and burrowed in holes of the earth? or will they strike at once for the institutions of Egypt, where, though the monkey was a god, there was still a sufficient distance between him and his human worshipper? But all such discussions are vain. The oak will as soon go back into the acorn, or the bird into its shell, as we return to the monarchical or aristocratic forms of by-gone ages.

Nor let it be forgotten, in contemplating our condition, that the human passions, as unfolded and invigorated by our institutions, are not only possessed of all the prerogatives, and equipped with all the implements of sovereignty; but that they are forever roused and spurred to the most vehement efforts. It is a law of the passions, that they exert strength in proportion to the causes which excite them—a law which holds true in cases of sanity, as well as in the terrible strength of insanity. And with what endless excitements are the passions of men here plied! With us, the Press is such a clarion, that it proclaims all the great movements of this great country, with a voice that sweeps over its whole surface, and comes back to us in echoes from its extremest borders. From the Atlantic to the Pacific, from the Lakes to the Gulf, men cheer, inflame, exasperate each other, as though they were neighbors in the same street. What the ear of Dionysius was to him, making report of every word uttered by friend or foe, our institutions have made this land to every citizen. It is a vast sounding gallery; and from horizon to horizon every shout of triumph and every cry of alarm are gathered up and rung in every man's dwelling. All objects which stimulate the passions of men are made to pass before the eyes of all, as in a circling panorama. In very truth we are all hung upon the same electrical wire, and if the ignorant and vicious get possession of the apparatus, the intelligent and the virtuous must take such shocks as the stupid or profligate experimenters may choose to administer.

Mark how the excitements which our institutions supply have wrought upon the love of gain and the love of place. Vast speculations —such as in other countries would require not only royal sanctions and charters, but the equipment of fleets, and princely outfits of gold and arms—are here rushed into, on flash paper, by clerks and apprentices, not out of their time. What party can affirm that it is exempt from members who prize office, rather than the excellence that deserves it? *Where* can I be—not *what* can I be—is the question suggested to aspirants for fame. How many have their eyes fixed upon posts of honor and emolument which but one only can fill! While few will be satisfied with occupying less than their portion of space in the public eye, thousands have marked out some great compartment of the sky for the blazonry of their names. And hence it is, that, wherever there is a signal of gain, or of power, the vultures of cupidity and of ambition darken the air. Young men launch into this tumultuous life, years earlier than has ever been witnessed elsewhere. They seek to win those prizes without delay, which, according to Nature's ordinances and appointments, are the rewards of a life of labor. Hence they find no time for studying the eternal principles of justice, veracity, equality, benevolence, and for applying them to the complicated affairs of men. What cares a young adventurer for the immutable laws of trade, when he has purchased a ticket in some lottery of speculation, from which he expects to draw a fortune? Out of such an unbridled, unchastened love of gain, whether it traffics in townships of land or in twopenny toys, do we not know beforehand, there will come infinite falsehoods, knavery and bankruptcy? Let this state of things continue, and he will be a happy man who dares to say of any article of food or of apparel, which he eats or wears, that it has not, at some period of its preparation, or in some of its transfers, been contaminated by fraud. And what a state of society would it argue, in other respects, if the people at large should ever become indifferent to the question, whether fraud be, or be not, inwoven into the texture, and kneaded into the substance of what they daily consume—whether what they eat or drink or wear be not an embodiment of the spirit of lies!

So the inordinate love of office will present the spectacle of gladiatorial contests, of men struggling for station as for life, and using against each other the poisonous weapons of calumny and vituperation; while the abiding welfare, the true greatness and prosperity of the people will be like the soil of some neutral Flanders, over which the hostile bands of partisans will march and countermarch, and convert it into battle-fields, so that, whichever side may triumph, the people will be ruined. . . .

Again; we hear good men, every day, bemoaning the *ignorance* of certain portions of our country, and of individuals in all parts of it. The use often made of the elective franchise, the crude, unphilosophical notions, sometimes advanced in our legislative halls on questions of political economy, the erroneous views entertained by portions of the people, respecting the relation between representative and constituent, and the revolutionary ideas of others in regard to the structure of civil society—these are cited as specimens and proofs of the *ignorance* that abounds amongst us. No greater delusion can blind us. This much-lamented ignorance, in the cases supposed, is a phantom, a spectre. The outcry against it is a false alarm, diverting attention from a real to an imaginary danger. Ignorance is not the cause of the evils referred to. With exceptions comparatively few, we have but two classes of ignorant persons amongst us, and they are harmless. Infants and idiots are ignorant; few others are so. Those whom we are accustomed to call ignorant, are full of false notions, as much worse than ignorance as wisdom is better. A merely ignorant man has no skill in adapting means to ends, whereby to jeopard the welfare of great interests or great numbers. Ignorance is blankness; or, at most, a lifeless, inert mass, which can, indeed, be moved and placed where you please, but will stay where it is placed. In Europe, there are multitudes of ignorant men—men into whose minds no idea ever entered respecting the duties of society or of government, or the conditions of human prosperity. They, like their work-fellows, the cattle, are obedient to their masters; and the range of their ideas on political or social questions is hardly more extensive than that of the brutes. But with our institutions, this state of things, to any great extent, is impossible. The very atmosphere we breathe is freighted with the ideas of property, of acquisition and transmission; of wages, labor and capital; of political and social rights; of the appointment to, and tenure of offices; of the reciprocal relations between the great departments of government—executive, legislative, and judicial. Every native-born child amongst us imbibes notions, either false or true, on these subjects. Let these notions be false; let an individual grow up, with false ideas of his own nature and destiny as an immortal being, with false views respecting what government, laws, customs, should be; with no knowledge of the works or the opinions of those great men who framed our government, and adjusted its various parts to each other; and when such an individual is invested with the political rights of citizenship, with power to give an authoritative voice and vote upon the affairs of his country, he will look upon all existing things as rubbish which it is his duty to sweep away, that he may have room for the erection of other structures, planned after the model of his own false ideas. No man that ever lived could, by mere intuition or instinct, form just opinions upon a thousand questions, pertaining to civil society, to its jurisprudence, its local, national and international duties. Many truths, vital to the welfare of the people, differ in their reality, as much from the appearances which they present to uninstructed minds, as the apparent size of the sun differs from its real size, which, in truth, is so many thousand times larger than the earth, while to the untaught eye it appears to be so many thousand times smaller. And if the human propensities are here to manifest themselves through the enlarged means of false knowledge which our institutions, unaided by special instruction, will furnish; if they are to possess all the instruments and furtherances which our doctrine of political equality confers; then the result must be, a power to do evil almost infinitely greater than ever existed before, instigated by impulses proportionately strong. Hence our dangers are to be, not those of ignorance, which would be comparatively tolerable, but those of false knowledge, which transcend the powers of mortal imagination to portray. Would you appreciate the amazing difference between ignorance and false knowledge, look at France, before and during her great revolution. Before the revolution, her people were merely ignorant; during the revolution, they acted under the lights of false knowledge. An idiot is ignorant, and does little harm; a maniac has false ideas, and destroys, burns and murders.

Looking again at the nature of our institutions, we find that it is not the material or corporeal interests of man alone that are here decided by the common voice; such, for instance, as those pertaining to finance, revenue, the adjustment of the great economical interests of society, the rival claims between agriculture, commerce and manufactures, the partition and distribution of legislative, judicial and executive powers, with a long catalogue of others of a kindred nature; but also those more solemn questions which pervade the innermost sanctuary of domestic life, and, for worship or for sacrilege, enter the Holy of Holies in the ark of society—these also are submitted to the general arbitrament. The haughty lordling, whose heart never felt one throb for the welfare of mankind, gives vote and verdict on the extent of popular rights; the libertine and debauchee give vote and verdict on the sanctity of the marriage covenant; the atheist on the definition of blasphemy. Nor is this great people invited merely to speculate, and frame abstract theories, on these momentous themes; to make picture models, on paper, in their closets; they are not invited to sketch Republics of Fancy only, but they are commissioned to make Republics of Fact; and in such Republics as they please to make, others, perforce, must please to live. If I do not like my minister, or my parish, I can *sign off* (as we term it), and connect myself with another; if I do not like my town, I can move out of it; but where shall a man sign to, or move to, out of a bad world? Nor do our people hold these powers, as an ornament merely, as some ostensible but useless badge of Freedom; but they keep them as instruments for use, and sometimes wield them as weapons of revenge. So closely indeed are we inwoven in the same web of fate, that a vote given on the banks of the Missouri or Arkansas may shake every plantation and warehouse on the Atlantic, and, reaching seaward, overtake and baffle enterprise, into whatever oceans it may have penetrated. . . .

Again, then, I ask, with unmitigated anxiety, what institutions we now possess, that can furnish defence or barrier against the action of those propensities, which each generation brings into the world as a part of its being, and which our institutions foster and stimulate into unparalleled activity and vigor? Can any Christian man believe, that God has so constituted and so governs the human race, that it is always and necessarily to be suicidal of its earthly welfare? No! the thought is impious. The same Almighty Power which implants in our nature the germs of these terrible propensities, has endowed us also with reason and conscience and a sense of responsibility to Him; and, in his providence, he has opened a way by which these nobler faculties can be elevated into dominion and supremacy over the appetites and passions. But if this is ever done, it must be mainly done during the docile and teachable years of childhood. I repeat it, my friends, *if this is ever done, it must be mainly done during the docile and teachable years of childhood.* Wretched, incorrigible, demoniac, as any human being may ever have become, there was a time when he took the first step in error and in crime; when, for the first time, he just nodded to his fall, on the brink of ruin. Then, ere he was irrecoverably lost, ere he plunged into the abyss of infamy and guilt, he might have been recalled, as it were by the waving of the hand. Fathers, mothers, patriots, Christians! it is this very hour of peril through which our children are now passing. They know it not, but we know it; and where the knowledge is, there rests the responsibility. Society is responsible; not society considered as an abstraction, but society as it consists of living members, which members we are. Clergymen are responsible; all men who have enjoyed the opportunities of a higher education in colleges and universities are responsible, for they can convert their means, whether of time or of talent, into instruments for elevating the masses of the people. The conductors of the public press are responsible, for they have daily access to the public ear, and can infuse just notions of this high duty into the public mind. Legislators and rulers are responsible. In our country, and in our times, no man is worthy the honored name of a statesman, who does not include the highest practicable education of the people in all his plans of administration. He may have eloquence, he may have a knowledge of all history, diplomacy, jurisprudence; and by these he might claim, in other countries, the elevated rank of a statesman; but, unless he speaks, plans, labors, at all times and in all places, for the culture and edification of the whole people, he is not, he cannot be, an American Statesman.

If this dread responsibility for the fate of our children be disregarded, how, when called upon, in the great eventful day, to give an account of the manner in which our earthly duties have been discharged, can we expect to escape the condemnation: "Inasmuch as ye have not done it to one of the least of these, ye have not done it unto me"?

4

WHIG MYTH–MAKING

Rufus Choate
ILLUSTRATING NEW ENGLAND HISTORY

When he was a college student, Rufus Choate (1799–1859) listened with awe to Daniel Webster's stirring courtroom performance in the celebrated Dartmouth College Case. Choate decided then to become a lawyer and ever after took the "Godlike Daniel" as his mentor. Some contemporaries thought Choate actually the greater advocate. Heroic orators like Webster and Choate raised the legal profession to such heights of influence that in the 1830s the French visitor de Tocqueville could call lawyers "the aristocracy of America." Choate lent his rhetorical powers to the cause of Whig politics as state legislator, congressman, and senator. He also lent them to the cause of Whig culture, as the following selection demonstrates.

There was a great deal of anxiety and self-consciousness in the early American republic regarding the creation of a native high culture to complete the achievement of independence. History and literature were regarded as helpful devices in fostering a sense of national identity. Choate addresses himself to both subjects here, linking them to his own cultural conservatism in his desire to foster a reverence for the past in a new society.

The history of the United States, from the planting of the several colonies out of which they have sprung, to the end of the war of the Revolution, is now as amply written, as accessible, and as authentic, as any other portion of the history of the world, and incomparably more so than an equal portion of the history of the origin and first ages of any other nation that ever existed. But there is one thing more which every lover of his country, and every lover of literature, would wish done for our early history. He would wish to see such a genius as Walter Scott, or rather a thousand such as he, undertake in earnest to

SOURCE. Rufus Choate, "The Importance of Illustrating New England History by a Series of Romances Like the Waverley Novels. Delivered at Salem, 1833." *The Works of Rufus Choate with a Memoir of His Life,* ed. Samuel Gilman Brown (Boston, 1862), I, 319–346.

illustrate that early history, by a series of romantic compositions, "in prose or rhyme," like the Waverley Novels, the Lay of the Last Minstrel, and the Lady of the Lake, the scenes of which should be laid in North America, somewhere in the time before the Revolution, and the incidents and characters of which should be selected from the records and traditions of that, our heroic age. He would wish at length to hear such a genius mingling the tones of a ravishing national minstrelsy with the grave narrative, instructive reflections, and chastened feelings of [the early American historians] Marshall, Pitkin, Holmes, and Ramsay. He would wish to see him giving to the natural scenery of the New World, and to the celebrated personages and grand incidents of its earlier annals, the same kind and degree of interest which Scott has given to the Highlands, to the Reformation, the Crusades, to Richard the Lion-hearted, and to Louis XI. He would wish to see him clear away the obscurity which two centuries have been collecting over it, and unroll a vast, conprehensive, and vivid panorama of our old New-England lifetimes, from its sublimest moments to its minutest manners. . . .

For our lawyers, politicians, and for most purposes of mere utility, business, and intellect, our history now perhaps unfolds a sufficiently "ample page." But, I confess, I should love to see it assume a form in which it should speak directly to the heart and affections and imagination of the whole people. I should love to see by the side of these formidable records of dates, and catalogues of British governors, and provincial acts of Assembly—these registers of the settlement of towns, and the planting of churches, and convocation of synods, and drawing up of platforms—by the side of these austere and simply severe narratives of Indian wars, English usurpations, French intrigues, colonial risings, and American independence; I should love to see by the side of these great and good books, about a thousand neat duodecimos of the size of Ivanhoe, Kenilworth, and Marmion, all full of pictures of our natural beauty and grandeur, the still richer pictures of our society and manners, the lights and shadows of our life, full of touching incidents, generous sentiments, just thoughts, beaming images, such as are scattered over everything which Scott has written, as thick as stars on the brow of night, and give to everything he has written that imperishable, strange charm, which will be on it and embalm it forever.

Perhaps it is worthy even of your consideration, whether this is not a judicious and reasonable wish. I propose, therefore, as the subject of a few remarks, this question: Is it not desirable that a series of compositions of the same general character with the novels and

poems of Scott, and of equal ability, should be written in illustration
of the history of the North American United States prior to the peace
of 1783? . . .

In the *first* place, they would embody, and thus would fix deep in
the general mind and memory of the whole people, a vast amount of
positive information quite as authentic and valuable and curious as
that which makes up the matter of professed history, but which the
mere historian does not and cannot furnish. They would thus be not
substitutes for history, but supplements to it. Let us dwell upon this
consideration for a moment. It is wonderful when you think closely
on it, how little of all which we should love to know, and ought to
know, about a former period and generation, a really standard history
tells us. From the very nature of that kind of composition it must be
so. Its appropriate and exclusive topics are a few prominent, engrossing and showy incidents—wars, conquests, revolutions, changes of
dynasties, battles and sieges—the exterior and palpable manifesta-
tions of the workings of the stormy and occasional passions of men
moving in large masses on the high places of the world. These topics it
treats instructively and eloquently. But what an inadequate conception does such a book give you of the time, the country, and the people
to which it relates! What a meagre, cold, and unengaging outline does
it trace; and how utterly deficient in minute, precise, and circumstantial, and satisfactory information! How little does it tell you of the
condition and character of the great body of the people—their occupations, their arts and customs, their joys and sorrows!—how little of the
origin, state, and progress of opinions, and of the spirit of the age!—
how misty, indistinct, and trantalizing are the glimpses you gain of
that old, fair, wonderful creation which you long to explore! It is like a
vast landscape painting in which nothing is represented but the clov-
en summit and grand sweep of the mountain, a portion of the sounding shore of the illimitable sea, the dim distant course of a valley,
traversed by the Father of Rivers two thousand miles in length—and
which has no place for the inclosed corn-field, the flocks upon a
thousand hills, the cheerful country-seat, the village spires, the
churchyard, the vintage, the harvest-home, the dances of peasants—
and the Cotter's Saturday night!

Now, the use, one use, of such romances as Scott's is to supply
these deficiencies of history. Their leading object, perhaps, may be to
tell an interesting story with some embellishments of poetry and
eloquence and fine writing and mighty dialogue. But the plan on
which they are composed requires that they should interweave into
their main design a near, distinct and accurate, but magnified and

ornamental view of the times, people, and country to which that story goes back. They are, as it were, telescope, microscope, and kaleidoscope all in one, if the laws of optics permit such an illustration. . . .

Let me remind you that Scott is not the only writer of romance who has made his fiction the vehicle of authentic and useful information concerning the past, and thus earned the praise of a great historian. Let me remind you of another instance, the most spendid in literature. The Iliad and Odyssey of Homer—what are they but great Waverley Novels! And yet what were our knowledge of the first 400 years of Grecian history without them! . . .

It is time now to turn to our early history, and consider more directly in what way and to what extent our Iliad and Odyssey, and Ivanhoe and Kenilworth, when they come to be written, will help to illustrate and to complete and to give attraction to that history. Select then, for this purpose, almost at random, any memorable event or strongly marked period in our annals. King Philip's War is as good an illustration as at this moment occurs to me. What do our historians tell us of that war? and of New England during that war? You will answer substantially this: It was a war excited by Philip—a bold, crafty, and perfidious Indian chief dwelling at Bristol, in Rhode Island—for the purpose of extirpating or expelling the English colonists of Massachusetts, Plymouth, Connecticut and New Haven. It began in 1675 by an attack on the people of Swansea as they were returning on Sunday from meeting. It ended in August, 1676, at Mount Hope by the death of Philip, and the annihilation of his tribe. In the course of these two years he had succeeded in drawing into his designs perhaps fifteen or twenty communities of Indians, and had at one time and another, perhaps, eight or ten thousand men in arms.

The scenes of the war shifted successively from Narraganset Bay to the northern line of Massachusetts in the valley of the Connecticut River. But there was safety nowhere; there was scarcely a family of which a husband, a son, a brother, had not fallen. The land was filled with mourning. Six hundred dwelling-houses were burned with fire. Six hundred armed young men and middle-aged fell in battle; as many others, including women and children, were carried away into that captivity so full of horrors to a New-England imagination; the culture of the earth was interrupted; the prayers, labors, and sufferings of half a century were nearly forever frustrated.

Such is about the whole of what history records, or rather, of what the great body of our well-educated readers know, of the New England of 1675, and of the severest and most interesting crisis through which, in any epoch, the colony was called to pass. Now, I say, commit this subject, King Philip's War, to Walter Scott, the poet, or the novelist. . . .

In the first place, he would collect and display a great many particulars of positive information concerning these old times, either not contained at all in our popular histories, or not in a form to fix the attention of the general reader. He would spread out before you the external aspects and scenery of that New England, and contrast them with those which our eyes are permitted to see, but which our fathers died without beholding. And what a contrast! . . . These ripened fruits of two hundred years of labor and liberty; these populous towns; this refined and affluent society; these gardens, orchards, and cornfields; these manufactories and merchant ships—where were they then? The whole colonial population of New England, including Massachusetts, Plymouth, Connecticut, New Haven, Maine, New Hampshire, at the breaking out of that war, has been variously estimated at from 40,000 to 120,000. I suppose that 80,000 may be a fair average of these estimates—a little less than the present population of the single county of Essex. They were planted along the coast from the mouth of the Kennebec to New Haven, upon a strip of country of a medium width, inwards from the sea, of forty or fifty miles—a great deal of which, however, was still wholly unreclaimed to cultivation, and much of it still occupied by its original and native owners. This belt of sea-coast—for it was no more than that—was the New England of 1675. . . .

On this narrow border were stretched along the low wooden houses with their wooden chimneys; the patches of Indian corn crossed and enclosed by the standing forest; the smooth-shaven meadow and salt marsh; the rocky pasture of horses, sheep, and neat cattle; the fish-flakes, lumber-yards, the fishing boats and coasting shallops; West India and Wine Islands merchant-ships; the meeting-houses, windmills, and small stockade forts—which made up the human, artificial, and visible exterior of the New England of that era. Altogether the whole scene, in its natural and in its cultivated elements, was in exact keeping with the condition and character and prospects of that generation of our ancestors. It was the dwelling place of the Pilgrims, and of the children of the Pilgrims. There lay—covered over as it were, partially sheltered, yet not wholly out of danger, like the sowing of a winter grain—the germs of this day's exceeding glory, beauty, and strength. There rose, plain, massive, and deep-set, the basement stories of our religious, civil, and literary institutions, beaten against and raged around by many a tempest and many a flood—yet not falling, for their foundation was a rock. Fifty years of continual emigration from England, and of general peace and general health, had swelled the handful of men who came passengers in the Mayflower to Plymouth, and in the Abigail to Salem, and in the Arbella to Boston, into an infant people. Independence of the mother country had hardly yet entered the waking or sleeping dreams of any man; but, as against all the world besides, they had begun to utter the language, put on the habits, and assume the port, of a nascent and asserted sovereignty and national existence. Some portion of the great work which they were sent hither to do they had already done. They had constructed a republican, representative government. They had made provision for the mental and moral culture of the rising nation. Something of the growth of a half-century of industry—"immature buds, blossoms fallen from the tree, and green fruit"—were beginning to gladden the natural and the moral prospect. Still the general aspect of the scenery of that day, even if surveyed from one of those eminences which now rise in so much beauty around Boston, would have seemed to the senses and imagination of a beholder wild, austere, and uninviting. . . . But when you contemplated the prospect a little more closely—when you saw what costly and dear pledges the Pilgrims had already given to posterity and the new world—when you saw the fixtures which they had settled into and incorporated with its soil, the brick college at Cambridge, and the meeting-houses sending up their spires from every clearing—when you surveyed the unostentatious but permanent and vast imporovements which fifty years had traced upon the face of that stern and wild land, and garnered up in its bosom—when you looked steadfastly into the countenances of those men, and read there that expression of calm resolve, high hope, and fixed faith—when you heard their prayers for that once pleasant England as for a land they no longer desired to see; for the new world, now not merely the scene of their duties but the home of their heart's adoption—you would no longer doubt that, though the next half century should be, as it proved, a long, bloody warfare—though the mother country should leave them, as she did, to contend single-handed with Indians, French, and an unpropitious soil and sky—though acts of navigation and boards of trade should restrain their enterprise and rob it of its rewards—that their triumph was still certain, and a later generation would partake of its fruits and be encompassed about by its glory. . . .

There are two or three subjects, among a thousand others of a different character, connected with the history of New England in that era, which deserve, and would reward, the fullest illustration which learning and genius and philosophy could bestow. They have been treated copiously and ably; but I am sure that whoso creates the romantic literature of the country will be found to have placed them in new lights, and to have made them for the first time familiar, intelligible, and interesting to the mass of the reading community.

Let me instance as one of these the *old Puritan character*. In every view of it, it was an extraordinary mental and moral phenomenon. The countless influences which have been acting on man ever since his creation, the countless variety of condition and circumstances, of climate, of government, of religion, and of social systems in which he has lived, never produced such a specimen of character as this before, and never will do so again. It was developed, disciplined, and perfected for a particular day and a particular duty. When that day was ended and that duty done, it was dissolved again into its elements, and disappeared among the common forms of humanity, apart from which it had acted and suffered, above which it had towered, yet out of which it had been by a long process elaborated. The *human* influences which combined to form the Puritan character from the general mind of England—which set this sect apart from all the rest of the community, and stamped upon it a system of manners, a style of dress and salutation and phraseology, a distinct, entire scheme of opinions upon religion, government, morality, and human life, marking it off from the crowds about it, as the fabled waters of the classical fountain passed underneath the sea, unmingled, unchanged in taste or color —these things are matters of popular history, and I need not enumerate or weigh them. What was the *final* end for which the Puritans were raised up, we also in some part all know. All things here in New England proclaim it.The works which they did, these testify of them and of the objects and reality of their mission, and they are inscribed upon all the sides of our religious, political, and literary edifices, legibly and imperishably.

But while we appreciate what the Puritans have done, and recognize the divine wisdom and purposes in raising them up to do it, something is wanting yet to give to their character and fortunes a warm, quick interest, a charm for the feelings and imagination, and abiding-place in the heart and memory and affections of all the generations of the people to whom they bequeathed these representative governments and this undefiled religion. It is time that literature and the arts should at least cooperate with history. Themes more inspiring or more instructive were never sung by old or modern bards in hall or bower. The whole history of the Puritans—of that portion which remained in England and plucked Charles from his throne and buried crown and mitre beneath the foundations of the Commonwealth, and of that other not less noble portion which came out hither from England, and founded a freer, fairer, and more enduring Commonwealth—all the leading traits of their religious, intellectual, and active character, their theological doctrines, their superstitions, their notions of the divine government and economy, and of the place they filled in it—everything about them, everything which befell them —was out of the ordinary course of life; and he who would adequately record their fortunes, display their peculiarities, and decide upon their pretensions, must, like the writer of the Pentateuch, put in requisition alternately music, poetry, eloquence, and history, and speak by turns to the senses, the fancy, and the reason of the world.

They were persecuted for embracing a purer Protestantism than the Episcopacy of England in the age of Elizabeth. Instead of ceasing to be Protestants, persecution made them republicans, also. They were nicknamed Puritans by their enemies; then afterward they became a distinct, solitary caste—*among*, but not of, the people of England. They were flattered, they were tempted, they were shut up in prison, they were baptized with the fire of martyrdom. Solicitation, violence, were alike unavailing, except to consolidate their energies, perfect their virtues, and mortify their human affections, to raise their thoughts from the kingdoms and kings of this world, and the glory of them, to the contemplation of that surpassing glory which is to be revealed. Some of them at length, not so much because these many years of persecution had wearied or disheartened them, as because they saw in it an intimation of the will of God, sought the freedom which there they found not, on the bleak sea-shore and beneath the dark pine-forest of New England. History, fiction, literature, does not record an incident of such moral sublimity as this. . . .

It was fit that the founders of our race should have been such men, that they should have so labored and so suffered, that their tried and strenuous virtues should stand out in such prominence and grandeur. It will be well for us when their story shall have grown"familiar as a household word," when it shall make even your children's bosoms glow and their eyes glisten in the ballad and nursery-tale, and give pathos and elevation to our whole higher national minstrelsy.

There is another subject connected with our early history eminently adapted to the nature and purposes of romantic literature, and worthy to be illustrated by such a literature—that is, the condition, prospects, and fate of the New England tribes of Indians at the epoch of Philip's War. . . . The history of man, like the roll of the Prophet, is full, within and without, of morning, lamentation, and woe; but I do not know that in all that history there is a situation of such mournful interest as this.

The terrible truth had at length flashed upon the Indian chief, that the presence of civilization, even of humane, peaceful, and moral civilization, was incompatible with the existence of Indians. He comprehended at length the tremendous power which knowledge, arts, law, government, confer upon social man. He looked in vain to the physical energies, the desperate, random, uncombined, and desultory exertions, the occasional individual virtues and abilities of barbarism, for an equal power to resist it. He saw the advancing population of the colonies. He saw shiploads of white men day after day coming ashore from some land beyond the sea, of which he could only know that it was over-peopled. Every day the woodman's axe sounded nearer and nearer. Every day some valuable fishing or hunting-ground, or corn-land or meadow, passed out of the Indian possession, and was locked up forever in the mortmain grasp of an English title. What then, where then, was the hope of the Indian? . . . Such were the condition and prospects of the Indians of New England at the beginning of Philip's war.

It is doubtful if that celebrated chief intended to provoke such a war, or if he ever anticipated for it a successful issue. But there is no doubt that after it had begun he threw his whole great powers into the conduct of it—that he formed and moved a confederacy of almost all the aborigines of New England to its support, that he exhausted every resource of bravery and Indian soldiership and statesmanship, that he died at last for a land and for a throne which he could not save. Our fathers called him King Philip, in jest. I would not wrong his warrior-shade by comparing him with any five in six of the kings of Europe, of his day or ours. . . .

Let me solicit your attention to another view of this subject. I have urged thus far, that our future Waverley Novels and poetry would contain a good deal of positive information which our histories do not contain—gleanings, if you please, of what the licensed reapers have, intentionally or unintentionally, let fall from their hands: and that this information would be authentic and valuable, I now add, that they would have another use. They would make the information which our histories do contain more accessible and more engaging to the great body of readers, even if they made no addition to its absolute quantity. They would melt down, as it were, and stamp the heavy bullion into a convenient, universal circulating medium. They would impress the facts, the lessons of history, more deeply, and incorporate them more intimately into the general mind and heart, and current and common knowledge of the people.

All history, all records of the past, of the acts, opinions and characters of those who have preceded us in the great procession of the generations, is full of instruction, and written for instruction. Especially may we say so of our own history. But of all which it teaches, its moral lessons are, perhaps, the most valuable. It holds up to our emulation and love great models of patriotism and virtue. It introduces us into the presence of venerated ancestors, "of whom the world was not worthy." It teaches us to appreciate and cherish this good land, these free forms of government, this pure worship of the conscience, these schools of popular learning, by reminding us through how much tribulation, not our own, but others, these best gifts of God to man have been secured to us. It corrects the cold selfishness which would regard ourselves, our day, and our generation, as a separate and insulated portion of man and time; and, awakening our sympathies for those who have gone before, it makes us mindful, also, of those who are to follow, and thus binds us to our fathers and to our posterity by a lengthening and golden cord. It helps us to realize the serene and august presence and paramount claims of our country, and swells the deep and full flood of American feeling.

Such are some of the moral influences and uses of our history. Now, I say that he who writes the romance of history, as Scott has written it, shall teach these lessons, and exert and diffuse these influences, even better than he who confines himself to what I may call the reality of history. In the first place, he could make a more select and discriminating choice of incidents and characters and periods of time. There is a story told of an epicure who never would eat more than one mouthful out of the sunny side of the peach. That is about the proportion, about the quality, of all which Scott culls out of history.

Much of what history relates produces no impression upon the moral sentiments or the imagination. Much of it rather chills, shames, and disgusts us, than otherwise. Throughout it is constantly exciting a succession of discordant and contradictory emotions—alternate pride and mortification, alternate love and anger, alternate commendation and blame. The persecutions of the Quakers, the controversies with Roger Williams and Mrs. Hutchinson, the perpetual synods and ecclesiastical surveillance of the old times; a great deal of this is too tedious to be read, or it offends and alienates you. It is truth, fact; but it is just what you do not want to know, and are none the wiser for knowing. Now, he who writes the romance of history takes his choice of all its ample but incongruous material. "Whatsover things are honest, whatsoever things are just, whatsoever things are pure, whatsoever things are lovely, whatsoever things are of good report, if there be any virtue and if there be any praise"—these things alone he thinks of and impresses. In this sense he accommodates the show of things to the desires and the needs of the immortal, moral nature. . . . He records the useful truth therefore, only, gathering only the wheat, wine, and oil, into his garner, leaving all the rest to putrefy or be burned.

But farther. Such a writer as I am supposing is not only privileged to be more select and felicitous in his topics, his incidents, characters, and eras, but he treats these topics differently, and in a way to give ten thousand-fold more interest and impressiveness to all the moral lessons they are adapted to teach. He tells the truth, to be sure; but he does not tell the whole truth, for that would be sometimes misplaced and discordant. He tells something more than the truth, too, remembering that though man is not of imagination *all compact*, he is yet, in part, a creature of imagination, and can be reached and perfected by a law of his nature in part only through the imagination. He makes the imagination, therefore, he makes art, wit, eloquence, philosophy, and poetry, invention, a skilful plot, a spirited dialogue, a happy play, balance and rivalry of characters—he makes all these contribute to embellish and recommend that essential, historical truth which is as the nucleus of the whole fair orb. Thus he gives a vividness, individuality, nearness, magnitude, to the remotest past, which hardly belongs to the engrossing and visible present, and which history gives to nothing. . . . Some things which history would show, you do not see. But you see the best of everything, all that is grand and beautiful of nature, all that is brilliant in achievement, all that is magnanimous in virtue, all that is sublime in self-sacrifice; and you see a great deal more of which history shows you nothing. To say that Scott's view of an age, a character, or a historical event, is not a true view, is not much more sensible than to say that nothing exists but what you can see in the dark, that he who brings a light into your room in the night, suddenly creates everything which you are enabled to discover by the light of it.

I do not know that I can better illustrate this difference between the romance and the reality of history, and in some respects the superiority of the former for teaching and impressing mere historical truth, than by going back to the ten years which immediately preceded the Battle of Lexington. If idle wishes were not sinful as well as idle, that of all time past is the period in which we might all wish to have lived. Yet how meagre and unsatisfactory is the mere written history. The tea was thrown overboard, to be sure, and the Gaspar burned; town meetings were held, and committees of correspondence chosen, and touching appeals, of pathos and argument and eloquence unequalled, addressed to the king and people of England in behalf of their oppressed subjects and brethren of America. And when history has told you this she is silent. . . . And how would Scott reveal to you the spirit of that age? He would place you in the middle of a group of citizens of Boston, going home from the Old South, perhaps, or Faneuil Hall, where James Otis, or Josiah Quincy, or Samuel Adams, had been speaking, and let you listen to their conversation. He would take you to their meeting on Sunday when the congregation stood up in prayer, and the venerable pastor adverted to the crisis, and asked for strength and guidance from above to meet it. He would remark to you that varied expression which ran instantaneously over the general countenance of the assembly, and show you in that varied expression—the varied fortunes of America—the short sorrow, the long joy, the strife, the triumph, the agony, and the glory. In that congregation you might see in one seat the worn frame of a mother whose husband followed the banners of Wolfe, and fell with him on the Plains of Abraham, shuddering with apprehension lest such a life and such a death await her only son, yet striving as became a matron of New England, for grace to make even that sacrifice. You might see old men who dragged Sir William Pepperell's cannon along the beach at Louisburg, now only regretting that they had not half so much youthful vigor left to fight their king as they then used up in fighting his enemies. . . .

Thus somewhat would Scott contrive to give you a perception of that indefinable yet real and operative existence—the spirit of a strongly agitated age. . . .

In leaving this subject, I cannot help suggesting, at the hazard of being thought whimsical, that a literature of such writings as these, embodying the romance of the whole revolutionary and ante-revolutionary history of the United States, might do *something* to perpetuate the Union itself. The influence of a rich literature of passion and fancy upon society must not be denied merely because you cannot measure it by the yard or detect it by the barometer. Poems and romances which shall be read in every parlor, by every fireside, in every schoolhouse, behind every counter, in every printing-office, in every lawyer's office, at every weekly evening club, in all the states of this confederacy, must do something, along with more palpable if not more powerful agents, toward moulding and fixing that final, grand, complex result—the national character. A keen, well-instructed judge of such things said, if he might write the ballads of a people, he cared little who made its laws. Let me say, if a hundred men of genius would extract such a body of romantic literature from our early history as Scott has extracted from the history of England and Scotland, and as Homer extracted from that of Greece, it perhaps would not be so alarming if demagogues should preach, or governors practise, or executives tolerate nullification. Such a literature would be common property of all the states, a treasure of common ancestral recollections, more noble and richer than our thousand million acres of public land; and, unlike that land, it would be indivisible. It would be as the opening of a great fountain for the healing of the nations. It would turn back our thoughts from these recent and overrated diversities of interest—these controversies about Negro-cloth, coarse-wooled sheep and cotton bagging—to the day when our fathers walked hand in hand together through the valley of the Shadow of Death in the War of Independence. Reminded of our fathers, we should remember that we are brethren. The exclusiveness of state pride, the narrow selfishness of a mere local policy, and the small jealousies of vulgar minds, would be merged in an expanded, comprehensive, constitutional sentiment of old, family, fraternal regard. It would reassemble, as it were, the people of America in one vast congregation. It would rehearse in their hearing all things which God had done for them in the old time; it would proclaim the law once more; and then it would bid them join in that grandest and most affecting solemnity—a national anthem of thanksgiving for deliverance, of honor for the dead, of proud prediction for the future!

Part Four
SOCIAL MORALITY

1

WHIG PHILANTHROPY

Joseph Tuckerman
FOURTH SEMIANNUAL REPORT

Joseph Tuckerman (1778–1840) typifies the sort of bourgeois philanthropy associated with American Whiggery. Like Nicholas Biddle, Tuckerman was a man of property, patrician family, and genteel tastes. But while Biddle went into the countinghouse, Tuckerman went into the church. In 1825 he was called to a new kind of urban pastorate: the ministry to the poor in Boston. There Tuckerman displayed talents for organization and innovation rivaling those of Horace Mann. Setting up his chapel in a tenement, he arranged for community activities and established a farm school for slum children and a training program for unskilled blacks. Soon he was cooperating with clergymen of several denominations in a common effort. His most important contribution was the practice of home visitations that combined material assistance with family counseling. If Mann is the father of professional public schoolteaching, Tuckerman is the father of modern social work.

The following selection is a report Tuckerman made to his financial supporters, the American Unitarian Association. It is a clear, matter-of-fact exposition of the methods and objectives of nineteenth-century charity. To twentieth-century ears, it sounds rather harsh.

Boston, Nov. 5th, 1829

Gentlemen,

The approaching winter will probably be one of more than usual suffering among the poor of our city; and in the anticipation of a consequent greater demand for charity, the inquiries have often been proposed within a month or two past, what are the best preparations

SOURCE. Joseph Tuckerman, "Fourth Semiannual Report to the Executive Committee of the American Unitarian Association," *Mr. Tuckerman's Semiannual Reports of His Service as a Minister At Large in Boston* (New York, 1832), pp. 58–77.

that can be made for the exercise of this charity? How may we at once most judiciously, and most effectually, provide for the wants, for which it will be absolutely necessary that we make some provision? These are important questions, and demand very serious attention.

One circumstance which will make the coming winter more than ordinarily trying to many, is, that they have not been able, during the past season, to obtain the employment, by which they could make the preparations they have been accustomed to make for the months of winter. There is scarcely a mechanic occupation pursued among us, in which large numbers, through the summer and autumn, have not found it very difficult, and often impracticable to obtain work enough to enable them to pay their rent, and to purchase absolutely necessary food and clothing; and we have had double the number of day-laborers, required for all the work on which they depend for support. The consequence of this state of things has been, that a larger number of these, and of mechanics, than has been usual within the same term, have left the city: and it would have been well for many more, as well as for the city, if they had sought elsewhere for the means of supporting themselves, which, for a considerable time yet to come, they will find it difficult to obtain here. While considering, therefore, how we may most wisely minister to those, whose wants we cannot disregard, and whose sufferings it is our duty to relieve, an enlarged view of the interests of the poor, as well as those of their benefactors, requires of us that we take good heed, in a time of more than ordinary demand for charity, that we do not adopt any measures, which will enlarge and perpetuate the evil of an excessive poor population. Will it not be well, then, first to look at the causes to which are to be ascribed the large number of the poor which we have among us? I will but glance at two of the most obvious of them.

The first of these causes is, the great demand for laborers which has been kept up for some years past among us, principally, perhaps in consequence of the new direction which was given to the employment of capital, by the checks and embarrassments that were experienced in its employment in commerce. We have had a very large amount of disposable capital in our city, and at least a proportionally active spirit of enterprise. It has not, therefore, been difficult to obtain credit, where any new enterprise opened a tolerably fair prospect of success. In this state of things, our capital, instead of being sent abroad, has been spread over the land; partly, in the establishment of manufactories; and partly, in an enlargement of the number of our expensive buildings, either for residence, or for places of business, beyond the demand of the city for them. Which of these appropriations of capital has conduced to the greatest amount of suffering on the whole, may admit of a doubt. But it is not doubtful whether hundreds of families have been drawn to our city, and have settled themselves here, in consequence of the demand which has been created for their labors, by the additions which have thus been made to our public and private buildings, and with whom it is not now an easy thing to return to the places whence they came; who have learned to prefer a city life, and who must now, to a considerable extent, be dependent on charity. I do not advert to these circumstances in the spirit of reproach. I would only account for the fact that we have now among us an extraordinary excess of those who are wanted for the labor of the city.

There is a large class of the poorest of those in the country, to whom the city has always attractions enough to bring them into it. Not a few of this class receive no small encouragement from some of the Overseers of the Poor in the country, as quickly as possible to find their way to the city, where they may either obtain work, or be assisted as they cannot be in the places from which they come to us.[1] And here, if they cannot find employment, they do not seek long without finding the associates they want. Here, too, they can live as they will in greater security, because they are scarcely known but to those who are in the same conditions with themselves. When once brought into the city, it is therefore extremely difficult to obtain their removal from it. A time of actual, or of apparent prosperity, when work is promised, or seems at least to be promised, to all who ask for it, will increase as well this class of its inhabitants, as that of the industrious mechanics who come here to raise themselves to competence and respectability. These are considerations, which admonish us of dangers that lie in the path of duty respecting the poor. The truth is, and we should understand it, that the greatest conceivable demand for labor in a city will soon be met by an abundant supply; for the materials of this supply are abundant every where. It is this dictate, therefore, of a wise policy, to forsee, and avoid whatever may give an artificial extension to the laboring class of a city. For, even if the

[1]Everyone in Massachusetts was a legal resident of the town where he was born, and all his life it remained the legal responsibility of that town to provide him with public assistance should he ever require it. The Overseers of the Poor in small towns were naturally quite happy to see their welfare recipients leave in search of employment. But a large town like Boston, where many moved to find work, would often try to send people back to their legal residences whenever they became unemployed. Thus the state had a guaranteed welfare system, but one not well suited to geographic mobility and urbanization. Ed.

numbers which are thus brought into it should bring down wages to the level of demand for their services, and thus apparently, for a time, advance the interest of the capitalist, or of the employer, a reaction will sooner or later occur, in which the employer and the capitalist, must make a return for this temporary advantage, in the form either of a poor tax, or of charity, considerably beyond the amount gained by the depression of wages. In illustration of what I mean by the excessive demand which has been made for laborers among us, it is enough to state the fact, which I think that I can state upon good authority, that there are now five or six hundred houses to be let in this city. And it is also a fact important to be considered in this connexion, that while the rents of the houses which are inhabited by the affluent, and by the middling classes, have fallen perhaps nearly to the level of the general depression of business, the rents of the poor are almost universally as high as they have been for some years past; for the very plain reason, that there is so great a demand for the rooms which are rented by them, that it is very difficult for a poor family that would remove from one part of the city to another, to make the desired exchange in their place of abode; and the difficulty is much increased, if the object be to find a room which is twelve and a half or twenty-five cents lower than that which they are occupying. As far as our excessive population of this class is attributable to this cause, it may be well to understand the fact, even if nothing can immediately be done for a remedy of the evil. I believe, however, that between two and three hundred have left the city within the last three or four months, from a conviction that they might elsewhere more easily find the means of support. And it will certainly be for their advantage, if many more, from the same cause, should be induced to spread themselves over the country.

The second of these causes is the widely spread fame of our charity.

This, I have no doubt, has been a means of bringing many to us, not only from the towns in our state, and from the neighboring states, but from the British dominions in America, and even from Europe. I do not refer to this circumstance, that I may check the current of benevolence in any heart; for we have, in truth, no excess of benevolent feeling among us. Nor will a reference to either of the causes to which I have adverted, restrain from one effort of kindness in any well ordered mind. But it will throw some light on the inquiry, how is the tendency to this redundant population to be checked? Ask the agents of any of our benevolent societies, whether there are not multitudes among the poor, who know as well the times of the meetings of these associations, their anniversary days, and the amount of their funds—or at least, of their public collections, as they are known to the officers of these societies? But without referring to the poor themselves as the heralds of these charities, see what a machinery is put into operation, whenever a public meeting is to be held of any of our benevolent associations, that as large a multitude as possible may be called together. And of whom does this multitude consist? Is it not principally of the poor? In view of these things, I would say then, let it be understood, and talked of, and *published,* that it is a mistaken conception that has been excited abroad, that there is a demand for laborers in our city. This may do something for us. And, let us learn to be less boastful of our charities, and less ostentatious in their exercise. We may do all that we are now doing, and far more, for the poor, and thus for our own virtue, and yet we may do all far more quietly, and effectually, and with less injury to ourselves and others, than by our present modes of exercising our public benevolence. . . .

Let us then return to the question, from which we have wandered for a moment. How may we most effectually, and most judiciously, provide for those necessities of the poor for which it will be absolutely necessary to make provision? . . .

Three means of relief have been proposed, either of which, if adopted, I believe would conduce to an ultimate and very considerable increase of the evil. Let us look at them.

A proposition has been repeatedly suggested, for relieving the poor in the important concern of their rent. This is indeed a very heavy part of their burden, and there are cases in which they must be assisted to bear it. It has therefore been asked, would it not even be a good investment of money, to build a number of houses expressly for the poor, which shall be rented to them for half or two thirds the sum, which they must now pay for rooms, far inferior to those that might be thus provided for them? This without doubt, would be to the families which should be so accommodated, a great good. But it must be considered that the high rents required of the poor arise from the excess in the number of the poor among us. If, then, we build more habitations for them, shall we lessen, or increase this excess? Ought we not rather to do what we may to induce those who can well be spared to leave the city, and to seek in the country for the employment which they cannot find here? I believe that an enlarged Christian kindness strongly requires of us, in this way to seek a diminution of the number of our poor. And let the number be diminished of those who want the rooms occupied by the poor, and the rents of these rooms will soon find their proper level. This is the only way in which I think that this evil is to be effectually remedied.

Another inquiry which has often been proposed is, may not some new modes be found of employing the poor? Or, may we not do something for the female poor, by establishing another house for employing those who cannot elsewhere find employment?

Here the same difficulty again occurs. We shall thus ultimately increase that very excess, which we should endeavor to lessen. We shall thus offer a most effectual encouragement to the poor of the country, to come here for the labor, with which we thus offer to supply them. . . . Unnecessary and useless work must occasion ultimate loss somewhere; and, indirectly at least, even to the laborers employed upon it; for it so far disenables their employers to continue to employ them. And the work, in any department even of useful labor, which has furnished a supply beyond demand must equally, if not still more, check the operations of employers; and thus bring distress on those, who depend for the means of subsistence on daily labor.

A third inquiry which has been made is, would it not be advisable to establish two or three soup-houses, and perhaps two or three depositories of vegetables, to which the greatly suffering part of the poor might go two or three times in a week, for the small supplies which might be dealt out to them?

Establishments of this kind are well known in Europe, and they have been adopted in some cities of our own country, in times of great distress among the poor. And they are, without doubt, means of relieving the necessities of many, who should in some way be assisted. But I have as little doubt whether they are means of increasing the pauperism of a city. It must be seen, at once, how direct will be their tendency to bring idlers and vagrants from the country, who would much rather, in this way be supplied with food at their own homes, however mean and miserable those homes might be, than live in subjection to the discipline of a country alms house. It will be impossible, too, in these establishments, to maintain a principle of discrimination. The indolent and intemperate will therefore not only obtain their full share of this bounty, but they will sell that which you give them for food, for the very means of indulging the intemperance, which is, perhaps, above all others, the cause of their poverty and sufferings. Nor is it an unimportant consideration, that these establishments having once begun, it will be believed by those for whom they are intended, will be *continued*; and they will be looked to for the means of living in the winter. The excitement to personal effort for provisions for the future will therefore be proportionally checked. There are not many who will put forth all their energies for their families if they can look with confidence to a foreign supply of their wants. This is as true indeed, of those in the more favored classes of society, as among the poor; and it would be happier for many of the young in these clases, if they were reared under a stronger sense of the dependence of their condition through life, upon their personal exertions for respectability and for fortune. We are not knowingly to entrench on the laws of God's providence, that every man shall do what he can for himself, and for those of his own household. In a century or two hence, if we are to go in the unchristian course in which other cities have gone, establishments of this kind may be necessary here. But it is hoped, before they shall be resorted to, that due inquiry will be made respecting their tendencies, and their consequences, where they have been adopted.

Is it asked, then, how should we act, or what is it our duty to do, in this very difficult work of provision for the poor of our city?

Before I give my opinion upon this question, I may be allowed to exonorate myself from a suspicion, to which I feel that I may be exposed, by the precautions which I have suggested in relation to the exercise of our charity. It may be said, that I have learned to look upon the poor, rather in the light in which they are seen by the political economist, than as a Christian. But I answer, that I should esteem that to be a false and injurious principle in political economy, which is not in perfect consistency with Christian morality. I would, however, consider the Christian precepts, in regard to the poor, as I would the language of the New Testament respecting the rich, in connexion with those qualifications, which other precepts of our religion, as well as good common sense require us to employ in the practical interpretation of them.—While, therefore, I would understand and feel that the poorest of human beings, equally as the richest, is a child of God; that every human being, however poor, and however degraded, has a common nature with him who is the most favoured, and is his *brother*; that for our means and opportunities of instructing the ignorant, of supplying the wants of the destitute, and of recovering the most debased to virtue and to God, we are finally to give account to him who has made us to differ, and who has entrusted us with these means, that we might be the instruments of his benevolence to our fellow-creatures; and while I would feel all the power of the words of our Lord Jesus Christ, and the blessedness of the privilege to which we may be advanced by them, "inasmuch as ye have fed the hungry, and clothed the naked, and visited the sick and the prisoner, ye have shown this kindness unto me"; I would yet remember also, that our religion, with equal distinctness, teaches us, if not in its letter, yet in its spirit, that we are not by our charity to encourage idleness and vice, and thus to increase and perpetuate pauperism and misery. As we are not to do evil that good may come, so neither are we to mistake that for goodness, which a little judgment and foresight might teach us would inevitably lead to evil. As, therefore, I think it to be the Christian duty of parishes in the country to take the charge of their own poor, and faithfully to provide for their own, who cannot provide for themselves, I would say, let us act upon this sentiment. And I think that the inhabitants of a city are acting for the best good of that part of the very poor among them, who belong to the country, by using all fair and Christian means of inducing them to return, or of sending them to the places from which they came, where they will be far less exposed to vice, and where their wants may at least be equally well supplied. And let us do what we thus may for the relief of the city, as long as our social institutions exist and human nature remains as it is, we shall always have a great number of poor among us, to whom it will not be more our duty, than it should be our happiness, to do good as far as God shall enable us. Nor is it desirable that we should have no poor among us. Nay, it is even desirable to awaken more of the spirit of Christian charity, than now exists among us. I have spoken of the fame of our benevolence. But, in truth, the more favored classes of our society are very far behind the requisitions of our religion in regard to their duties towards the poor. But I comprehend in the term charity, as does our religion, far more than almsgiving. I shall have occasion, however, again to refer to this subject. I would now only say, that as Christians we may, and should aim, not alone at the greatest immediate, but at the greatest ultimate good. We should do good at the expense, and even at the hazard, of the least possible evil. We should make almsgiving, as far as possible, to minister not only to comfort, but to piety and virtue. This will be found at once to be the truest economy, as well as a just exposition of Christian duty. And in proportion as we can rise to this benevolence, it will doubly bless both him that gives, and him that receives.

That we may most effectually meet the wants of the poor, I would say then, first, that it should be insisted upon, *that there shall be a discrimination in the distribution of alms by our charitable societies.*

It is objected to these societies, that while the good which they do is partial and temporary, the evils to which they conduce are extensive and permanent. It is said that they are known to the poor, and have consequently a direct tendency to increase a willingness to be dependent; that they do, and often must, support the idle in their indolence, and furnish to the intemperate the means of living in their sin; that they are exposed to almost every species of deception, which they have not the means of detecting; and that they are among the most powerful of the influences, by which the most dependent, and often the worst among the poor, are brought into the city, and are retained here. I have stated these objections strongly, and I am aware that these societies are exposed to them. Acting as they do, independently of each other, they must often commit great mistakes, and occasion no inconsiderable evil. But is this evil necessary? It cannot be denied, that these societies give great relief to many of the poor, who could hardly, in any other way, be so efficiently assisted. They are useful, also, to the several members who compose them, by calling forth, and exercising, an excellent spirit of Christian benevolence. And they give a frequently renewed excitement to the benevolence of those who contribute to their support. These are circumstances of good too important to be lost, if the evils to which we have referred may be remedied. And is there no adequate remedy for these evils? Or, may they not so far be checked that they shall no longer be considered as powerful objections to this mode of exercising charity? I am not willing to believe that the case is hopeless.

It should be known that our benevolent societies profess, and really endeavour to maintain the principle of discrimination in the exercise of their charities. They *visit* the families which apply for their bounty, and learn what they can respecting their characters, as well as their wants. The difficulty however is, that, as they now act without any communication with each other, they do, and necessarily must, interfere with each other. They must depend alone on those whom they relieve, for a knowledge of what is done for them by others; and they do, and can know, little more of those who receive their bounty, than may be learned from themselves, or from their poor neighbors, who may be interested either to uphold, or to injure them. But is it not practicable, that there should be an understanding, and a concert of action, between these societies? Can no plan be devised for *their closer union with each other*; or, by which they may know what is done by each other, and by the overseers of the poor in the wards in which they severally act? . . .

In the *second* place, I think it to be of great importance, that *immediate, and more vigorous measures should be adopted, for preventing the accumulation of foreign poor in the city.*

There would, in truth, be no difficulty in providing for all our native poor, if it were for them only that we were called to make provision. But vast numbers of the poor of other countries are thrown upon us; and—I say it not in the spirit of reproach—they are taking the bread of

our own children. They are here, and must have their share of the
labors of the poor, and of the bounty which we have to bestow upon
the poor. But a remedy for this evil is not more demanded for the
virtue and well being of a city, than it is for the best good of those
whom we would thus restrain from seeking a dwelling place among
us. Unhappily it has been thought to be good policy to encourage
emigration to our country; and we have held out the lure to the
restless and discontented throughout the world, as well as to the
enterprising and virtuous, that, after two years declaration of their
intention to be citizens, and five years residence, they may be naturalized, if two individuals will testify that, in the sense of law, they are
moral men. The grossest impositions, too, it is well known, have been
practiced by some of the poorest who come to our country, in order to
bring here others of their own countrymen. Is it asked, what remedy is
proposed for this evil? I answer, we require new legislative provisions
in regard to the foreign poor who are brought among us. Masters of
vessels are now alone liable for the passengers they may land upon our
shores; and bonds can be required of them, only by the authorities of
the towns in which they may land their passengers. The laws, therefore, respecting these poor, are easily evaded; for passengers of this
description, I am told, are put on shore at places, from which they can
easily come to the city, while those who bring them, being thus
exempted from the bonds that would be required if they were landed
here, are under little or no check upon the question, whether they
may bring as many as can collect money enough to pay for their
voyage to our country. So, however, it would not be—certainly not to
an equal extent—if owners of vessels shall be made liable for the
passengers that are brought out in their vessels; and if the selectmen,
or the civil authorities of any town, by ascertaining in what vessels
any vagrant poor were brought to our country, may prosecute these
owners for damages, whether the men were landed in their town or
city, or any where else within the state. Let a remedy of the evil be
sought here, and the example will probably be followed by other
states. If the object can be attained by any other, and better course, let
it be adopted. But something should be done in the cause, and something must be done, or the evil may, in no long time, be irremediable.
Measures also should be taken in regard to those who come to the city
from different parts of our own state, and from the neighboring states.
If the officers of other towns are but too much inclined to cast off their
burdens upon us may we not give them some lessons in the principles
of political justice, which they will find it for their interest to remember and to practice?

And in the third place, I would say, that means should be employed to impress our community with a deeper sense of the relation which Christianity recognises between the more and less favored classes of society; between the rich and the poor.

It is not to be forgotten, that, after all the vigilance that can be exercised, and all the judgment and caution that can be maintained, for the prevention of pauperism, and for security against deceptions, and the abuse of charity, there will still be many, very many, even in a compact community of only 60 or 65,000 who must be more or less dependent for subsistence on the care and kindness of others. And in view of the gospel of Jesus Christ, if not of the doctrines of political economists, these have claims, unquestionable claims, upon those who are able to provide for them. I go further, and say, that if there must be, as there certainly are, many who are comparatively unworthy of the bounty which they seek, they have yet, if Christianity be true, strong claims upon beings around them, who are in happier conditions than their own. These claims may in part be answered by public institutions for their relief, in times of their great distress; and in part, by the benevolent associations that are formed to visit and relieve them. But there is no public provision, or associated exercise of charity, that can supercede, or be substituted for, individual obligation, and individual responsibility. This obligation, and this responsibility, as I am happy to know, are felt to an important extent among us. But if it were felt as it should be, we should not need benevolent societies, nor should we ever have occasion for the adoption of extraordinary measures for the poor, even in times of peculiarly pressing necessity. Here, then, is the great end at which we should aim. And I am doubtful whether the blessing so obtained would be greater to the many hundreds, who would thus be saved from the severest of the sufferings to which they are exposed, or to the favored instruments of extending this relief to them.

Is it asked, what are the duties of the intelligent, and the rich, in regard to the poor? What is it that it is desired should be done in our capacity as private Christians?

I answer, and I think it is contemplated by our religion, that the more favored classes should feel, and strongly feel, that they have a common nature with those in the less favored conditions of life; that opportunities and means are responsibilities; and that it is God's will, that they should be his instruments for accomplishing the purposes of his benevolence to the poor. They should therefore visit the widow, the fatherless, and the prisoner, and do what they can to assist, and to improve them. Or, to be yet more explicit, every individual who has the means of assisting a few families, should feel his obligation to seek out, and to know, a few families, with which he shall connect himself as a Christian friend. One may be able to maintain this intercourse with only two or three families, and another may do it with ten or a dozen. But every man who is disposed for this intercourse, may find leisure for it. Let him visit these families once in a week; and, if he cannot do it with convenience on other days, let him do it on Sunday, in the intervals from public worship. And let him feel that, in forming this connexion, he has taken upon himself a moral charge; that he is to be the adviser, and to seek the imporovement, of parents and children; to aid parents in keeping their children at school, and in placing them out as apprentices; to promote temperance, industry, order and cleanliness among them; to connect them, when it shall be practicable, with some congregation of worshippers; to inspire them with a proper self-respect, in times of sickness and sorrow to be their comforter; and in seasons of want, so to minister to their necessities, that their energies for self-support may be increased, rather than lessened, by the bounty they may receive. Is there any thing in all this that is merely theoretical, or visionary? The simplest principles of Christianity, carried into full exercise, would perfectly secure the permanency of all this good amongst us. We have means enough, intellectual, moral, and pecuniary, to meet all the demands of our city in regard to the poor. The whole difficulty of the case, is that of bringing these means into use for the purpose. In other words, our great want on this subject is, that of a greater prevalence of the true spirit of our religion among the intelligent and the rich, in regard in their relation to the poor, and to the Christian duties which grow out of this relation. Let the objects of Christianity be accomplished in the rich and the poor will be *blessed*. None will then withhold the kindness they can exercise, and there will be no complaining in our streets.

My visits, during the last six months, have been divided between three hundred and seventy families; and during the last year, between nearly five hundred families. In looking back upon this intercourse, I am sensible that, in some of these families, I have probably been instrumental of no good. There are others in which, though no very perceptible change has been effected, I have reason to believe that there has been some amelioration of condition, arising from improvement of character. And I feel assured that there are not a few who have been encouraged and strengthened, and carried on in the ways of well doing by this ministry. I have great happiness in my knowledge of the numbers towards whom I have been enabled to act as a Christian friend in these exigencies, in which some at least would hardly have known where to have looked for a friend to advise, and to act for them. This, indeed, is a very interesting and delightful part of my service. There are occasions, to themselves of great importance, in which the poor want advice and the interposition of a friend, quite as much as the hungry want bread. Mothers want this assistance in regard to their children, who are beyond their control, and are on the verge of moral ruin. And husbands and fathers want it, that they may make the provision which they would, but know not how to make, for their families. There are, too, circumstances of temptation and of trial, wholly of a personal nature, but of deep concern to the individuals suffering under them, which call for, and in this ministry receive, sympathy and assistance. And I believe that there are those who have been advanced by it in the Christian life; and some, who have been recovered from great and gross transgression. My objections to detail on these subjects are insuperable. They might awaken interest, but they would do no good: and probably, if they should come to the knowledge of those referred to in them, would conduce to evil. Many children have been placed in our schools, who otherwise would not have been there; and others have been kept in school, who might have been lost as vagrants. There is, however, much to be done for the salvation of a large number of children in the city, concerning whom a heavy responsibility rests somewhere. The whole community ought to be alive to the moral dangers of these children. If neglected, they will as assuredly furnish the future supplies for our prisons, as the well educated and well disciplined portion of the children of the city will furnish supplies for the various useful professions, and occupations among us. . . .

I am not willing to close this report without availing myself of the opportunity which it offers, to express to you my sense of the loss, which I, in common with many of the poor in our city, have sustained in the death of the late Mrs. Samuel Eliot, and of recording the respect, and gratitude, and affection, with which I shall not cease to remember her, as one of the best benefactors and supporters of my office as a minister of the poor. I know that she has been a subject of the prayers of the poor, and that they have mourned for her death with the tears of most unfeigned sorrow. . . .

Respectfully,
JOSEPH TUCKERMAN.

P.S. I am informed, that one or two persons have availed themselves of my name in begging, by saying that I have sent them to the families to which they have applied for charity. But I never so sent any one to an individual, or to a family, but in a single instance, and a long while ago; and then with a written recommendation. But this I shall not do again; and any one thus using my name, may be known as an impostor.

2

THE RIGHTS OF THE INDIANS

Theodore Frelinghuysen
THE CHEROKEE LANDS

One of the sharpest issues dividing the parties of the Jackson era was Indian policy. The most dramatic confrontation arose from the expropriation and forced migration of the so-called Five Civilized Tribes: Cherokee, Choctaw, Chickasaw, Creek, and Seminole. White settlers in Alabama, Georgia, and Mississippi demanded that these Indians be dispossessed of lands that had been guaranteed to them by treaty. The state governments, disregarding the treaties, asserted sovereignty over the Indian lands. When Andrew Jackson entered the White House, he avowed his sympathies with the white settlers. A bill to commence arrangements for Indian removal, backed by the administration, occasioned the following speech by one of the president's opponents.

Theodore Frelinghuysen (1787–1862) was an attorney and senator from New Jersey. He later served as mayor of Newark and in 1844 was Henry Clay's vice-presidential running mate. The following speech caused William Lloyd Garrison, always a friend to nonwhites, to cite him as a "patriot and Christian." (Frelinghuysen was a very active lay churchman and temperance advocate.) In their defense of the Indians, Frelinghuysen and his allies failed; the removal bill narrowly passed Congress. The United States Supreme Court under Chief Justice John Marshall vindicated the right of the Indians to their lands in 1832, but Jackson simply defied the court. Most of the Indians were rounded up and driven by the army to what is now Oklahoma. Some, especially the Seminoles, managed to escape into impenetrable areas from which they waged guerrilla warfare.

The Senate resumed the bill to provide for an exchange of lands with the Indians residing in any of the States or Territories, and for their removal west of the Mississippi.

Mr. Frelinghuysen moved to add to the bill the following:

"Sec. 9. That, until the said tribes or nations shall choose to

SOURCE. Theodore Frelinghuysen, "Speech on the Cherokee Lands," U.S. Congress, *Register of Debates*, Vol. VI; Part I (April 9, 1830), 309–320.

remove, as by this act is contemplated, they shall be protected in their present possessions, and in the enjoyment of all their rights of territory and government, as heretofore exercised and enjoyed, from all interruptions and encroachments.

"Sec. 10. That, before any removal shall take place of any of the said tribes or nations, and before any exchange or exchanges of land be made as aforesaid, that the rights of any such tribes or nations, in the premises, shall be stipulated for, secured, and guarantied, by treaty or treaties, as heretofore made." . . .

(His speech, as delivered on the three several days, was as follows:)

I propose an amendment, Mr. President, to this bill, by the addition of two sections in the forms of provisos. The first of which brings up to our consideration the nature of our public duties, in relation to the Indian nations; and the second provides for the continuance of our future negotations, by the mode of treaties, as in our past intercourse with them. . . .

God, in his providence, planted these tribes on this Western continent, so far as we know, before Great Britain herself had a political existence. I believe, sir, it is not now seriously denied that the Indians are men, endowed with kindred faculties and powers with ourselves; that they have a place in human sympathy, and are justly entitled to a share in the common bounties of a benignant Providence. And, with this conceded, I ask in what code of the law of nations, or by what process of abstract deduction, their rights have been extinguished?

Where is the decree or ordinance that has stripped these early and first lords of the soil? Sir, no record of such measure can be found. And I might triumphantly rest the hopes of these feeble fragments of once great nations upon this impregnable foundation. However mere human policy, or the law of power, or the tyrant's plea of expediency, may have found it convenient at any or in all times to recede from the unchangeable principles of eternal justice, no argument can shake the political maxim, that, where the Indian always has been, he enjoys an absolute right still to be, in the free exercise of his own modes of thought, government, and conduct.

In the light of natural law, can a reason for a distinction exist in the mode of enjoying that which is my own? If I use it for hunting, may another take it because he needs it for agriculture? I am aware that some writers have, by a system of artificial reasoning, endeavored to justify, or rather excuse the encroachments made upon Indian territory; and they denominate these abstractions the law of nations, and, in this ready way, the question is despatched. Sir, as we trace the sources of this law, we find its authority to depend either upon the conventions or common consent of nations. And when, permit me to inquire, were the Indian tribes ever consulted on the establishment of such a law? Whoever represented them or their interests in any congress of nations, to confer upon the public rules of intercourse, and the proper foundations of dominion and property? The plain matter of fact is, that all these partial doctrines have resulted from the selfish plans and pursuits of more enlightened nations; and it is not matter for any great wonder, that they should so largely partake of a mercenary and exclusive spirit toward the claims of the Indians.

It is, however, admitted, sir, that, when the increase of population and the wants of mankind demand the cultivation of the earth, a duty is thereby devolved upon the proprietors of large and uncultivated regions, of devoting them to such useful purposes. But such appropriations are to be obtained by fair contract, and for reasonable compensation. It is, in such a case, the duty of the proprietor to sell: we may properly address his reason to induce him; but we cannot rightfully compel the cession of his lands, or take them by violence, if his consent be withheld. It is with great satisfaction that I am enabled, upon the best authority, to affirm, that this duty has been largely and generously met and fulfilled on the part of the aboriginal proprietors of this continent. Several years ago, official reports to Congress stated the amount of Indian grants to the United States to exceed two hundred and fourteen millions of acres. Yes, sir, we have acquired, and now own, more land as the fruits of their bounty than we shall dispose of at the present rate to actual settlers in two hundred years. For, very recently, it has been ascertained, on this floor, that our public sales average not more than about one million of acres annually. It greatly aggravates the wrong that is now meditated against these tribes, to survey the rich and ample districts of their territories, that either force or persuasion have incorporated into our public domains. As the tide of our population has rolled on, we have added purchase to purchase. The confiding Indian listened to our professions of friendship: we called him brother, and he believed us. Millions after millions he has yielded to our importunity, until we have acquired more than can be cultivated in centuries—and yet we crave more. We have crowded the tribes upon a few miserable acres on our southern frontier: it is all that is left to them of their once boundless forests: and still, like the horse-leech, our insatiated cupidity cries, give! give!

Before I proceed to deduce collateral confirmations of this original title, from all our political intercourse and conventions with the Indian tribes, I beg leave to pause a moment, and view the case as it lies beyond the treaties made with them: and aside also from all conflicting claims between the confederation, and the colonies, and the Congress of the states. Our ancestors found these people, far removed from the commotions of Europe, exercising all the rights, and enjoying the privileges, of free and independent sovereigns of this new world. They were not a wild and lawless horde of banditti, but lived under the restraints of government, patriarchal in its character, and energetic in its influence. They had chiefs, head men, and councils. The white men, the authors of all their wrongs, approached them as friends—they extended the olive branch; and being then a feeble colony and at the mercy of the native tenants of the soil, by presents and professions,propitiated their good will. The Indian yielded a slow, but substantial confidence; granted to the colonists an abiding place; and suffered them to grow up to man's estate beside him. He never raised the claim of elder title: as the white man's wants increased, he opened the hand of his bounty wider and wider. By and by, conditions are changed. His people melt away; his lands are constantly coveted; millions after millions are ceded. The Indian bears it all meekly; he complains, indeed, as well he may; but suffers on: and now he finds that this neighbor, whom his kindness had nourished, has spread an adverse title over the last remains of his patrimony, barely adequate to his wants, and turns upon him, and says, "Away! We cannot endure you so near us! These forests and rivers, these groves of your fathers, these firesides and hunting grounds, are ours by the right of power, and the force of numbers." Sir, let every treaty be blotted from our records, and in the judgment of natural and unchangeable truth and justice, I ask, who is the injured, and who is the aggressor? Let conscience answer, and I fear not the result. Sir, let those who please, denounce the public feeling on this subject as the morbid excitement of a false humanity; but I return with the inquiry, whether I have not presented the case truly, with no feature of it overcharged or distorted? And, in view of it, who can help feeling, sir? Do the obligations of justice change with the color of the skin? Is it one of the prerogatives of the white man, that he may disregard the dictates of moral principles, when an Indian shall be concerned? No, sir. In that severe and impartial scrutiny which futurity will cast over this subject, the righteous award will be, that those very causes which are now pleaded for the relaxed enforcement of the rules of equity, urged upon us not only a rigid execution of the highest justice, to the very letter, but claimed at our hands a generous and magnanimous policy.

Standing here, then, on this unshaken basis, how is it possible that even a shadow of claim to soil, or jurisdiction, can be derived, by forming a collateral issue between the State of Georgia and the General Government? Her complaint is made against the United States, for encroachments on her sovereignty. Sir, the Cherokees are no parties to this issue; they have no part in this controversy. They hold by better title than either Georgia or the Union. They have nothing to do with State sovereignty, or United States, sovereignty. They are above and beyond both. True, sir, they have made treaties with both, but not to acquire title or jurisdiction; these they had before—ages before the evil hour to them, when their white brothers fled to them for an asylum. They treated to secure protection and guarantee for subsisting powers and privileges; and so far as those conventions raise obligations, they are willing to meet, and always have met, and faithfully performed them; and now expect from a great people, the like fidelity to plighted covenants.

I have thus endeavored to bring this question up to the control of first principles. I forget all that we have promised, and all that Georgia has repeatedly conceded, and, by her conduct, confirmed. Sir, in this abstract presentation of the case, stripped of every collateral circumstance—and these only the more firmly established the Indian claims—thus regarded, if the contending parties were to exchange positions; place the white man where the Indian stands; load him with all these wrongs, and what path would his outraged feelings strike out for his career? Twenty shillings tax, I think it was, imposed upon the immortal Hampden, roused into activity the slumbering fires of liberty in the Old World, from which she dates a glorious epoch, whose healthful influence still cherishes the spirit of freedom. A few pence of duty on tea, that invaded no fireside, excited no fears, disturbed no substantial interest whatever, awakened in the American colonies a spirit of firm resistance; and how was the tea tax met, sir? Just as it should be. There was lurking beneath this trifling imposition of duty, a covert assumption of authority, that led directly to oppressive exactions. "No taxation without representation," became our motto. We would neither pay the tax nor drink the tea. Our fathers buckled on their armor, and, from the water's edge, repelled the encroachments of a misguided cabinet. We successfully and triumphantly contended for the very rights and privileges that our Indian neighbors now implore us to protect and preserve to them. Sir, this thought invests the subject under debate with most singular and momentous interest. We, whom God has exalted to the very summit of prosperity—whose brief career forms the brightest page in history; the wonder and praise of the world; freedom's hope, and her consolation; we, about to turn traitors to our principles and our fame—about to become the opressors of the feeble, and to cast away our birthright! Sir, I hope for better things.

It is a subject full of grateful satisfaction, that, in our public intercourse with the Indians, ever since the first colonies of white men found an abode on these western shores, we have distinctly recognized their title; treated with them as owners, and in all our acquisitions of territory, applied ourselves to these ancient proprietors, by purchase and cession alone, to obtain the right of soil. Sir, (said Mr. F.) I challenge the record of any other or different pretension. When, or where, did any assembly or convention meet which proclaimed, or even suggested to these tribes, that the right of discovery contained a superior efficacy over all prior titles?

And our recognition was not confined to the soil merely. We regarded them as nations—far behind us indeed in civilization, but still we respected their forms of government—we conformed our conduct to their notions of civil policy. We were aware of the potency of any edict that sprang from the deliberations of the council fire; and when we desired lands, or peace, or alliances, to this source of power and energy, to this great lever of Indian government we addressed our proposals —to this alone did we look; and from this alone did we expect aid or relief.

I now proceed, very briefly, to trace our public history in these important connexions. As early as 1763, a proclamation was issued by the King of Great Britain to his American colonies and dependencies, which, in clear and decided terms, and in the spirit of honorable regard for Indian privileges, declared the opinions of the Crown and the duties of its subjects. The preamble to that part of this document which concerns Indian affairs, is couched in terms that cannot be misunderstood. I give a little extract: "And whereas it is just and reasonable and essential to our interest and the security of our colonies, that the several nations or tribes of Indians with whom we are connected, and who live under our protection, should not be molested or disturbed in the possession of such parts of our dominions and territories, as, not having been ceded to or purchased by us, are reserved to them or any of them as their hunting grounds," therefore, the Governors of colonies are prohibited, upon any pretence whatever, from granting any warrants of survey, or passing any patents for lands, "upon any lands whatever, which, not having been ceded or purchased, were reserved to the said Indians:" and, by another injunction in the same proclamation, "all persons whatever, who have either wilfully or inadvertently seated themselves upon any lands, which, not having been ceded to, or purchased by the crown, were reserved to the Indians as aforesaid, are strictly enjoined and required to remove themselves from such settlements."

This royal ordinance is an unqualified admission of every principle that is now urged in favor of the liberties and rights of these tribes. It refers to them as nations that had put themselves under the protection of the crown; and adverting to the fact that their lands had not been ceded or purchased, it freely and justly runs out the inevitable conclusion, that they are reserved to these nations as their property; and forbids all surveys and patents, and warns off all intruders and trespassers. Sir, this contains the epitome of Indian history and title. No king, colony, state, or territory, ever made, or attempted to make, a grant or title to the Indians, but universally and perpetually derived their titles from them. This one fact, that stands forth broadly on the page of Indian history, which neither kings nor colonies—neither lords, proprietors, nor diplomatic agents, have, on any single occasion, disputed, is alone sufficient to demolish the whole system of political pretensions, conjured up in modern times, to drive the poor Indian from the last refuge of his hopes. . . .

Under the confederation of the old thirteen states, and shortly before the adoption of the Constitution, on the 20th of November, 1785, a treaty was made with the Cherokee nation, at Hopewell. This treaty according to its title, was concluded between "Commissioners Plenipotentiary of the United States of America, of the one part, and the Headmen and Warriors of all the Cherokees, of the other." It gives "peace to all the Cherokees," and receives them into the favor and protection of the United States. And, by the first article, the Cherokees agree to restore all the prisoners, citizens of the United States, or subjects of their allies, to their entire liberty. Here, again, we discover the same magnanimous policy of renouncing any pretended rights of a conqueror in our negotiations with the allies of our enemy. We invite them to peace; we engage to become their protectors, and in the stipulation for the liberation of prisoners, we trace again the broad line of distinction between citizens of the United States and the Cherokee people.

Who, after this, sir, can retain a single doubt as to the unquesioned political sovereignty of these tribes? It is very true, that they were not absolutely independent. As they had become comparatively feeble, and as they were, in the mass, an uncivilized race, they chose to depend upon us for protection; but this did not destroy or affect their sovereignty. The rule of public law is clearly stated by Vattel—"one community may be bound to another by a very unequal alliance, and still be a sovereign State. Though a weak State, in order to provide for.

its safety, should place itself under the protection of a more powerful one, yet, if it reserves to itself the right of governing its own body, it ought to be considered as an independent State." If the right of self-government is retained, the state preserves its political existence; and permit me to ask, when did the southern Indians relinquish this right? Sir, they have always exercised it, and were never disturbed in the enjoyment of it, until the late legislation of Georgia and the States of Alabama and Mississippi.

The treaty next proceeds to establish territorial domains, and to forbid all intrusions upon the Cherokee country, by any of our citizens, on the pains of outlawry. It provides, that, if any citizen of the United States shall remain on the lands of the Indians for six months "after the ratification of the treaty, such person shall forfeit the protection of the United States, and the Indians may punish him, or not, as they please." What stronger attribute of sovereignty could have been conceded to this tribe, than to have accorded to them the power of punishing our citizens according to their own laws and modes; and, sir, what more satisfactory proof can be furnished to the Senate, of the sincere and inflexible purpose of our government to maintain the rights of the Indian nations, than the annexation of such sanctions as the forfeiture of national protection? . . .

The next important event, in connexion with the Cherokees, is the treaty of Holston, made with them on the 2d July, 1791. This was the first treaty negotiated with the Cherokees after the constitution. And it is only necessary to consider the import of its preamble, to become satisfied of the constancy of our policy, in adhering to the first principles of our Indian negotiations. . . .

The preamble to this treaty I will now recite:

"The parties being desirous of establishing permanent peace and friendship between the United States and the said Cherokee nation, and the citizens and members thereof, and to remove the causes of war, by ascertaining their limits, and making other necessary, just, and friendly arrangements: the President of the United States, by William Blount, Governor of the territory of the United States of America, south of the river Ohio, and Superintendent of Indian affairs for the Southern District, who is vested with full powers for these purposes, by and with the advice and consent of the Senate of the United States; and the Cherokee nation, by the undersigned chiefs and warriors, representing the said nation, have agreed to the following articles," &c.

The first article stipulates that there shall be "perpetual peace and friendship" between the parties; a subsequent article provides, that the boundary between the United States and Cherokees " shall be ascertained and marked plainly, by three persons appointed by the United States, and three Cherokees on the part of their nation."

In pursuance of the advice of the Senate, by the seventh article of this treaty, "The United States solemnly guarantee to the Cherokee nation all their lands not hereby ceded."

And after several material clauses, the concluding article suspends the effect and obligation of the treaty upon its ratification "by the President of the United States, with the advice and consent of the Senate of the United States."

Now, sir, it is a most striking part of this history, that every possible incident, of form, deliberation, advisement, and power, attended this compact. The Senate was consulted when our plenipotentiary was commissioned; full powers were then given to our commissioner; the articles were agreed upon; the treaty referred to the Executive and Senate for their ratification, and, with all its provisions, by them solemnly confirmed.

It requires a fullness of self-respect and self-confidence, the lot of a rare few, after time has added its sanctions to this high pledge of national honor, to attempt to convict the illustrious men of that Senate of gross ignorance of constitutional power; to charge against them that they strangely mistook the charter under which they acted; and violated almost the proprieties of language, as some gentlemen contend, by dignifying with the name and formalities of a treaty "mere bargains to get Indian lands." Sir, who so well understood the nature and extent of the powers granted in the constitution, as the statemen who aided by their personal counsels to establish it?

Every administration of this Government, from President Washington's, have, with like solemnities and stipulations, held treaties with the Cherokees; treaties, too, by almost all of which we obtained further acquisitions of their territory. Yes, sir, whenever we approached them in the language of friendship and kindness, we touched the chord that won their confidence; and now, when they have nothing left with which to satisfy our cravings, we propose to annul every treaty—to gainsay our word—and by violence and perfidy, drive the Indian from his home. . . . Under the influence of this rule of common fairness, how can we ever dispute the sovereign right of the Cherokees to remain east of the Mississippi, when it was in relation to that very location that we promised our patronage, aid, and good neighborhood? Sir, is this high-handed encroachment of Georgia to be the commentary upon the national pledge here given, and the obvious import of these terms? How were these people to remain, if not as they then existed, and as we then acknowledged them to be, a distinct and separate community, governed by their own peculiar laws and customs? We can never deny these principles, while fair dealing retains any hold of our conduct. Further, sir, it appears from this treaty, that the Indians who preferred to remain east of the river, expressed "to the President an anxious desire to engage in the pursuits of agriculture and civilized life in the country they then occupied," and we engaged to encourage those laudable purposes. Indeed, such pursuits had been recommended to the tribes, and patronized by the United States, for many years before this convention. . . .

It will not be necessary (said Mr. F.) to pursue the details of our treaty negotiations further. I beg leave to state, before I leave them, however, that with all the southwestern tribes of Indians we have similar treaties, not only the Cherokees, but the Creeks, Choctaws, and Chickasaws, in the neighborhood of Georgia, Tennessee, Alabama, and Mississippi, hold our faith, repeatedly pledged to them, that we would respect their boundaries, repel aggressions, and protect and nourish them as our neighbors and friends; and to all these public and sacred compacts Georgia was a constant party. They were required, by an article never omittted, to be submitted to the Senate of the United States for their advice and consent. They were so submitted; and Georgia, by her able Representatives in the Senate, united in the ratification of these same treaties, without, in any single instance, raising an exception, or interposing a constitutional difficulty or scruple. . . .

How can Georgia, after all this, desire or attempt, and how can we quietly permit her, "to invade and disturb the property, rights, and liberty of the Indians?" And this, not only not "in just and lawful wars authorized by Congress," but in the time of profound peace, while the Cherokee lives in tranquil prosperity by her side. I press on the inquiry—How can we tamely suffer these States to make laws, not only not "founded in justice and humanity," "for preventing wrongs being done to the Indians," but for the avowed purpose of inflicting the gross and wanton injustice of breaking up their Government—of abrogating their long cherished customs, and of annihilating their existence as a distinct people?

The Congress of the United States, in 1799, in an act to regulate trade and intercourse with the Indian tribes; and again, by a similar act in 1802, still in force, distinctly recognized every material stipulation contained in the numerous treaties with the Indians. In fact, sir, these acts of legislation were passed expressly to effectuate our treaty stipulations.

These statutes refer to "the boundaries, as established by treaties, between the United States and the various Indian tribes"; they next direct such "lines to be clearly ascertained, and distinctly marked," prohibit any citizen of the United States from crossing these lines, to hunt or settle, and authorize the employment of the public and military force of the Government, to prevent intrusion, and to expel trespassers upon Indian lands. The twelfth section of this important law most wisely guards the great object of Indian title from all public and private imposition, by enacting "that no purchase, grant, lease, or other conveyance of lands, or of any title or claim thereto, from any Indian or nation, or tribe of Indians, within the bounds of the United States, shall be of any validity in law or equity, unless the same be made by treaty or convention, entered into pursuant to the constitution."

I trust, sir, that this brief exposition of our policy, in relation to Indian affairs, establishes, beyond all controversy, the obligation of the United States to protect these tribes in the exercise and enjoyment of their civil and political rights. Sir, the question has ceased to be—What are our duties? An inquiry much more embarrassing is forced upon us: How shall we most plausibly, and with the least possible violence, break our faith? Sir, we repel the inquiry—we reject such an issue—and point the guardians of public honor to the broad, plain faith of faithful performance, and to which they are equally urged by duty and by interest. .

Here I might properly rest, as the United States are the only party that the Indians are bound to regard. But, if farther proofs be wanting to convince us of the unwarrantable pretentions of Georgia, in her late violent legislation, they are at hand, cogent, clear, and overwhelming. This state, sir, was not only a party to all these conventions with the General Government; she made as solemn treaties with the Creeks and Cherokees for herself, when a colony, and after she became a state. These form a part of her title, and are bound up with her public laws. . . .

And yet, now we hear that these Indians have been for all the time, since Georgia had existence, a component part of her population; within the full scope of her jurisdiction and sovereignty, and subject to the control of her law!

The people of this country will never acquiesce in such violent constructions. They will read for themselves; and when they shall learn the history of all our intercourse with these nations; when they shall perceive the guaranties so often renewed to them, and under what solemn sanctions, the American community will not seek the aids of artificial speculations on the requisite formalities to a technical treaty. No, sir, I repeat it: They will judge for themselves, and proclaim, in language that the remotest limit of this republic will understand—"call these sacred pledges of a nation's faith by what name you please, our word has been given, and we should live and die by our word." . . .

I have complained of the legislation of Georgia. I will now refer the Senate to the law of that state, passed on the 19th December, 1829, that the complaint may be justified. The title of the law would suffice for such purpose without looking further into its sections. After stating its object of adding the territory in the occupancy of the Cherokee nation of Indians to the adjacent counties of Georgia, another distinct office of this oppressive edict of arbitrary power is avowed to be, "to annul all laws and ordinances made by the Cherokee nation of Indians." And, sir, the act does annul them effectually. For the seventh section enacts, "that after the first day of June next, all laws, ordinances, orders, and regulations of any kind whatever, made, passed, or enacted by the Cherokee Indians, either in general council, or in any other way whatever, or by any authority whatever, of said tribe, be, and the same are hereby declared to be, null and void and of no effect, as if the same had never existed." Sir, here we find a whole people outlawed—laws, customs, rules, government, all, by one short clause, abrogated and declared to be void as if they never had been. History furnishes no example of such high handed usurpation—the dismemberment and partition of Poland was a deed of humane legislation compared with this. . . .

It is not surprising that our agents advertised the War Department, that if the general government refused to interfere, and the Indians were left to the law of the states, they would soon exchange their lands and remove. To compel, by harsh and cruel penalties, such exchange, is the broad purpose of this act of Georgia, and nothing is wanting to fill up the picture of this disgraceful system, but to permit the bill before us to pass without amendment or proviso. Then it will all seem fair on our statute books. It legislates for none but those who may choose to remove, while we know that grinding, heart-breaking exactions are set in operation elsewhere, to drive them to such a choice. By the modification I have submitted, I beg for the Indian the poor privilege of the exercise of his own will. But the law of Georgia is not yet satisfied. The last section declares, "that no Indian, or descendant of any Indian, residing within the Creek or Cherokee nations of Indians, shall be deemed a competent witness in any Court of this State, to which a white person may be a party, except such white person resides within the said nation." It did not suffice to rob these people of the last vestige of their own political rights and liberties; the work was not complete until they were shut out of the protection of Georgia laws. For, sir, after the first day of June next, a gang of lawless white men may break into the Cherokee country, plunder their habitations, murder the mother with the children, and all in the sight of the wretched husband and father, and no law of Georgia will reach the atrocity. It is vain to tell us, sir, that murder may be traced by circumstantial probabilities. The charge against this State is, you have, by force and violence, stripped these people of the protection of their government, and now refuse to cast over them the shield of your own. The outrage of the deed is, that you leave the poor Indian helpless and defenceless, and in this cruel way hope to banish him from his home. Sir, if this law be enforced, I do religiously believe that it will awaken tones of feeling that will go up to God, and call down the thunders of his wrath. . . .

Sir, our fears have been addressed in behalf of those states whose legislation we resist: and it is inquired with solicitude, would you urge us to arms with Georgia? No, sir. This tremendous alternative will not be necessary. Let the general government come out, as it should, with decided and temperate firmness, and officially announce to Georgia, and the other states, that if the Indian tribes choose to remain, they will be protected against all interference and encroachment; and such is my confidence in the sense of justice in the respect for law, prevailing in the great body of this portion of our fellow-citizens, that I believe they would submit to the authority of the nation. I can expect no other issue. But if the general government be urged to the crisis, never to be anticipated, of appealing to the last resort of her powers; and when reason, argument, and persuasion fail, to raise her strong arm to repress the violations of the supreme law of the land, I ask, is it not in her bond, sir? Is her guaranty a rope of sand? This effective weapon has often been employed to chastise the poor Indians, sometimes with dreadful vengeance, I fear; and shall not their protection avail to draw it from the scabbard? . . .

Let such decided policy go forth in the majesty of our laws now, and sir, Georgia will yield. She will never encounter the responsibilities or the horrors of a civil war. But if she should, no stains of blood will be on our skirts; on herself the guilt will abide forever.

Sir, (said Mr. F.) if we abandon these aboriginal proprietors of our soil, these early allies and adopted children of our forefathers, how shall we justify it to our country? to all the glory of the past, and the promise of the future? Her good name is worth all else besides that contributes to her greatness. And, as I regard this crisis in her history; the time has come when this unbought treasure shall be plucked from dishonor, or abandoned to reproach.

How shall we justify this trespass to ourselves? Sir, we may deride it, and laugh it to scorn now; but the occasion will meet every man, when he must look inward, and make honest inquisition there. Let us beware how, by oppressive encroachments upon the sacred privileges of our Indian neighbors, we minister to the agonies of future remorse.

3

AN UNJUST WAR

Thomas Corwin
THE MEXICAN WAR

The Mexican War was waged by a Democratic administration under President Polk. Whigs generally regarded it as an unjust war of aggression provoked by our side. Antiwar feeling ran especially strong in the northern states. In Congress, the Whigs had resisted the initial involvement but were faced with a troublesome dilemma once fighting began. Should they oppose appropriations to finance the war, or would it be unpatriotic to withhold support from American soldiers in the field? Most Whig congressmen voted reluctantly for military appropriations. One who did not explains his position here.

Thomas Corwin (1794–1865), born in a poor Kentucky family, educated himself to be a lawyer and became active in Ohio politics at an early age. He moved naturally from supporting the Adams-Clay faction of the 1820s into the Whig party. At various times he served as state legislator, congressman, governor of Ohio, and secretary of the treasury. Only reluctantly did he leave the moribund Whig party in 1858 to become a Republican. Lincoln gave him the important, and appropriate, post of minister to Mexico. At the time he delivered this speech Corwin was United States senator from Ohio.

Anxious as I know all are to act, rather than debate, I am compelled . . . to solicit the attention of the Senate. I do this chiefly that I may discharge the humble duty of giving to the Senate, and through this medium to my constituents, the motives and reasons which have impelled me to occupy a position always undesirable, but, in times like the present, painfully embarrassing.

I have been compelled, from convictions of duty which I could not disregard, to differ not merely with those on the other side of the chamber, with whom I seldom agree, but also to separate, on one or

SOURCE. Thomas Corwin, "On the Mexican War. In the Senate of the United States, February 11th, 1847," *Life and Speeches of Thomas Corwin,* ed. Josiah Morrow (Cincinnati, 1896), pp. 277–314.

two important questions, from a majority of my friends on this side—those who compose here that Whig party, of which, I suppose, I may yet call myself a member. . . .

I sincerely wish it were in my power to cherish those placid convictions of security which have settled upon the mind of the Senator from Michigan [Lewis Cass]. So far from this, I have been, in common with the Senator from South Carolina [John C. Calhoun], oppressed with melancholy forebodings of evils to come, and not unfrequently by a conviction that each step we take in this unjust war, may be the last in our career; that each chapter we write in Mexican blood, may close the volume of our history as a free people. . . .

Sir, if any one could sit down, free from the excitements and biases which belong to public affairs—could such a one betake himself to those sequestered solitudes, where thoughtful men extract the philosophy of history from its facts, I am quite sure no song of "all's well" would be heard from his retired cell. No, sir, looking at the events of the last twelve months, and forming his judgment of these by the suggestions which history teaches, and which she alone *can* teach, he would record another of those sad lessons which, though often taught, are, I fear, forever to be disregarded. He would speak of a republic, boasting that its rights were secured, and the restricted powers of its functionaries bound up in the chains of a written Constitution; he would record on his page, also, that such a people, in the wantonness of strength or the fancied security of the moment, had torn that written Constitution to pieces, scattered its fragments to the winds, and surrendered themselves to the usurped authority of ONE MAN.

He would find written in that Constitution, *Congress* shall have power to declare war; he would find everywhere, in that old charter, proofs clear and strong, that they who framed it intended that Congress, composed of two Houses, the representatives of the states, and the people, should (if any were pre-eminent) be the controlling power. He would find there a President designated; whose general and almost exclusive duty it is to *execute*, not to *make* the law. Turning from this to the history of the last ten months, he would find that the President alone, without the advice or consent of Congress, had, by a bold usurpation, made war on a neighboring republic; and what is quite as much to be deplored, that Congress, whose high powers were thus set at naught and defied, had, with ready and tame submission, yielded to the usurper the wealth and power of the nation to execute his will, as if to swell his iniquitous triumph over the very Constitution which he and they had alike sworn to support.

If any one should inquire for the cause of a war in this country, where should he resort for an answer? Surely to the journals of both Houses of Congress, since Congress alone has power to declare war; yet, although we have been engaged in war for the last ten months, a war which has tasked all the fiscal resources of the country to carry it forward, you shall search the records and the archives of both Houses of Congress in vain for any detail of its causes, any resolve of Congress that war shall be waged. How is it, then, that a peaceful and peace-loving people, happy beyond the common lot of man, busy in every laudable pursuit of life, have been forced to turn suddenly from these and plunge into the misery, the vice and crime which ever have been, and ever shall be, the attendant scourges of war? The answer can only be, it was by the act and will of the President *alone,* and not by the act or will of Congress, the war-making department of the government. . . .

When the makers of that Constitution assigned to Congress alone, the most delicate and important power—to declare war—a power more intimately affecting the interests, immediate and remote, of the people, than any which a government is ever called on to exert—when they withheld this great prerogative from the Executive and confided it to Congress alone, they but consulted in this, as in every other work of their hands, the gathered wisdom of all preceding times. Whether they looked to the stern despotisms of the ancient Asiatic world, or the military yoke of imperial Rome, or the feudal institutions of the middle ages, or the more modern monarchies of Europe, in each and all of these, where the power to wage war was held by one or by a few, it had been used to sacrifice, not to protect the many. The caprice or ambition of the tyrant had always been the cause of bloody and wasting war, while the subject millions had been treated by their remorseless masters, only as "tools in the hands of him who knew how to use them." They therefore declared that this fearful power should be confided to those who represent the people, and those who here in the Senate represent the sovereign states of the republic. After securing this power to Congress, they thought it safe to give the command of the armies in peace and war to the President. We shall see hereafter, how by an abuse of his power as commander-in-chief, the President has drawn to himself that of declaring war, or commencing hostilities with a people with whom we were on terms of peace, which is substantially the same.

The men of former times took very good care that your standing army should be exceedingly small, and they who had the most lively apprehensions of investing in one man the power to command the army, always inculcated upon the minds of the people the necessity of keeping that army within limits, just as small as the necessity of the external relations of the country would possibly admit. It has happened, Mr. President, that when a little disturbance on your Indian frontier took place, Congress was invoked for an increase of your military force. Gentlemen came here who had seen partial service in the armies of the United States. They tell you that the militia of the country is not to be relied upon—that it is only in the regular army of the United States that you are to find men competent to fight the battles of the country, and from time to time when that necessity has seemed to arise, forgetting this old doctrine, that a large standing army in time of peace was always dangerous to human liberty, we have increased that army from six thousand up to about sixteen thousand men. Mr. President, the other day we gave ten regiments more; and for not giving it within the quick time demanded by our master, the commander-in-chief, some minion, I know not who, for I have not looked into this matter until this morning, feeding upon the fly-blown remnants that fall from the Executive shambles and lie putrefying there, has denounced us as Mexicans, and called the American republic to take notice, that there was in the Senate, a body of men chargeable with incivism—Mexicans in heart—traitors to the United States. . . .

It must have occurred to everybody how utterly impotent the Congress of the United States *now* is for any purpose whatever, but that of yielding to the President every demand which he makes for men and money, unless they assume that *only* position which is left—that which, in the history of other countries, in times favorable to human liberty, has been so often resorted to as a check upon arbitrary power —withholding money, refusing to grant the services of men when demanded for purposes which are not deemed to be proper.

When I review the doctrines of the majority here, and consider their application to the existing war, I confess I am at a loss to determine whether the world is to consider our conduct as a ridiculous farce, or be lost in amazement at such absurdity in a people calling themselves free. The President, without asking the consent of Congress, involves us in war, and the majority here, without reference to the justice or necessity of the war, call upon us to grant men and money at the pleasure of the President, who they say, is charged with the duty of carrying on the war and responsible for its result. If we grant the means thus demanded, the President can carry forward this war for any end, or from any motive, without limit of time or place.

With these doctrines for our guide, I will thank any Senator to furnish me with any means of escaping from the prosecution of this or any other war for a hundred years to come, if it pleased the President who shall be, to continue it so long. Tell me, ye who contend that being in war, duty demands of Congress for its prosecution, all the money and every able-bodied man in America to carry it on if need be; who also contend that it is the right of the President, without the control of Congress, to march your embodied hosts to Monterey, to Yucatan, to Mexico, to Panama, to China, and that under penalty of death to the officer who disobeys him—tell me, I demand it of you, tell me, tell the American people, tell the nations of Christendom, what is the difference between your American democracy and the most odious, most hateful despotism, that a merciful God has ever allowed a nation to be afflicted with since government on earth began? . . .

I have looked at this subject with a painful endeavor to come to the conclusion, if possible, that it was my duty, as a Senator of the United States, finding the country in war, to "fight it out," as we say in the common and popular phrase of the times, to a just and honorable peace! I could very easily concede that to be my duty if I found my country engaged in a just war—in a war necessary even to protect that fancied honor of which you talk so much. . . .

But when I am asked to say whether I will prosecute a war, I cannot answer that question, yea or nay, until I have determined whether that was a *necessary* war; and I cannot determine whether it was necessary until I know how it was that my country was involved in it. And it is to that particular point, Mr. President—without reading documents, but referring to a few facts which I understand not to be denied on either side of this chamber—that I wish to direct the attention of the American Senate, and so far as may be, that of any of the noble and honest-hearted constituents whom I represent here. I know, Mr. President, the responsibility which I assume in undertaking to determine that the President of the United States has done a great wrong to the country, whose honor and whose interest he was required to protect. I know the denunciations which await every one who shall dare to put himself in opposition to that high power—that idol god—which the people of this country have made to themselves and called a President. . . .

Sir, I know that the *people* of the United States neither sought nor forced Mexico into this war, and yet I know that the President of the United States, with the command of your standing army, did seek that war, and that *he* forced the war upon Mexico. . . .

Mr. President, I trust we shall abandon the idea, the heathen, barbarian notion, that our true national glory is to be won, or retained, by military prowess or skill in the art of destroying life. And, while I cannot but lament, for the permanent and lasting renown of my country, that she should command the service of her children in what I must consider wanton, unprovoked, *unnecessary*, and, therefore, unjust war, I can yield to the brave soldier, whose trade is war, and whose duty is obedience, the highest meed of praise for his courage, his enterprise and perpetual endurance of the fatigues and horrors of war. I know the gallant men who are engaged in fighting your battles possess personal bravery equal to any troops, in any land, anywhere engaged in the business of war. I do not believe we are less capable in the art of destruction than others, or less willing, on the slightest pretext, to unsheath the sword, and consider "revenge a virtue." I could wish, also, that your brave soldiers, while they bleed and die on the battle-field, might have (what in this war is impossible) the consolation to feel and know that their blood flowed in defense of a great right—that their lives were a meet sacrifice to an exalted principle.

But sir, I return to our relations with Mexico. Texas, . . . having won her independence, and torn from Mexico about one-fourth part of her territory, comes to the United States, sinks her national character into the less elevated, but more secure, position of *one* of the United States of America. The revolt of Texas, her successful war with Mexico, and a consequent loss of a valuable province, all inured to the ultimate benefit of our Government and our country. While Mexico was weakened and humbled, we, in the same proportion, were strengthened and elevated. All this was done against the wish, the interest and the earnest remonstrance of Mexico.

Every one can feel, if he will examine himself for a moment, what must have been the mingled emotions of pride, humiliation and bitter indignation, which raged in the bosoms of the Mexican people, when they saw one of their fairest provinces torn from them by a revolution, moved by a foreign people; and that province, by our act and our consent, annexed to the already enormous expanse of our territory. It is idle, Mr. President, to suppose that the Mexican people would not feel as deeply for the dismemberment and disgrace of their country as you would for the dismemberment of the Union of ours. Sir, there is not a race, nor tribe, nor people on the earth, who have an organized social or political existence, who have clung with more obstinate affection to every inch of soil they could call their own, than this very Spanish, this Mexican, this Indian race, in that country. . . . Do you wonder, therefore, after all this, that when Texas did thus forcibly pass away from them and come to us, that prejudice amounting to hate, resentment implacable as revenge toward us, should seize and possess and madden the entire population of a country thus weakened, humbled, contemned?

Mr. President, how would the fire of indignation have burned in every bosom here if the government of Canada, with the connivance of the Crown of England, had permitted its people to arm themselves, or it might be, had allowed its regiments of trained mercenary troops stationed there to invade New York and excite her to revolt, telling them that the Crown of England was the natural and paternal ruler of any people desiring to be free and happy—that your government was weak, factious, oppressive—that man withered under its baleful influence—that your stars and stripes were only emblems of degradation and symbols of faction—that England's lion, rampant on his field of gold, was the appropriate emblem of power and symbol of national glory—and they succeeded in alienating the weak or wicked of your people from you—should we not then have waged exterminating war upon England, in every quarter of the globe, where her people were to be found? . . . Yet, the question being reversed, that is precisely the condition in which Mexico stood toward you after San Jacinto was fought, and on the day Texas was annexed.

Your people did go to Texas. I remember it well. They went to Texas to fight for their rights. They could not fight for them in their own country. Well, they fought for their rights. They conquered them! They "conquered a peace!" They were your citizens—not Mexicans. They were recent emigrants to that country. They went there for the very purpose of seizing on that country and making it a free and independent republic, with a view, as some of them said, of bringing it into the American confederacy in due time. . . . Is the Mexican man sunk so low that he cannot hear what fills the mouth and ear of rumor all over this country? He knows that this was the settled purpose of some of your people. He knows that your avarice had fixed its eagle glance on these rich acres in Mexico, and that your proud power counted the number that could be brought against you, and that your avarice and your power together marched on to the subjugation of the third or fourth part of the Republic of Mexico, and took it from her. We knew this, and knowing it, what should have been the feeling and sentiment in the mind of the President of the United States toward such a people—a people at least in their own opinion so deeply injured by us as were these Mexicans.

The Republic of Texas comes under the government of the United States, and it happens that the minister resident at your court—and it is a pretty respectable court, Mr. President,—we have something of a king—not for life, it is true, but a quadrennial sort of a monarch, who does very much as he pleases—the minister resident at that court of yours stated at the time that this revolted province of Texas was claimed by Mexico, and that if you received it as one of the sovereign states of this Union, right or wrong, it was impossible to reason with his people about it—they would consider it as an act of hostility. Did you consult the national feeling of Mexico then? . . .

But this was not agreeable to the lofty conceptions of the President. He preferred a vigorous war to the tame process of peaceful adjustment. He now throws down the pen of the diplomat, and grasps the sword of the warrior. Your army, with brave old "Rough and Ready" at its head, is ordered to pass the Nueces, and advance to the east bank of the Rio Grande. There, sir, between these two rivers, lies that slip of territory, that chapparal thicket, interspersed with Mexican haciendas, out of which this wasteful, desolating war arose. Was this territory beyond the river Nueces in the State of Texas?

Now I have said, that I would not state any disputable fact. It is known to every man who has looked into this subject, that a revolutionary government can claim no jurisdiction anywhere when it has not defined and exercised its power with the sword. It was utterly indifferent to Mexico and the world what legislative enactments Texas made. She extended her revolutionary government and her revolutionary dominion not one inch beyond the extent to which she had carried the power of Texas in opposition to the power of Mexico.

It is therefore a mere question of fact; and how will it be pretended that that country, lying between the Nueces and the Del Norte, to which your army was ordered, and of which it took possession, was subject to Texan law and not Mexican law? What did your general find there? What did he write home? Do you hear of any trial by jury on the east bank of the Rio Grande—of Anglo-Saxons making cotton there with their Negroes? No! You hear of Mexicans residing peacefully there, but fleeing from their cottonfields at the approach of your army—no slaves, for it had been a decree of the Mexican government, years ago, that no slaves should exist there. If there were a Texan population on the east bank of the Rio Grande, why did not General Taylor hear something of those Texans hailing the advent of the American army, coming to protect them from the ravages of the Mexicans! . . .

Do you hear anything of that? No ! On the contrary, the population fled at the approach of your army. In God's name, I wish to know if it has come to this, that when an American army goes to protect American citizens on American territory, they flee from it as if from the most barbarous enemy? Yet such is the ridiculous assumption of those who pretend that, on the east bank of the Rio Grande, where your arms took possession, there were Texan population, Texan power, Texan laws, and American United States power and law! No, Mr. President, when I see that stated in an Executive document, written by the finger of a President of the United States, and when you read in those documents, with which your tables groan, the veracious account of that noble old General Taylor, of his reception in that country, and of those men—to use the language of one of his officers—fleeing before the invaders; when you compare these two documents together, is it not a biting sarcasm upon the *sincerity* of public men—a bitter satire upon the *gravity* of all public affairs?

Can it be, Mr. President, that the honest, generous, Christian people of the United States will give countenance to this egregious, palpable misrepresentation of fact—this bold falsification of history? Shall it be written down in your public annals, when the world looking on and you yourselves know, that Mexico, and not Texas, possessed this territory to which your armies marched? As Mexico had never been dispossessed by Texan power, neither Texas nor your Government had any more claim to it than you now have to California, that other possession of Mexico over which your all-grasping avarice has already extended its remorseless dominion. . . .

All this mass of undeniable fact, known even to the careless reader of the public prints, is so utterly at war with the studiously-contrived statements in your cabinet documents, that I do not wonder at all that an amiable national pride, however misplaced here, has prevented hitherto a thorough and fearless investigation of their truth. Nor, sir, would I probe this feculent mass of misrepresentation, had I not been compelled to it in defense of votes which I was obliged to record here, within the last ten days. Sir, with my opinions as to facts connected with this subject, and my deductions, unavoidable, from them, I should have been unworthy the high-souled State I represent, had I voted men and money to prosecute further a war commenced, as it now appears, in aggression, and carried on by repetition only of the original wrong. Am I mistaken in this? If I am, I shall hold him the dearest friend I can own, in any relation of life, who shall show me my error. If I am wrong in this question of fact, show me how I err, and gladly will I retrace my steps; satisfy me that my country was in peaceful and rightful possession between the Nueces and Rio Grande when General Taylor's army was ordered there; show me that at Palo Alto and Resaca de las Palmas blood was shed on American soil in American possession, and then, for the *defense* of that possession, I will vote away the last dollar that power can wring from the people, and send every man able to bear a musket to the ranks of war. But until I shall be thus convinced, duty to myself, to truth, to conscience, to public justice, requires that I persist in every lawful opposition to this war.

While the American President can command the army, thank Heaven I can command the purse. While the President, under the penalty of death, can command your officers to proceed, I can tell them to come back, or the President can supply them as he may. He shall have no funds from me in the prosecution of a war which I cannot approve. That I conceive to be the duty of a Senator. I am not mistaken in that. If it be my duty to grant whatever the President demands, for what am I here? Have I no will upon the subject? Is it not placed at my discretion, understanding, judgement? Have an American Senate and House of Representatives nothing to do but obey the bidding of the President, as the army he commands is compelled to obey under penalty of death? No! The representatives of the sovereign people and sovereign States were never elected for such purposes as that. . . .

When, in 1688, [the] doctrine of specific appropriations became a part of the British constitution, the King could safely be trusted with the control of the army. If war is made there by the Crown, and the Commons do not approve of it, refusal to grant supplies is the easy remedy—one, too, which renders it impossible for a king of England to carry forward any war which may be displeasing to the English people. Yes, sir, in England, since 1688, it has not been in the power of a British sovereign to do that, which in your boasted republic, an American president, under the auspices of what you call democracy, has done—make war, without consent of the legislative power. In England, supplies are at once refused, if Parliament does not approve the objects of the war. *Here*, we are told, we must not look to the objects of the war, being *in the war*—made by the President—we must help him to fight it out, should it even please him to carry it to the utter extermination of the Mexican race. Sir, I believe it must proceed to this shocking extreme, if you are, by war, to "conquer a peace." Here, then, is your condition. The President involves you in war without your consent. Being *in* such a war, it is demanded as a duty, that we grant men and money to carry it on. The President tells us he shall prosecute this war, till Mexico pays us, or agrees to pay us, all its expenses. I am not willing to scourge Mexico thus; and the only means left me is to say to the commander-in-chief, "Call home your army, I will feed and clothe it no longer; you have whipped Mexico in three pitched battles, this is revenge enough; this is punishment enough."

The President has said he does not expect to hold Mexican territory by conquest. Why then conquer it? Why waste thousands of lives and millions of money fortifying towns and creating governments, if, at the end of the war, you retire from the graves of your soldiers and the desolated country of your foes, only to get money from Mexico for the expense of all your toil and sacrifice? Who ever heard, since Christianity was propagated among men, of a nation taxing its people, enlisting its young men and marching off two thousand miles to fight a people merely to be paid for it in money? What is this but hunting a market for blood, selling the lives of your young men, marching them in regiments to be slaughtered and paid for, like oxen and brute beasts? Sir, this is, when stripped naked, that atrocious idea first promulgated in the President's message, and now advocated here, of fighting on till we can get our indemnity for the past as well as the present slaughter. We have chastised Mexico, and if it were worth while to do so, we have, I dare say, satisfied the world that we can fight. What now? Why the mothers of America are asked to send another of their sons to blow out the brains of Mexicans because they refuse to pay the price of the first who fell there, fighting for glory! And what if the second fall, too? The Executive, the parental reply, is,"we shall have him paid for, we shall get full indemnity!" Sir, I have no patience with this flagitious notion of fighting for indemnity, and this under the equally absurd and hypocritical pretense of securing an honorable peace. An honorable peace! If you have accomplished the objects of the war (if indeed you had an object which you dare to avow), cease to fight, and you will have peace. . . .

You may wrest provinces from Mexico by war—you may hold them by the right of the strongest—you may rob her, but a treaty of peace to that effect with the people of Mexico, legitimately and freely made, you never will have! I thank God that it is so, as well for the sake of the Mexican people as ourselves, for, unlike the Senator from Alabama [Mr. Bagby], I do not value the life of a citizen of the United States above the lives of a hundred thousand Mexican women and children—a rather cold sort of philanthropy, in my judgment. For the sake of Mexico then, as well as our own country, I rejoice that it is an impossibility, that you can obtain by treaty from her those territories, under the existing state of things. . . .

What is the territory, Mr. President, which you propose to wrest from Mexico? It is consecrated to the heart of the Mexican by many a well-fought battle, with his old Castilian master. His Bunker Hills, and Saratogas, and Yorktowns are there. The Mexican can say, "There I bled for liberty! and shall I surrender that consecrated home of my affections to the Anglo-Saxon invaders? What do they want with it? They have Texas already. They have possessed themselves of the territory between the Nueces and the Rio Grande. What else do they want? To what shall I point my children as memorials of that independence which I bequeath to them, when those battle-fields shall have passed from my possession?"

Sir, had one come and demanded Bunker Hill of the people of Massachusetts, had England's lion ever showed himself there, is there a man over thirteen, and under ninety who would not have been ready to meet him—is there a river on this continent that would not have run red with blood—is there a field but would have been piled high with the unburied bones of slaughtered Americans before these conse-crated battle-fields of liberty should have been wrested from us? But this same American goes into a sister republic, and says to poor, weak Mexico, "Give up your territory—you are unworthy to possess it— I have got one-half already—all I ask of you is to give up the other!" . . . Why, my worthy Christian brother, on what principle of justice? "I want room!"

Sir, look at this pretense of want of room. With twenty millions of people, you have about one thousand millions of acres of land, invit-ing settlement by every conceivable argument—bringing them down to a quarter of a dollar an acre, and allowing every man to squat where he pleases. But the Senator from Michigan says we will be two hun-dred millions in a few years, and we want room. If I were a Mexican I would tell you, "Have you not room in your own country to bury your dead men? If you come into mine we will greet you with bloody hands, and welcome you to hospitable graves."

Why, says the Chairman of this Committee on Foreign Relations, it is the most reasonable thing in the world! We ought to have the Bay of San Francisco. Why? Because it is the best harbor on the Pacific! It has been my fortune, Mr. President, to have practiced a good deal in criminal courts in the course of my life, but I never yet heard a thief, arraigned for stealing a horse, plead that it was the best horse that he could find in the country! . . .

Sir, I have read, in some account of your battle of Monterey, of a lovely Mexican girl, who, with the benevolence of an angel in her bosom, and the robust courage of a hero in her heart, was busily engaged, during the bloody conflict, amid the crash of falling houses, the groans of the dying, and the wild shriek of battle, in carrying water to slake the burning thirst of the wounded of either host. While bending over a wounded American soldier, a cannon-ball struck her and blew her to atoms! Sir, I do not charge my brave, generous-hearted countrymen who fought that fight with this. No, no! We who send them—we who know that scenes like this, which might send tears of sorrow "down Pluto's iron cheek," are the invariable, inevitable attendants on war—we are accountable for this. And this—this is the way we are to be made known to Europe. This—*this* is to be the undying renown of free, republican America! "She has stormed a city—killed many of its inhabitants of both sexes—she has room!" *So* it will read. Sir, if this were our only history, then may God of His mercy grant that its volume may speedily come to a close. . . .

Do we not know, Mr. President, that it is a law never to be repealed, that falsehood shall be short lived? Was it not ordained of old that truth only shall abide forever? Whatever we may say to-day, or whatever we may write in our books, the stern tribunal of history will review it all, detect falsehood, and bring us to judgment before that posterity which shall bless or curse us, as we may act *now*, wisely or otherwise. We may hide in the grave (which awaits us all) in vain; we may hope there, like the foolish bird that hides its head in the sand, in the vain belief that its body is not seen, yet even there this preposterous excuse of want of "room" shall be laid bare, and the quick-coming future will decide that it was a hypocritical pretense, under which we sought to conceal the avarice which prompted us to covet and to seize by force *that* which was not ours.

Mr. President, this uneasy desire to augment our territory has depraved the moral sense and blunted the otherwise keen sagacity of our people. What has been the fate of all nations who have acted upon the idea that they must advance! Our young orators cherish this notion with a fervid, but fatally mistaken zeal. They call it by the mysterious name of "destiny." "Our destiny," they say is "onward," and hence they argue, with ready sophistry, the propriety of seizing upon any territory and any people that may lie in the way of our "fated" advance. Recently these progressives have grown classical; some assiduous student of antiquities has helped them to a patron saint. They have wandered back into the desolated Pantheon, and there, among the Polytheistic relics of that "pale mother of dead empires," they have found a god whom these Romans, centuries gone by, baptized "Terminus." . . .

Whoever would know the further fate of this Roman deity, so recently taken under the patronage of American democracy, may find ample gratification of his curiosity in the luminous pages of Gibbon's "Decline and Fall." Such will find that Rome thought as you now think, that it was her destiny to conquer provinces and nations, and no doubt she sometimes said as you say, "I will conquer a peace," and where now is she, the Mistress of the World? The spider weaves his web in her palaces, the owl sings his watch-song in her towers. Teutonic power now lords it over the servile remnant, the miserable momento of old and once omnipotent Rome. Sad, very sad, are the lessons which time has written for us. Through and in them all, I see nothing but the inflexible execution of that old law, which ordains as eternal, that cardinal rule, "Thou shalt not covet thy neighbor's goods, nor *anything* which is his." . . .

Mr. President, if the history of our race has established any truth, it is but a confirmation of what is written, "the way of the transgressor is hard." Inordinate ambition, wantoning in power and spurning the humble maxims of justice has—ever has—and ever shall end in ruin. Strength cannot always trample upon weakness—the humble shall be exalted, the bowed down will at length be lifted up. It is by faith in the law of strict justice, and the practice of its precepts, that nations alone can be saved. All the annals of the human race, sacred and profane, are written over with this great truth, in characters of living light. It is my fear, my fixed belief, that in this invasion, this war with Mexico, we have forgotten this vital truth. . . .

But, Mr. President, if further acquisition of territory is to be the result either of conquest or treaty, then I scarcely know which should be preferred, eternal war with Mexico, or the hazards of internal commotion at home, which last, I fear, *may* come if another province is to be added to our territory. There is one topic connected with this subject which I tremble when I approach, and yet I cannot forbear to notice it. It meets you in every step you take. It threatens you which way soever you go in the prosecution of this war. I allude to the question of slavery. Opposition to its further extension, it must be obvious to every one, is a deeply-rooted determination with men of all parties in what we call the non-slaveholding states. New York, Pennsylvania and Ohio, three of the most powerful, have already sent their legislative instructions here—so it will be, I doubt not, in all the rest. It is vain now to speculate about the reasons for this. Gentlemen of the south may call it prejudice, passion, hypocrisy, fanaticism. I shall not dispute with them now on that point. The great fact that it is so, and not otherwise, is what it concerns us to know. You nor I cannot alter or change this opinion if we would. These people only say, we will not, cannot consent that you shall carry slavery where it does not already exist. They do not seek to disturb you in that institution, as it exists in your states. Enjoy it if you will, and as you will. This is their language, this their determination. How is it in the south? Can it be expected that they should expend in common, their blood and their treasure, in the acquisition of immense territory, and then willingly forego the right to carry thither their slaves, and inhabit the conquered country if they please to do so? Sir, I know the feelings and opinions of the south too well to calculate on this. Nay, I believe they would even contend to any extremity for the mere *right*, had they no wish to exert it. I believe (and I confess I tremble when the conviction presses upon me) that there is equal obstinacy on both sides of this fearful question. If then, we persist in war, which if it terminate in anything short of a mere wanton waste of blood as well as money, must end (as this bill proposes) in the acquisition of territory, to which at once this controversy must attach—this bill would seem to be nothing less than a bill to produce internal commotion. Should we prosecute this war another moment or expend one dollar in the purchase or conquest of a single acre of Mexican land, the north and the south are brought into collision on a point where neither will yield. Who can foresee or foretell the result? Who so bold or reckless as to look such a conflict in the face unmoved? I do not envy the heart of him who can realize the possibility of such a conflict without emotions too painful to be endured. Why then shall we, the representatives of the sovereign states of this Union—the chosen guardians of this confederated republic, why should we precipitate this fearful struggle, by continuing a war, the results of which must be to force us at once upon it? Sir, rightly considered, *this* is treason, treason to the Union, treason to the dearest interests, the loftiest aspirations, the most cherished hopes of our constituents. It is a crime to risk the possibility of such a contest. . . .

Let us abandon all idea of acquiring further territory, and by consequence cease at once to prosecute this war. Let us call home our armies, and bring them at once within our own acknowledged limits. Show Mexico that you are sincere when you say you desire nothing by conquest. She has learned that she cannot encounter you in war, and if she had not, she is too weak to disturb you here. Tender her peace, and my life on it, she will then accept it. But whether she shall or not, you will have peace without her consent. It is your invasion that has made war, your retreat will restore peace. Let us then close forever the approaches of internal feud, and so return to the ancient concord and the old way of national prosperity and permanent glory. Let us here, in this temple consecrated to the Union, perform a solemn lustration; let us wash Mexican blood from our hands, and on these altars, in the presence of that image of the Father of his country that looks down upon us, swear to preserve honorable peace with all the world, and eternal brotherhood with each other.

4

CONSCIENCE WHIGGERY

Charles Sumner
ANTISLAVERY DUTIES OF THE WHIG PARTY

The remaining selections all deal with the sectional controversy over slavery that disrupted the Union and permanently destroyed the Whig party. As the party which had emphasized both national unity and national morality, the Whigs were torn apart by an issue that seemed to force them to choose one or the other.

Charles Sumner (1811–1874) was one of America's most courageous and principled statesmen. He turned his back on a lucrative Boston law practice to take up the banner of reform. He fought to improve conditions in prisons and to promote the cause of peace. As the following speech indicates, he belonged to the antislavery wing of the Whig party, the "Conscience" Whigs. Disappointed by the refusal of Webster and other prominent party members to take the strong stand against slavery here demanded, Sumner left the Whigs in 1848 to support the Free Soil movement. A United States senator from 1851 until his death, Sumner proved himself a consistent opponent of slavery and advocate of rights for the emancipated blacks. On a famous occasion in 1856 he was savagely clubbed on the Senate floor by a South Carolina congressman who crept up behind him while he was sitting at his desk.

MR. PRESIDENT AND FELLOW-CITIZENS, WHIGS OF MASSACHUSETTS:—
Grateful for the honor done me in this early call to address the convention, I shall endeavor to speak with sincerity and frankness on the duties of the Whig party. . . .

I am happy that the convention is convoked in Faneuil Hall—a place vocal with inspiring accents. . . . Whigs of Massachusetts, in

SOURCE. Charles Sumner, "Antislavery Duties of the Whig Party. Speech at the Whig State Convention of Massachusetts, in Faneuil Hall, Boston, September 23, 1846," *Works* (Boston, 1870), I, 304—316.

Faneuil Hall assembled, must be true to this early scene of patriot struggles; they must be true to their own name, which has descended from the brave men who took part in those struggles.

We are a convention of Whigs. And who are the Whigs? Some may say they are supporters of the tariff; others, that they are advocates of internal improvements, of measures to restrict the veto power, or it may be of a Bank. All these are now, or have been, prominent articles of the party. But this enumeration does not do justice to the Whig character.

The Whigs, as their name imports, are, or ought to be, the party of freedom. They seek, or should seek, on all occasions, to carry out fully and practically the principles of our institutions. Those principles which our fathers declared, and sealed with their blood, their Whig children should seek to manifest in acts. The Whigs, therefore, reverence the Declaration of Independence, as embodying the vital truths of freedom, especially that great truth, "that all men are created equal." They reverence the Constitution of the United States, and seek to guard it against infractions, believing that under the Constitution freedom can be best preserved. They reverence the Union, believing that the peace, happiness, and welfare of all depend upon this blessed bond. They reverence the public faith, and require that it shall be punctiliously kept in all laws, charters, and obligations. They reverence the principles of morality, truth, justice, right. They seek to advance their country rather than individuals, and to promote the welfare of the people rather than of leaders. . . .

Such is, as I trust, the Whig party of Massachusetts. It refuses to identify itself exclusively with those measures of transient policy which, like the Bank, may become "obsolete ideas," but connects itself with everlasting principles which can never fade or decay. Doing this, it does not neglect other things, as the tariff, or internal improvements; but it treats them as subordinate. Far less does it show indifference to the Constitution or the Union; for it seeks to render these guardians and representatives of the principles to which we are attached.

The Whigs have been called by you, Mr. President, *conservatives*. In a just sense, they should be conservatives—not of forms only, but of substance—not of the letter only, but of the living spirit. The Whigs should be conservators of the ancestral spirit, conservators of the animating ideas in which our institutions were born. They should profess that truest and highest conservatism which watches, guards, and preserves the great principles of Truth, Right, Freedom, and Humanity. Such a conservatism is not narrow and exclusive, but broad and expansive. It is not trivial and bigoted, but manly and generous. It is the conservatism of '76.

Let me say, then, that the Whigs of Massachusetts are—I hope it is not my wish only that is father to the thought—the party which seeks the establishment of Truth, Freedom, Right, and Humanity, under the Constitution of the United States, and by the Union of the states. They are Unionists, Constitutionalists, Friends of the Right.

The question here arises, How shall this party, inspired by these principles, now act? The answer is easy. In strict accordance with their principles. It must utter them with distinctness, and act upon them with energy.

The party will naturally express opposition to the present Administration for its treacherous course on the tariff; and for its interference by veto with internal improvements; but it will be more alive to evils of greater magnitude—the unjust and unchristian war with Mexico, which is not less absurd than wicked, and, beyond this, the institution of slavery.

The time, I believe, has gone by, when the question is asked, *What has the North to do with slavery?* It might almost be answered, that, politically, it has little to do with anything else—so are all the acts of our government connected, directly or indirectly, with this institution. Slavery is everywhere. Appealing to the Constitution, it enters the halls of Congress, in the disproportionate representation of the slave states. It holds its disgusting mart at Washington, in the shadow of the Capitol, under the legislative jurisdiction of the Nation—of the north as well as the south. It sends its miserable victims over the high seas, from the ports of Virginia to the ports of Louisiana, beneath the protecting flag of the republic. It presumes to follow into the free states those fugitives who, filled with the inspiration of freedom, seek our altars for safety; nay, more, with profane hands it seizes those who have never known the name of slave, freemen of the north, and dooms them to irremediable bondage. It insults and expels from its jurisdiction honored representatives of Massachusetts, seeking to secure for her colored citizens the peaceful safeguard of the Union. It assumes at pleasure to build up new slaveholding states, striving perpetually to widen its area, while professing to extend the area of freedom. It has brought upon the country war with Mexico, with its enormous expenditures and more enormous guilt. By the spirit of union among its supporters, it controls the affairs of government—interferes with the cherished interests of the north, enforcing and then refusing protection to her manufactures—makes and unmakes presidents—usurps to itself the larger portion of all offices of honor and profit, both in the army and navy, and also in the civil department—and stamps upon our whole country the character, before the world, of that monstrous anomaly and mockery, *a slaveholding republic,* with the living truths of freedom on its lips and the dark mark of slavery on its brow.

In opposition to slavery, Massachusetts has already, to a certain extent, done what becomes her character as a free commonwealth. By successive resolutions of her legislature, she has called for the abolition of slavery in the District of Columbia, and for the abolition of the slave-trade between the states; and she has also proposed an amendment of the Constitution, putting the south upon an equality with the north in congressional representation. More than this, her judiciary, always pure, fearless, and upright, has inflicted upon slavery the brand of reprobation. I but recall a familiar fact, when I refer to the opinion of the Supreme Court of Massachusetts, where it is expressly declared that "slavery is contrary to natural right, to the principles of justice, humanity, and sound policy." This is the law of Massachusetts.

And shall this commonwealth continue in any way to sustain an institution which its laws declare to be contrary to natural right, justice, humanity, and sound policy? Shall Whigs support what is contrary to the fundamental principles of the party? Here the consciences of good men respond to the judgment of the Court. If it be wrong to hold a single slave, it must be wrong to hold many. If it be wrong for an individual to hold a slave, it must be wrong for a state. If it be wrong for a state in its individual capacity, it must be wrong also in association with other states. Massachusetts does not allow any of her citizens within her borders to hold slaves. Let her be consistent, and call for the abolition of slavery wherever she is any way responsible for it, not only where she is a party to it, but wherever it may be reached by her influence—that is, everywhere beneath the Constitution and laws of the national government. "If any practices exist," said Mr. Webster, in one of those earlier efforts which commended him to our admiration, his Discourse at Plymouth in 1820—"if any practices exist contrary to the principles of justice and humanity, within the reach of our laws or our influence, *we are inexcusable, if we do not exert ourselves to restrain and abolish them.*" This is correct, worthy of its author, and of Massachusetts. It points directly to Massachusetts as inexcusable for not doing her best to restrain and abolish slavery everywhere within the reach of her laws or her influence.

Certainly, to labor in this cause is far higher and nobler than to strive for *repeal of the Tariff,* once the tocsin to rally the Whigs. REPEAL OF SLAVERY UNDER THE CONSTITUTION AND LAWS OF THE

NATIONAL GOVERNMENT is a watchword more Christian and more potent, because it embodies a higher sentiment and a more commanding duty.

The time has passed when this can be opposed on constitutional grounds. It will not be questioned by any competent authority, that Congress may, by express legislation, abolish slavery: first, in the District of Columbia; secondly, in the territories, if there should be any; thirdly, that it may abolish the slave-trade on the high seas between the states; fourthly, that it may refuse to admit new states with a constitution sanctioning slavery. Nor can it be questioned that the people of the United States may, in the manner pointed out by the Constitution, proceed to its amendment. It is, then, by constitutional legislation, and even by amendment of the Constitution, that slavery may be reached.

Here the question arises, Is there any *compromise* in the Constitution of such a character as to prevent action? This word is invoked by many honest minds as the excuse for not joining in this cause. Let me meet this question frankly and fairly. The Constitution, it is said, was the result of compromise between the free states and the slave states, which good faith will not allow us to break. To this it may be replied, that the slave states, by their many violations of the Constitution, have already overturned all the original compromises, if any there were of perpetual character. But I do not content myself with this answer. I wish to say, distinctly, that there is no compromise on slavery not to be reached *legally and constitutionally*, which is the only way in which I propose to reach it. Wherever powers and jurisdiction are secured to Congress, they may unquestionably be exercised in conformity with the Constitution; even in matters beyond existing powers and jurisdiction there is a constitutional method of action. The Constitution contains an article pointing out how, at any time, amendments may be made. This is an important element, giving to the Constitution a *progressive* character, and allowing it to be moulded according to new exigencies and conditions of feeling. The wise framers of this instrument did not treat the country as a Chinese foot—never to grow after its infancy—but anticipated the changes incident to its advance. "*Provided*, that no amendment which may be made prior to the year one thousand eight hundred and eight shall in any manner affect the first and fourth clauses in the ninth section of the first article, and that no state, without its consent, shall be deprived of its equal suffrage in the Senate." These are the words of the Constitution. They expressly designate what shall be sacred from amendment—what compromise shall be perpetual—and so doing, according to a familiar rule of law and of logic, virtually declare that the remainder of the Constitution may be amended. Already, since its adoption, twelve amendments have been made, and every year produces new projects. There has been a pressure on the floor of Congress to abrogate the veto, and also to limit the tenure of the presidential office. Let it be distinctly understood, then—and this is my answer to the pretension of binding compromise—that, in conferring upon Congress certain specified powers and jurisdiction, and also in providing for the amendment of the Constitution, its framers expressly established the means for setting aside what are vaguely called compromises of the Constitution. They openly declare, "Legislate as you please, in conformity with the Constitution; and even make amendments rendered proper by change of opinion or circumstances, following always the manner prescribed."

Nor can we dishonor the revered authors of the Constitution by supposing that they set their hands to it, believing that under it slavery was to be *perpetual*,—that the republic, which they had reared to its giant stature, snatched from heaven the sacred fire of freedom, only to be bound, like another Prometheus, in adamantine chains of Fate, while slavery, like another vulture, preyed upon its vitals. Let Franklin speak for them. He was President of the earliest Abolition Society in the United States, and in 1790, only two years after the adoption of the Constitution, addressed a petition to Congress, calling upon them to "step to the very verge of the power vested in them for discouraging every species of traffic in the persons of our fellow-men." Let Jefferson speak for them. His desire for the abolition of slavery was often expressed with philanthropic warmth and emphasis, and is too familiar to be quoted. Let Washington speak for them. "It is among my first wishes," he said, in a letter to John F. Mercer, "to see some plan adopted by which slavery in this country *may be abolished by law.*" And in his will, penned with his own hand, during the last year of his life, he bore his testimony again, by providing for the emancipation of all his slaves. . . .

I assume, then, that it is the duty of Whigs professing the principles of the fathers to express themselves openly, distinctly, and solemnly against slavery,—*not only against its further extension, but against its longer continuance under the Constitution and Laws of the Union.* But while it is their duty to enter upon this holy warfare, it should be their aim to temper it with moderation, with gentleness, with tenderness, towards slave-owners. These should be won, if possible, rather than driven, to the duties of emancipation. But emancipation should always be presented as the cardinal object of our national policy.

It is for the Whigs of Massachusetts now to say whether the republican edifice shall indeed be one where all the Christian virtues will be fellow-workers with them. The resolutions which they adopt, the platform of principles which they establish, must be the imperishable foundation of a true glory.

But it will not be sufficient to pass *resolutions* opposing slavery; we must choose *men* who will devote themselves earnestly, heartily, to the work,—who will enter upon it with awakened conscience, and with that valiant faith before which all obstacles disappear,—who will be ever loyal to truth, freedom, right, humanity,—who will not look for rules of conduct down to earth, in the mire of expediency, but with heaven-directed countenance seek those great "primal duties" which "shine aloft like stars," to illumine alike the path of individuals and of nations. They must be true to the principles of Massachusetts. They must not be northern men with southern principles, nor northern men under southern influences. They must be courageous and willing on all occasions to stand alone, provided right be with them. "Were there as many devils in Worms as there are tiles upon the roofs," said Martin Luther, "yet would I enter." Such a spirit is needed now by the advocates of right. They must not be ashamed of the name which belongs to Franklin, Jefferson, and Washington,—expressing the idea which should be theirs—Abolitionist. They must be thorough, uncompromising advocates of the repeal of slavery—of its abolition under the laws and Constitution of the United States. They must be Repealers, Abolitionists.

There are a few such now in Congress. Massachusetts has a venerable Representative [John Quincy Adams] whose aged bosom still glows with inextinguishable fires, like the central heats of the monarch mountain of the Andes beneath its canopy of snow. To this cause he dedicates the closing energies of a long and illustrious life. Would that all might join him!

There is a Senator of Massachusetts we had hoped to welcome here to-day, whose position is of commanding influence [Daniel Webster]. Let me address him with the respectful frankness of a constituent and friend. Already, Sir, by various labors, you have acquired an honorable place in the history of our country. By the vigor, argumentation, and eloquence with which you upheld the Union, and that interpretation of the Constitution which makes us a Nation, you have justly earned the title of *Defender of the Constitution.* By masterly and successful negotiation, and by efforts to compose the strife concerning Oregon, you have earned another title,—*Defender of Peace.* Pardon me, if I add, that there are yet other duties claiming your care, whose performance will be the crown of a long life in the public service. Do not forget them. Dedicate, Sir, the years happily in store for you, with all that precious experience which is yours, to grand endeavor, in the name of human freedom, for the overthrow of that terrible evil which now afflicts our country. . . . Do not shrink from the task. With the marvellous powers that are yours, under the auspicious influences of an awakened public sentiment, and under God, who smiles always upon conscientious labor for the welfare of man, we may hope for beneficent results. Assume, then, these unperformed duties. The aged shall bear witness to you; the young shall kindle with rapture, as they repeat the name of Webster; the large company of the ransomed shall teach their children and their children's children, to the latest generation, to call you blessed; and you shall have yet another title, never to be forgotten on earth or in heaven—*Defender of Humanity*,—by the side of which that earlier title will fade into insignificance, as the Constitution, which is the work of mortal hands, dwindles by the side of Man, created in the image of God.

To my mind it is clear that the time has arrived when the Whigs of Massachusetts, the party of freedom, owe it to their declared principles, to their character before the world, and to conscience, that they should place themselves firmly on this honest ground. They need not fear to stand alone. They need not fear separation from brethren with whom they have acted in concert. Better be separated even from them than from the right. Massachusetts can stand alone, if need be. The Whigs of Massachusetts can stand alone. Their motto should not be, "Our party, *howsoever bounded*," but "Our party, bounded always by the right." They must recognize the dominion of Right, or there will be none who will recognize the dominion of the party. Let us, then, in Faneuil Hall, beneath the images of our fathers, vow perpetual allegiance to the right, and perpetual hostility to slavery. Ours is a noble cause, nobler even than that of our fathers, inasmuch as it is more exalted to struggle for the freedom of *others* than for *our own*. The love of right, which is the animating impulse of our movement, is higher even than the love of freedom. But right, freedom, and humanity all concur in demanding the abolition of slavery.

5

THE HIGHER LAW

William H. Seward
FREEDOM IN THE NEW TERRITORIES

William H. Seward (1801–1872), a central figure in Whig history, came from western New York. He joined the Whigs from the Antimasonic party, a populistic movement that swept his region in the late 1820s and early 1830s. Together with Thurlow Weed and Horace Greeley he built a strong Whig organization. Seward compiled a progressive record as governor of New York from 1839 to 1843, promoting prison reform and state-financed internal improvements. Unlike many leaders of his party, Seward enjoyed good relations with the Roman Catholic hierarchy and supported (vainly) state aid for parochial schools. He did not succeed, however, in breaking the Democratic hold on Catholic immigrant voters.

The following was Seward's maiden speech on the floor of the United States Senate. It was delivered against the proposed Compromise of 1850, opening the territory acquired from Mexico to slavery. Webster and Clay were backing the Compromise, but Seward, in company with most northern Whigs, had become unalterably opposed to any further extension of slavery. The Compromise passed, revealing a severe split between the Conscience Whigs like Seward and the temporizing, harmonizing "Cotton" Whigs who composed most of the party leadership. In 1854 and 1855, realizing that the division could not be healed, Seward led his antislavery Whigs into the new Republican party.

It is insisted that the admission of California shall be attended by a COMPROMISE of questions which have arisen out of SLAVERY!

I AM OPPOSED TO ANY SUCH COMPROMISE, IN ANY AND ALL THE FORMS IN WHICH IT HAS BEEN PROPOSED; because, while admitting the purity and the patriotism of all from whom it is my misfortune to differ, I think all legislative compromises, which are not absolutely

SOURCE. William Henry Seward, "Freedom in the New Territories. A Speech in the Senate of the United States. March 11, 1850." *Works,* ed. George E. Baker (New York, 1853), I, 60–93.

necessary, radically wrong and essentially vicious. They involve the surrender of the exercise of judgment and conscience on distinct and separate questions, at distinct and separate times, with the indispensable advantages it affords for ascertaining truth. They involve a relinquishment of the right to reconsider in future the decisions of the present, on questions prematurely anticipated. And they are acts of usurpation as to future questions of the province of future legislators.

Sir, it seems to me as if slavery had laid its paralyzing hand upon myself, and the blood were coursing less freely than its wont through my veins, when I endeavor to suppose that such a compromise has been effected, and that my utterance forever is arrested upon all the great questions—social, moral, and political—arising out of a subject so important, and as yet so incomprehensible.

What am I to receive in this compromise? Freedom in California. It is well; it is a noble acquisition; it is worth a sacrifice. But what am I to give as an equivalent? A recognition of the claim to perpetuate slavery in the District of Columbia; forbearance toward more stringent laws concerning the arrest of persons suspected of being slaves found in the free states; forbearance from the *proviso* of freedom in the charters of new territories. None of the plans of compromise offered demand less than two, and most of them insist on all of these conditions. The equivalent, then, is, some portion of liberty, some portion of human rights in one region for liberty in another region. But California brings gold and commerce as well as freedom. I am, then, to surrender some portion of human freedom in the District of Columbia, and in East California and New Mexico, for the mixed consideration of liberty, gold, and power, on the Pacific coast. . . .

Why, sir, . . . California ought to come in, and must come in, whether slavery stand or fall in the District of Columbia; whether slavery stand or fall in New Mexico and Eastern California; and even whether slavery stand or fall in the slave states. California ought to come in, being a free state; and, under the circumstances of her conquest, her compact, her abandonment, her justifiable and necessary establishment of a constitution, and the inevitable dismemberment of the empire consequent upon her rejection, I should have voted for her admission even if she had come as a slave state. California ought to come in, and must come in at all events. It is, then, an independent, a paramount question. What, then, are these questions arising out of slavery, thus interposed, but collateral questions? They are unnecessary and incongruous, and therefore false issues, not introduced designedly, indeed, to defeat that great policy, yet unavoidably tending to that end. . . .

It is now avowed by the honorable senator from South Carolina [Mr. Calhoun] that nothing will satisfy the slave states but a compromise that will convince them that they can remain in the Union consistently with their honor and their safety. And what are the concessions which will have that effect. Here they are, in the words of that senator:

"The north must do justice by conceding to the south an equal right in the acquired territory, and do her duty by causing the stipulations relative to fugitive slaves to be faithfully fulfilled—cease the agitation of the slave question, and provide for the insertion of a provision in the Constitution, by an amendment, which will restore to the south in substance the power she possessed, of protecting herself, before the equilibrium between the sections was destroyed by the action of this government."

These terms amount to this: that the free states having already, or although they may hereafter have, majorities of population, and majorites in both houses of Congress, shall concede to the slave states, being in a minority in both, the unequal advantage of an equality. That is, that we shall alter the Constitution so as to convert the Government from a national democracy, operating by a constitutional majority of voices, into a federal alliance, in which the minority shall have a veto against the majority. And this would be nothing less than to return to the original Articles of Confederation.

I will not stop to protest against the injustice or the inexpediency of an innovation which, if it was practicable, would be so entirely subversive of the principle of democratic institutions. It is enough to say that it is totally impracticable. The free states, northern and western, have acquiesced in the long and nearly unbroken ascendency of the slave states under the Constitution, because the result happened under the Constitution. But they have honor and interests to preserve, and there is nothing in the nature of mankind, or in the character of that people to induce an expectation that they, loyal as they are, are insensible to the duty of defending them. But the scheme would still be impracticable, even if this difficulty were overcome. What is proposed is a *political* equilibrium. Every political equilibrium requires a *physical* equilibrium to rest upon, and is valueless without it. To constitute a physical equilibrium between the slave states and the free states, requires, first, an equality of territory, or some near approximation. And this is already lost. But it requires much more than this. It requires an equality or a proximate equality in the number of slaves and freemen. And this must be perpetual.

But the census of 1840 gives a slave basis of only 2,500,000, and a free basis of 14,500,000. And the population on the slave basis increases in the ratio of 25 per cent for ten years, while that on the free basis advances at the rate of 38 per cent. The accelerating movement of the free population, now complained of, will occupy the new territories with pioneers, and every day increases the difficulty of forcing or insinuating slavery into regions which freemen have pre-occupied. And if this were possible, the African slave trade is prohibited, and the domestic increase is not sufficient to supply the new slave states which are expected to maintain the equilibrium. The theory of a new political equilibrium claims that it once existed, and has been lost. When lost, and how? It began to be lost in 1787, when preliminary arrangements were made to admit five new free states in the northwest territory, two years before the Constitution was finally adopted; that is, it began to be lost two years before it began to exist!

Sir, the equilibrium, if restored, would be lost again, and lost more rapidly than it was before. The progress of the free population is to be accelerated by increased emigration, and by new tides from South America and from Europe and Asia, while that of the slaves is to be checked and retarded by inevitable partial emancipation. "Nothing," says Montesquieu, "reduces a man so low as always to see freemen, and yet not be free. Persons in that condition are natural enemies of the state, and their numbers would be dangerous if increased too high." Sir, the fugitive slave colonies and the emancipated slave colonies in the free states, in Canada, and in Liberia, are the best guaranties South Carolina has for the perpetuity of slavery.

Nor would success attend any of the details of this compromise. And, first, I advert to the proposed alteration of the law concerning fugitives from service or labor. I shall speak on this as on all subjects, with due respect, but yet frankly and without reservation. The Constitution contains only a compact, which rests for its execution on the states. Not content with this, the slave states induced legislation by Congress; and the Supreme Court of the United States have virtually decided that the whole subject is within the province of Congress, and exclusive of state authority. Nay, they have decided that slaves are to be regarded not merely as persons to be claimed, but as property and chattels, to be seized without any legal authority or claim whatever. The compact is thus subverted by the procurement of the slave states. With what reason, then, can they expect the states *ex gratia* to reassume the obligations from which they caused those states to be discharged? I say, then, to the slave states, you are entitled to no more stringent laws; and that such laws would be useless. The cause of the inefficiency of the present statute is not at all the leniency of its provisions. It is a law that deprives the alleged refugee from a legal obligation not assumed by him, but imposed upon him by laws enacted before he was born, of the writ of *habeas corpus*, and of any certain judicial process of examination of the claim set up by his pursuer, and finally degrades him into a chattel which may be seized and carried away peaceably wherever found, even although exercising the rights and responsibilities of a free citizen of the commonwealth in which he resides, and of the United States—a law which denies to the citizen all the safeguards of personal liberty, to render less frequent the escape of the bondman. And since complaints are so freely made against the one side, I shall not hesitate to declare that there have been even greater faults on the other side. Relying on the perversion of the Constitution, which makes slaves mere chattels, the slave states have applied to them the principles of the criminal law, and have held that he who aided the escape of his fellow-man from bondage was guilty of a larceny in stealing him. I speak of what I know. Two instances came within my own knowledge, in which governors of slave states, under the provision of the Constitution relating to fugitives from justice, demanded from the governor of a free state the surrender of persons as thieves whose alleged offences consisted in constructive larceny of the rags that covered the persons of female slaves, whose attempt at escape they had permitted or assisted.

We deem the principle of the law for the recapture of fugitives, as thus expounded, therefore, unjust, unconstitutional, and immoral; and thus, while patriotism withholds its approbation, the consciences of our people condemn it.

You will say that these convictions of ours are disloyal. Grant it for the sake of argument. They are, nevertheless, honest; and the law is to be executed among us, not among you; not by us, but by the federal authority. Has any government ever succeeded in changing the moral convictions of its subjects by force? But these convictions imply no disloyalty. We reverence the Constitution, although we perceive this defect, just as we acknowledge the splendor and the power of the sun, although its surface is tarnished with here and there an opaque spot.

Your constitution and laws convert hospitality to the refugee from the most degrading oppression on earth into a crime, but all mankind except you esteem that hospitality a virtue. . . . We are not slave-holders. We cannot, in our judgment, be either true Christians or real freemen, if we impose on another a chain that we defy all human power to fasten on ourselves. You believe and think otherwise, and doubtless with equal sincerity. We judge you not, and He alone who ordained the conscience of man and its laws of action can judge us. Do we, then, in this conflict of opinion, demand of you an unreasonable thing in asking that, since you will have property that can and will exercise human powers to effect its escape, you shall be your own police, and in acting among us as such you shall conform to principles indispensable to the security of admitted rights of freemen? If you will have this law executed, you must alleviate, not increase, its rigors.

Another feature in most of these plans of compromise is a bill of peace for slavery in the District of Columbia; and this bill of peace we cannot grant. We of the free states are, equally with you of the slave states, responsible for the existence of slavery in this district, the field exclusively of our common legislation. I regret that, as yet, I see little reason to hope that a majority in favor of emancipation exists here. The legislature of New York, from whom, with great deference, I dissent, seems willing to accept now the extinction of the slave trade, and waive emancipation. But we shall assume the whole responsibility if we stipulate not to exercise the power hereafter when a majority shall be obtained. Nor will the plea with which you would furnish us be of any avail. If I could understand so mysterious a paradox myself, I never should be able to explain to the apprehension of the people whom I represent, how it was that an absolute and express power to legislate in all cases over the District of Columbia was embarrassed and defeated by an implied condition not to legislate for the abolition of slavery in this district. . . .

I apply the same observations to the proposition for a waiver of the proviso of freedom in territorial charters. Thus far you have only direct popular action in favor of that ordinance, and there seems even to be a partial disposition to await the action of the people of the new territories, as we have compulsorily waited for it in California. But I must tell you, nevertheless, in candor and in plainness, that the spirit of the people of the free states is set upon a spring that rises with the pressure put upon it. That spring, if pressed too hard, will give a recoil that will not leave here one servant who knew his master's will, and did it not.

You will say that this implies violence. Not at all. It implies only peaceful, lawful, constitutional, customary action. . . .

There is another aspect of the principle of compromise which deserves consideration. It assumes that slavery, if not the only institution in a slave state, is at least a ruling institution, and that this characteristic is recognized by the Constitution. But *slavery* is only *one* of many institutions there. Freedom is equally an institution there. Slavery is only a temporary, accidental, partial, and incongruous one. Freedom, on the contrary, is a perpetual, organic, universal one, in harmony with the Constitution of the United States. The slaveholder himself stands under the protection of the latter, in common with all the free citizens of the state. But it is, moreover, an indispensable institution. You may separate slavery from South Carolina, and the state will still remain; but if you subvert freedom there, the state will cease to exist. But the principle of this compromise gives complete ascendency in the slave states, and in the Constitution of the United States, to the subordinate, accidental, and incongruous institution, over its paramount antagonist. To reduce this claim of slavery to an absurdity, it is only necessary to add that there are only two states in which slaves are a majority, and not one in which the slaveholders are not a very disproportionate minority.

But there is yet another aspect in which this principle must be examined. It regards the domain only as a possession, to be enjoyed either in common or by partition by the citizens of the old states. It is true, indeed, that the national domain is ours. It is true it was acquired by the valor and with the wealth of the whole nation. But we hold, nevertheless, no arbitrary power over it. We hold no arbitrary authority over anything, whether acquired lawfully or seized by usurpation. The Constitution regulates our stewardship; the Constitution devotes the domain to union, to justice, to defence, to welfare, and to liberty.

But there is a higher law than the Constitution, which regulates our authority over the domain, and devotes it to the same noble purposes. The territory is a part, no inconsiderable part, of the common heritage of mankind, bestowed upon them by the Creator of the universe. We are his stewards, and must so discharge our trust as to secure in the highest attainable degree their happiness. . . . Shall we, who are founding institutions, social and political, for countless millions; shall we, who know by experience the wise and the just, and are free to choose them, and to reject the erroneous and unjust; shall we establish human bondage, or permit it by our sufferance to be established? Sir, our forefathers would not have hesitated an hour. They found slavery existing here, and they left it only because they could not remove it. There is not only no free state which would now establish it, but there is no slave state, which, if it had had the free alternative as we now have, would have founded slavery. Indeed, our revolutionary predecessors had precisely the same question before them in establishing an organic law under which the states of Ohio, Indiana, Michigan, Illinois, and Wisconsin, have since come into the Union, and they solemnly repudiated and excluded slavery from those states forever. I confess that the most alarming evidence of our degeneracy which has yet been given is found in the fact that we even debate such a question.

Sir, there is no Christian nation, thus free to choose as we are, which would establish slavery. I speak on due consideration, because Britain, France, and Mexico, have abolished slavery, and all other European states are preparing to abolish it as speedily as they can. We cannot establish slavery, because there are certain elements of the security, welfare, and greatness of nations, which we all admit, or ought to admit, and recognize as essential; and these are the security of natural rights, the diffusion of knowledge, and the freedom of industry. Slavery is incompatible with all of these; and, just in proportion to the extent that it prevails and controls in any republican state, just to that extent it subverts the principle of democracy, and converts the state into an aristocracy or a despotism. . . . Of all slavery, African slavery is the worst, for it combines practically the features of what is distinguished as real slavery or serfdom with the personal slavery known in the oriental world. Its domestic features lead to vice, while its political features render it injurious and dangerous to the state.

I cannot stop to debate long with those who maintain that slavery is itself practically economical and humane. I might be content with saying that there are some axioms in political science that a statesman or a founder of states may adopt, especially in the Congress of the United States, and that among those axioms are these: That all men are created equal, and have inalienable rights of life, liberty, and the choice of pursuits of happiness; that knowledge promotes virtue, and righteousness exalteth a nation; that freedom is preferable to slavery, and that democratic governments, where they can be maintained by acquiescence, without force, are preferable to institutions exercising arbitrary and irresponsible power. . . . These are my reasons for declining to compromise the question relating to slavery as a condition of the admission of California. . . .

And this brings me to the great and all-absorbing argument that the Union is in danger of being dissolved, and that it can only be saved by compromise. I do not know what I would not do to save the Union; and therefore I shall bestow upon this subject a very deliberate consideration. . . .

I see nothing of that conflict between the southern and northern states, or between their representative bodies, which seems to be on all sides of me assumed. Not a word of menace, not a word of anger, not an intemperate word, has been uttered in the northern legislatures. They firmly but calmly assert their convictions; but at the same time they assert their unqualified consent to submit to the common arbiter, and for weal or woe abide the fortunes of the Union.

What if there be less of moderation in the legislatures of the south? It only indicates on which side the balance is inclining, and that the decision of the momentous question is near at hand. I agree with those who say that there can be no peaceful dissolution—no dissolution of the Union by the secession of states; but that disunion, dissolution, happen when it may, will and must be revolution. I discover no omens of revolution. . . .

Sir, in any condition of society there can be no revolution without a cause, an adequate cause. What cause exists here? We are admitting a new state; but there is nothing new in that: we have already admitted seventeen before. But it is said that the slave states are in danger of losing political power by the admission of the new state. Well, sir, is there anything new in that? The slave states have always been losing political power, and they always will be while they have any to lose. At first, twelve of the thirteen states were slave states; now only fifteen out of the thirty are slave states. Moreover, the change is constitutionally made, and the government was constructed so as to permit changes of the balance of power, in obedience to changes of the forces of the body politic. . . .

We hear on one side demands—absurd, indeed, but yet unceasing— for an immediate and unconditional abolition of slavery—as if any power, except the people of the slave states, could abolish it, and as if they could be moved to abolish it by merely sounding the trumpet loudly and proclaiming emancipation, while the institution is interwoven with all their social and political interests, constitutions, and customs.

On the other hand, our statesmen say that "slavery has always existed, and, for aught they know or can do, it always must exist, God permitted it, and he alone can indicate the way to remove it." As if the Supreme Creator, after giving us the instructions of his providence and revelation for the illumination of our minds and consciences, did not leave us in all human transactions, with due invocations of his Holy Spirit, to seek out his will and execute it for ourselves.

Here, then, is the point of my separation from both of these parties. I feel assured that slavery must give way, and will give way, to the salutary instructions of economy, and to the ripening influences of humanity; that emancipation is inevitable, and is near; that it may be hastened or hindered; and that whether it shall be peaceful or violent, depends upon the question whether it be hastened or hindered; that all measures which fortify slavery or extend it, tend to the consummation of violence; all that check its extension and abate its strength, tend to its peaceful extirpation. But I will adopt none but lawful, constitutional, and peaceful means, to secure even that end; and none such can I or will I forego. Nor do I know any important or responsible political body that proposes to do more than this. No free state claims to extend its legislation into a slave state. None claims that Congress shall usurp power to abolish slavery in the slave states. None claims that any violent, unconstitutional, or unlawful measure shall be embraced. And, on the other hand, if we offer no scheme or plan for the adoption of the slave states, with the assent and cooperation of Congress, it is only because the slave states are unwilling as yet to receive such suggestions, or even to entertain the question of emancipation in any form. . . .

Sir, the slave states have no reason to fear that this inevitable change will go too far or too fast for their safety or welfare. It cannot well go too fast or too far, if the only alternative is a war of races.

But it cannot go too fast. Slavery has a reliable and accommodating ally in a party in the free states, which, though it claims to be, and doubtless is in many respects, a party of progress, finds its sole security for its political power in the support and aid of slavery in the slave states. Of course, I do not include in that party those who are now cooperating in maintaining the cause of freedom against slavery. I am not of that party of progress which in the north thus lends its support to slavery. But it is only just and candid that I should bear witness to its fidelity to the interests of slavery.

Slavery has, moreover, a more natural alliance with the aristocracy of the north and with the aristocracy of Europe. So long as slavery shall possess the cotton fields, the sugar fields, and the rice fields of the world, so long will commerce and capital yield it toleration and sympathy. Emancipation is a democratic revolution. It is capital that arrests all democratic revolutions. It was capital that, so recently, in a single year, rolled back the tide of revolution from the base of the Carpathian Mountains, across the Danube and the Rhine, into the streets of Paris. It is capital that is rapidly rolling back the throne of Napoleon into the chambers of the Tuilleries.[1]

Slavery has a guaranty still stronger than these in the prejudices of caste and color, which induce even large majorities in all the free states to regard sympathy with the slave as an act of unmanly humiliation and self-abasement, although philosophy meekly expresses her

[1]Seward is referring to the defeat of the European Revolutions of 1848 and to the subversion of the Second French Republic by Napoleon III. Ed.

distrust of the asserted natural superiority of the white race, and confidently denies that such a superiority, if justly claimed, could give a title to oppression. . . .

With these alliances to break the force of emancipation, there will be no disunion and no secession. I do not say that there may not be disturbance, though I do not apprehend even that. . . . Senators speak of the Union as if it existed only by consent, and, as it seems to be implied, by the assent of the legislatures of the states. On the contrary, the union was not founded in voluntary choice, nor does it exist by voluntary consent.

A union was proposed to the colonies by Franklin and others, in 1754; but such was their aversion to an abridgment of their own importance, respectively, that it was rejected even under the pressure of a disastrous invasion by France.

A union of choice was proposed to the colonies in 1775; but so strong was their opposition, that they went through the war of independence without having established more than a mere council of consultation.

But with independence came enlarged interests of agriculture—absolutely new interests of manufactures—interests of commerce, of fisheries, of navigation, of a common domain, of common debts, of common revenues and taxation, of the administration of justice, of public defence, of public honor; in short, interests of common nationality and sovereignty—interests which at last compelled the adoption of a more perfect union—a national government.

The genius, talents, and learning of Hamilton, of Jay, and of Madison, surpassing perhaps the intellectual power ever exerted before for the establishment of a government, combined with the serene but mighty influence of Washington, were only sufficient to secure the reluctant adoption of the Constitution that is now the object of all our affections and of the hopes of mankind. No wonder that the conflicts in which that Constitution was born, and the almost desponding solemnity of Washington, in his farewell address, impressed his countrymen and mankind with a profound distrust of its perpetuity! No wonder that while the murmurs of that day are yet ringing in our ears, we cherish that distrust, with pious reverence, as a national and patriotic sentiment!

But it is time to prevent the abuses of that sentiment. It is time to shake off that fear, for fear is always weakness. It is time to remember that government, even when it arises by chance or accident, and is administered capriciously and oppressively, is ever the strongest of all human institutions, surviving many social and ecclesiastical changes and convulsions; and that this Constitution of ours has all the inherent strength common to governments in general, and added to them has also the solidity and firmness derived from broader and deeper foundations in national justice, and a better civil adaptation to promote the welfare and happiness of mankind.

The Union, the creature of necessities, physical, moral, social, and political, endures by virtue of the same necessities; and these necessities are stronger than when it was produced—stronger by the greater amplitude of territory now covered by it—stronger by the sixfold increase of the society living under its beneficent protection—stronger by the augmentation ten thousand times of the fields, the workshops, the mines, and the ships, of that society; of its productions of the sea, of the plow, of the loom, and of the anvil, in their constant circle of internal and international exchange—stronger in the long rivers penetrating regions before unknown—stronger in all the artificial roads, canals, and other channels and avenues essential not only to trade but to defence—stronger in steam navigation, in steam locomotion on the land, and in telegraph communications, unknown when the Constitution was adopted—stronger in the freedom and in the growing empire of the seas, stronger in the element of national honor in all lands, and stronger than all in the now settled habits of veneration and affection for institutions so stupendous and so useful.

The Union, then, is, not because merely that men choose that it shall be, but because some government must exist here, and no other government than this can. If it could be dashed to atoms by the whirlwind, the lightning, or the earthquake, to-day, it would rise again in all its just and magnificent proportions tomorrow. This nation is a globe, still accumulating upon accumulation, not a dissolving sphere.

I have heard somewhat here, and almost for the first time in my life, of divided allegiance—of allegiance to the south and to the Union—of allegiance to states severally and to the Union. Sir, if sympathies with state emulation and pride of achievement could be allowed to raise up another sovereign to divide the allegiance of a citizen of the United States, I might recognize the claims of the state to which, by birth and gratitude, I belong—to the state of Hamilton and Jay, of Schuyler, of the Clintons, and of Fulton—the state which, with less than two hundred miles of natural navigation connected with the ocean, has, by her own enterprise, secured to herself the commerce of the continent, and is steadily advancing to the command of the commerce of the world. But for all this I know only one country and one sovereign—the

United States of America and the American people. And such as my allegiance is, is the loyalty of every other citizen of the United States. As I speak, he will speak when his time arrives. He knows no other country and no other sovereign. He has life, liberty, property, and precious affections, and hopes for himself and for his posterity, treasured up in the ark of the Union. He knows as well and feels as strongly as I do, that this government is his own government; that he is a part of it; that it was established for him, and that it is maintained by him; that it is the only truly wise, just, free, and equal government, that has ever existed; that no other government could be so wise, just, free, and equal; and that it is safer and more beneficent than any which time or change could bring into its place.

You may tell me, sir, that although all this may be true, yet the trial of faction has not yet been made. Sir, if the trial of faction has not been made, it has not been because faction has not always existed, and has not always menaced a trial, but because faction could find no fulcrum on which to place the lever to subvert the Union, as it can find no fulcrum now; and in this is my confidence. I would not rashly provoke the trial; but I will not suffer a fear, which I have not, to make me compromise one sentiment, one principle of truth or justice, to avert a danger that all experience teaches me is purely chimerical. Let, then, those who distrust the Union make compromises to save it. I shall not impeach their wisdom, as I certainly cannot their patriotism; but, indulging no such apprehensions myself, I shall vote for the admission of California directly, without conditions, without qualifications, and without compromise.

For the vindication of that vote, I look not to the verdict of the passing hour, disturbed as the public mind now is by conflicting interests and passions, but to that period, happily not far distant, when the vast regions over which we are now legislating shall have received their destined inhabitants.

While looking forward to that day, its countless generations seem to me to be rising up and passing in dim and shadowy review before us; and a voice comes forth from their serried ranks, saying: "Waste your treasures and your armies, if you will; raze your fortifications to the ground; sink your navies into the sea; transmit to us even a dishonored name, if you must; but the soil you hold in trust for us—give it to us free. You found it free, and conquered it to extend a better and surer freedom over it. Whatever choice you have made for yourselves, let us have no partial freedom; let us all be free; let the reversion of your broad domain descend to us unincumbered, and free from the calamities and from the sorrows of human bondage."

6

THE MYSTIC CHORDS OF UNION

Abraham Lincoln
FIRST INAUGURAL ADDRESS

As a rising young attorney in Illinois, Abraham Lincoln (1809–1865) followed the Whig party line on banking, the tariff, and internal improvements. He once called Henry Clay "my beau ideal of a statesman." Lincoln became Whig minority leader in the lower house of the state legislature, and during a brief term in Congress from 1846 to 1848, he vigorously denounced the Mexican War. He remained a faithful Whig until the party disintegrated; then in 1856 he joined the Republicans. In 1858 Lincoln called America "a house divided against itself"; the same year William H. Seward foresaw "an irrepressible conflict" that would make the country either all slave or all free. They proved right—within three years the crisis had arrived.

Lincoln's first inaugural address shows how strongly Whig political ideas continued to influence him after he became president. Under circumstances of impending civil war, it must have seemed almost impossible to combine an appeal for social harmony with dedication to moral principle; but these were two of the highest values of Whiggery and Lincoln was committed to both. Here he joins firmness of principle with conciliatory rhetoric, resolving the two in his dedication to maintain the Union. Lincoln's position is a logical development from Seward's in the preceding selection. The resemblance, indeed, is no accident: Secretary of State-designate Seward had gone over the draft of the speech with his new chief. Seward's emendations (notably in the last paragraph) gave an especially Whiggish tone to Lincoln's text.

Fellow-Citizens of the United States:

In compliance with a custom as old as the Government itself, I appear before you to address you briefly and to take in your presence the oath prescribed by the Constitution of the United States to be

SOURCE. Abraham Lincoln, "First Inaugural Address," March 4, 1861, *Messages and Papers of the Presidents*, ed. James D. Richardson (Washington, D.C., 1900), VI, 5–12.

taken by the President "before he enters on the execution of his office."

I do not consider it necessary at present for me to discuss those matters of administration about which there is no special anxiety or excitement.

Apprehension seems to exist among the people of the southern states that by the accession of a Republican Administration their property and their peace and personal security are to be endangered. There has never been any reasonable cause for such apprehension. Indeed, the most ample evidence to the contrary has all the while existed and been open to their inspection. It is found in nearly all the published speeches of him who now addresses you. I do but quote from one of those speeches when I declare that "I have no purpose, directly or indirectly, to interfere with the institution of slavery in the States where it exists. I believe I have no lawful right to do so, and I have no inclination to do so." . . .

I now reiterate these sentiments, and in doing so I only press upon the public attention the most conclusive evidence of which the case is susceptible that the property, peace, and security of no section are to be in any wise endangered by the now incoming Administration. I add, too, that all the protection which, consistently with the Constitution and the laws, can be given will be cheerfully given to all the states when lawfully demanded, for whatever cause—as cheerfully to one section as to another. . . .

I take the official oath today with no mental reservations and with no purpose to construe the Constitution or laws by any hypercritical rules; and while I do not choose now to specify particular acts of Congress as proper to be enforced, I do suggest that it will be much safer for all, both in official and private stations, to conform to and abide by all those acts which stand unrepealed than to violate any of them trusting to find impunity in having them held to be unconstitutional.

It is seventy-two years since the first inauguration of a President under our national Constitution. During that period fifteen different and greatly distinguished citizens have in succession administered the executive branch of the government. They have conducted it through many perils, and generally with great success. Yet, with all this scope of precedent, I now enter upon the same task for the brief constitutional term of four years under great and peculiar difficulty. A disruption of the Federal Union, heretofore only menaced, is now formidably attempted.

I hold that in contemplation of universal law and of the Constitution the Union of these states is perpetual. Perpetuity is implied, if not expressed, in the fundamental law of all national governments. It is safe to assert that no government proper ever had a provision in its organic law for its own termination. Continue to execute all the express provisions of our National Constitution, and the Union will endure forever, it being impossible to destroy it except by some action not provided for in the instrument itself.

Again: If the United States be not a government proper, but an association of states in the nature of contract merely, can it, as a contract, be peaceably unmade by less than all the parties who made it? One party to a contract may violate it—break it, so to speak—but does it not require all to lawfully rescind it?

Descending from these general principles, we find the proposition that in legal contemplation the Union is perpetual confirmed by the history of the Union itself. The Union is much older than the Constitution. It was formed, in fact, by the Articles of Association in 1774. It was matured and continued by the Declaration of Independence in 1776. It was further matured, and the faith of all the then thirteen states expressly plighted and engaged that it should be perpetual, by the Articles of Confederation in 1778. And finally, in 1787, one of the declared objects for ordaining and establishing the Constitution was "to form a more perfect Union."

But if destruction of the Union by one or by a part only of the states be lawfully possible, the Union is *less* perfect than before the Constitution, having lost the vital element of perpetuity.

It follows from these views that no state upon its own mere motion can lawfully get out of the Union; that *resolves* and *ordinances* to that effect are legally void, and that acts of violence within any state or states against the authority of the United States are insurrectionary or revolutionary, according to circumstances.

I therefore consider that in view of the Constitution and the laws the Union is unbroken, and to the extent of my ability I shall take care, as the Constitution itself expressly enjoins upon me, that the laws of the Union be faithfully executed in all the states. Doing this I deem to be only a simple duty on my part, and I shall perform it so far as practicable unless my rightful masters, the American people, shall withhold the requisite means or in some authoritative manner direct the contrary. I trust this will not be regarded as a menace, but only as the declared purpose of the Union that it *will* constitutionally defend and maintain itself.

In doing this there needs to be no bloodshed or violence, and there shall be none unless it be forced upon the national authority. The power confided to me will be used to hold, occupy, and possess the property and places belonging to the government and to collect the duties and imposts; but beyond what may be necessary for these objects, there will be no invasion, no using of force against or among the people anywhere. Where hostility to the United States in any interior locality shall be so great and universal as to prevent competent resident citizens from holding the federal offices, there will be no attempt to force obnoxious strangers among the people for that object. While the strict legal right may exist in the government to enforce the exercise of these offices, the attempt to do so would be so irritating and so nearly impracticable withal that I deem it better to forego for the time the uses of such offices.

The mails, unless repelled, will continue to be furnished in all parts of the Union. So far as possible the people everywhere shall have that sense of perfect security which is most favorable to calm thought and reflection. The course here indicated will be followed unless current events and experience shall show a modification or change to be proper; and in every case and exigency my best discretion will be exercised, according to circumstances actually existing and with a view and a hope of a peaceful solution of the national troubles and the restoration of fraternal sympathies and affections.

That there are persons in one section or another who seek to destroy the Union at all events and are glad of any pretext to do it I will neither affirm nor deny; but if there be such, I need address no word to them. To those, however, who really love the Union may I not speak?

Before entering upon so grave a matter as the destruction of our national fabric, with all its benefits, its memories, and its hopes, would it not be wise to ascertain precisely why we do it? Will you hazard so desperate a step while there is any possibility that any portion of the ills you fly from have no real existence? Will you, while the certain ills you fly to are greater than all the real ones you fly from, will you risk the commission of so fearful a mistake?

All profess to be content in the Union if all constitutional rights can be maintained. Is it true, then, that any right plainly written in the Constitution has been denied? I think not. Happily, the human mind is so constituted that no party can reach to the audacity of doing this. Think, if you can, of a single instance in which a plainly written provision of the Constitution has ever been denied. If by the mere force of numbers a majority should deprive a minority of any clearly written constitutional right, it might in a moral point of view justify revolution; certainly would if such right were a vital one. But such is not our case. All the vital rights of minorities and of individuals are so plainly assured to them by affirmations and negations, guaranties and prohibitions, in the Constitution that controversies never arise concerning them. But no organic law can ever be framed with a provision specifically applicable to every question which may occur in practical administration. No foresight can anticipate nor any document of reasonable length contain express provisions for all possible questions. Shall fugitives from labor be surrendered by national or by State authority? The Constitution does not expressly say. *May* Congress prohibit slavery in the territories? The Constitution does not expressly say. *Must* Congress protect slavery in the territories? The Constitution does not expressly say.

From questions of this class spring all our constitutional controversies, and we divide upon them into majorities and minorities. If the minority will not acquiesce, the majority must, or the government must cease. There is no other alternative, for continuing the government is acquiescence on one side or the other. If a minority in such case will secede rather than acquiesce, they make a precedent which in turn will divide and ruin them, for a minority of their own will secede from them whenever a majority refuses to be controlled by such minority. For instance, why may not any portion of a new confederacy a year or two hence arbitrarily secede again, precisely as portions of the present Union now claim to secede from it? All who cherish disunion sentiments are now being educated to the exact temper of doing this.

Is there such perfect identity of interests among the states to compose a new union as to produce harmony only and prevent renewed secession?

Plainly the central idea of secession is the essence of anarchy. A majority held in restraint by constitutional checks and limitations, and always changing easily with deliberate changes of popular opinions and sentiments, is the only true sovereign of a free people. Whoever rejects it does of necessity fly to anarchy or to despotism. Unanimity is impossible. The rule of a minority, as a permanent arrangement, is wholly inadmissible; so that, rejecting the majority principle, anarchy or despotism in some form is all that is left.

I do not forget the position assumed by some that constitutional questions are to be decided by the Supreme Court, nor do I deny that such decisions must be binding in any case upon the parties to a suit as to the object of that suit, while they are also entitled to very high respect and consideration in all parallel cases by all other departments of the government. And while it is obviously possible that such decision may be erroneous in any given case, still the evil effect following it, being limited to that particular case, with the chance that it may be overruled and never become a precedent for other cases, can better be borne than could the evils of a different practice. At the same time, the candid citizen must confess that if the policy of the government upon vital questions affecting the whole people is to be irrevocably fixed by decisions of the Supreme Court, the instant they are made in ordinary litigation between parties in personal actions the people will have ceased to be their own rulers, having to that extent practically resigned their government into the hands of that eminent tribunal. Nor is there in this view any assault upon the court or the judges. It is a duty from which they may not shrink to decide cases properly brought before them, and it is no fault of theirs if others seek to turn their decisions to political purposes.

One section of our country believes slavery is *right* and ought to be extended, while the other believes it is *wrong* and ought not to be extended. This is the only substantial dispute. The fugitive-slave clause of the Constitution and the law for the suppression of the foreign slave trade are each as well enforced, perhaps, as any law can ever be in a community where the moral sense of the people imperfectly supports the law itself. The great body of the people abide by the dry legal obligation in both cases, and a few break over in each. This, I think, can not be perfectly cured, and it would be worse in both cases *after* the separation of the sections than before. The foreign slave trade, now imperfectly suppressed, would be ultimately revived without restriction in one section, while fugitive slaves, now only partially surrendered, would not be surrendered at all by the other.

Physically speaking, we can not separate. We can not remove our respective sections from each other nor build an impassable wall between them. A husband and wife may be divorced and go out of the presence and beyond the reach of each other, but the different parts of our country can not do this. They can not but remain face to face, and intercourse, either amicable or hostile, must continue between them. Is it possible, then, to make that intercourse more advantageous or more satisfactory *after* separation than *before*? Can aliens make treaties easier than friends can make laws? Can treaties be more faithfully enforced between aliens than laws can among friends? Suppose you go to war, you can not fight always; and when, after much loss on both sides and no gain on either, you cease fighting, the identical old questions, as to terms of intercourse, are again upon you.

This country, with its institutions, belongs to the people who inhabit it. Whenever they shall grow weary of the existing government, they can exercise their *constitutional* right of amending it or their *revolutionary* right to dismember or overthrow it. I can not be ignorant of the fact that many worthy and patriotic citizens are desirous of having the national Constitution amended. While I make no recommendation of amendments, I fully recognize the rightful authority of the people over the whole subject, to be exercised in either of the modes prescribed in the instrument itself; and I should, under existing circumstances, favor rather than oppose a fair opportunity being afforded the people to act upon it. I will venture to add that to me the convention mode seems preferable, in that it allows amendments to originate with the people themselves, instead of only permitting them to take or reject propositions originated by others, not especially chosen for the purpose, and which might not be precisely such as they would wish to either accept or refuse. I understand a proposed amendment to the Constitution—which amendment, however, I have not seen—has passed Congress, to the effect that the federal government shall never interfere with the domestic institutions of the States, including that of persons held to service. To avoid misconstruction of what I have said, I depart from my purpose not to speak of particular amendments so far as to say that, holding such a provision to now be implied constitutional law, I have no objection to its being made express and irrevocable.

The Chief Magistrate derives all his authority from the people, and they have conferred none upon him to fix terms for the separation of the states. The people themselves can do this also if they choose, but the Executive as such has nothing to do with it. His duty is to administer the present government as it came to his hands and to transmit it unimpaired by him to his successor.

Why should there not be a patient confidence in the ultimate justice of the people? Is there any better or equal hope in the world? In our present differences, is either party without faith of being in the right? If the Almighty Ruler of Nations, with His eternal truth and justice, be on your side of the North, or on yours of the South, that truth and that justice will surely prevail by the judgment of this great tribunal of the American people.

By the frame of the government under which we live this same people have wisely given their public servants but little power for mischief, and have with equal wisdom provided for the return of that little to their own hands at very short intervals. While the people retain their virtue and vigilance no Administration by any extreme of wickedness or folly can very seriously injure the government in the short space of four years.

My countrymen, one and all, think calmly and *well* upon this whole subject. Nothing valuable can be lost by taking time. If there be an object to *hurry* any of you in hot haste to a step which you would never take *deliberately*, that object will be frustrated by taking time; but no good object can be frustrated by it. Such of you as are now dissatisfied still have the old Constitution unimpaired, and, on the sensitive point, the laws of your own framing under it; while the new Administration will have no immediate power, if it would, to change either. If it were admitted that you who are dissatisfied hold the right side in the dispute, there still is no single good reason for precipitate action. Intelligence, patriotism, Christianity, and a firm reliance on Him who has never yet forsaken this favored land are still competent to adjust in the best way all our present difficulty.

In *your* hands, my dissatisfied fellow-countrymen, and not in *mine*, is the momentous issue of civil war. The government will not assail *you*. You can have no conflict without being yourselves the aggressors. *You* have no oath registered in heaven to destroy the government, while *I* shall have the most solemn one to "preserve, protect, and defend it."

I am loath to close. We are not enemies, but friends. We must not be enemies. Though passion may have strained it must not break our bonds of affection. The mystic chords of memory, stretching from every battlefield and patriot grave to every living heart and hearthstone all over this broad land, will yet swell the chorus of the Union, when again touched, as surely they will be, by the better angels of our nature.

SUGGESTIONS FOR FURTHER READING

Though most books written about the Jacksonian era focus on the Democrats, in doing so they often include valuable information and ideas regarding the Whigs. Arthur M. Schlesinger, Jr., *The Age of Jackson* (Boston: Little, Brown, 1945); Marvin Meyers, *The Jacksonian Persuasion* (Stanford, Calif.: Stanford University Press, 1957); and Lee Benson, *The Concept of Jacksonian Democracy: New York as a Test Case* (Princeton, N.J.: Princeton University Press, 1961) are three fascinating interpretive works that tell a great deal about Whiggery in the course of trying to define Jacksonianism. They are probably the first places readers of this anthology should turn for further stimulation. The different perspectives and conclusions of the authors are readily apparent.

For a general orientation to the events of the period, a good account is Glyndon G. Van Deusen, *The Jacksonian Era* (Boston: Harper Brothers, 1959). Two wider ranging surveys of the American past that contain provocative remarks on the Whigs are Vernon L. Parrington, *Main Currents in American Thought*, Vol. II (New York: Harcourt, Brace, 1927), and William Appleman Williams, *The Contours of American History* (Cleveland: World, 1961).

The development of the Whig party can be studied through E. Malcolm Carroll, *Origins of the Whig Party* (Durham, N.C.: Duke University Press, 1925); George Rawlings Poage, *Henry Clay and the Whig Party* (Chapel Hill, N.C.: University of North Carolina Press, 1936); and the careful state-by-state analysis of Richard P. McCormick, *The Second American Party System* (Chapel Hill, N.C.: University of North Carolina Press, 1966). Charles Grier Sellers, Jr., "Who Were the Southern Whigs?" *American Historical Review*, LIX (1954), 335–346, is a valuable supplement to Arthur C. Cole, *The Whig Party in the South* (Washington, D.C.: American Historical Association, 1913). Joel Silbey, *The Shrine of Party: Congressional Voting Behavior, 1841–1852* (Pittsburgh: University of Pittsburgh Press, 1967); and Robert F. Dalzell, Jr., *Daniel Webster and the Trial* of American Nationalism (Boston: Houghton Mifflin, 1973) are important for understanding the mature Whig party.

The Whig leaders have not suffered for want of biographies. Among the best and most readable are Richard N. Current, *Daniel Webster and the Rise of National Conservatism* (Boston: Little, Brown, 1955); Clement Eaton, *Henry Clay and the Art of American Politics* (Boston: Little, Brown, 1957); Samuel Flagg Bemis, *John Quincy Adams and the Union* (New York: Knopf, 1956); Thomas P. Govan, *Nicholas Biddle, Nationalist and Public Banker* (Chicago: University of Chicago Press, 1959); Glyndon G. Van Deusen, *William Henry Seward* (New York: Oxford University Press, 1967); and Jonathan Messerli, *Horace Mann* (New York: Knopf, 1971). It is said that more books have been written about Lincoln than anyone else except Napoleon and Christ. Reinhard Luthin, *The Real Abraham Lincoln* (Englewood Cliffs, N.J.: Prentice Hall, 1960), is a very useful volume, while David Donald, *Lincoln Reconsidered* (New York: Knopf, 1956); and Kenneth Stampp, *The Era of Reconstruction* (New York: Knopf, 1965), illuminate the first Republican President's persistent Whiggery.

The economic issues of the Whig-Democratic era have been examined extensively, often at the state level. The classic is Oscar and Mary Handlin, *Commonwealth: A Study of the Role of Government in the American Economy: Massachusetts, 1774–1861* (Cambridge, Mass.: Harvard University Press, 1947; revised 1969). Carter Goodrich, *Government Promotion of American Canals and Railroads* (New York: Columbia University Press, 1960), and Peter Temin, *The Jacksonian Economy* (New York: Norton, 1969), are quite sophisticated. The best nontechnical overview of economic developments in the period is George Rogers Taylor, *The Transportation Revolution* (New York: Rinehart, 1951). For economic thinking, the standard work is Joseph Dorfman, *The Economic Mind in American Civilization*, Vol. II (New York: Viking, 1946). The "Bank War" is still being re-fought, as one can tell from Bray Hammond, *Banks and Politics in America* (Princeton, N.J.: Princeton University Press, 1957), and Robert Remini, *Andrew Jackson and the Bank War* (New York: Norton, 1967).

The religious and reform movements of mid-nineteenth-century America have been a favorite topic of historical inquiry in recent years. Especially useful for an understanding of Whiggery are Whitney Cross, *The Burned-Over District* (Ithaca, N.Y.: Cornell University Press, 1950); Louis Filler, *The Crusade Against Slavery* (New York: Harper Brothers, 1960); and Joseph Gusfield, *Symbolic Crusade: Status Politics and the American Temperance Movement* (Urbana, Ill.: University of Illinois Press, 1963). On ethno-religious conflict, see

Oscar Handlin, *Boston's Immigrants* (Cambridge, Mass.: Harvard University Press, 1941, revised 1959); and Michael F. Holt, *Forging a Majority: The Formation of the Republican Party in Pittsburgh* (New Haven: Yale University Press, 1969).

For background in the political thought to which the American Whigs fell heir, see Gordon Wood, *The Creation of the American Republic* (Chapel Hill, N.C.: University of North Carolina Press, 1969); and Richard Hofstadter, *The Idea of a Party System* (Berkeley, Calif.: University of California Press, 1970). Other studies in American intellectual history relevant to the Whigs include Merrill D. Peterson, *The Jefferson Image in the American Mind* (New York: Oxford University Press, 1960); William R. Taylor, *Cavalier and Yankee* (New York: Braziller, 1961); Fred Somkin, *Unquiet Eagle* (Ithaca, N.Y.: Cornell University Press, 1967); Paul Nagel, *This Sacred Trust* (New York: Oxford University Press, 1971); and Daniel Walker Howe, *The Unitarian Conscience* (Cambridge, Mass.: Harvard University Press, 1970).